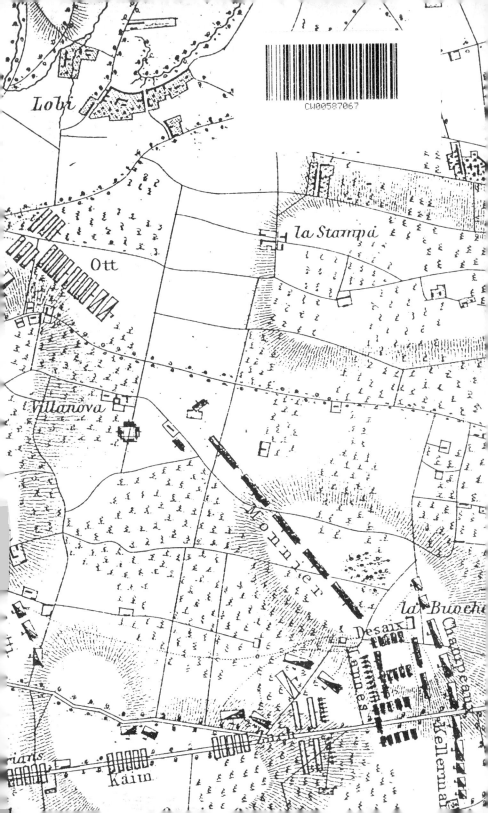

1800
MARENGO AND HOHENLINDEN

MARENGO
AND
HOHENLINDEN

Volume I

COLONEL GEORGE ARMAND FURSE, C.B.

LATE OF THE BLACK WATCH

WITH PLANS AND ILLUSTRATIONS

IN TWO VOLUMES

WORLEY PUBLICATIONS
1993
with
BRIGADE LIBRARY

Facsimile Edition Published 1993
by Worley Publications
10 Rectory Road East
Felling
Tyne & Wear NE10 9DN
Tel: (091) 469 2414

Published from 1903 Edition

Vol. I ISBN 1 869804 26 0
Vol. II ISBN 1 869804 27 9
Set ISBN 1 869804 28 7

Printed and Bound in Great Britain by
Antony Rowe Ltd, Bumper's Farm,
Chippenham, Wiltshire.

1800.

MARENGO AND HOHENLINDEN.

CHAPTER I.

BONAPARTE BECOMES FIRST CONSUL.

Bonaparte receives the news of the landing of a Turkish army—Defeats Mustapha Pasha at Aboukir—Decides to quit Egypt—Reasons he gives to Marmont for doing so—Anxiety of his family during his absence in Egypt—Bruix gets out of Brest—Friction between Lord Keith and Nelson—Tragic affairs at Naples—Bonaparte sails for France and lands at Fréjus—Enthusiastic reception—People rush in crowds to behold him—Arrives in Paris—Prevailing discontent in France—A change of Government desired—The 18th Brumaire—Bonaparte becomes First Consul—His great qualities and ability—His power of fascination—Chooses capable coadjutors—Excellence of his rule during the Consulate—His restless activity.

THE year 1799 had been very disastrous for France. The Republican armies in Germany and in Italy had met with a series of glaring reverses, and even in the East the French, under their most renowned leader, had been compelled to retire from the battered walls of the little fortified town of Saint Jean d'Acre. The last year of the eighteenth century was fast approaching, and in that year fortune was to smile again on the French nation; the disasters of the previous year were to be driven into utter oblivion by splendid victories gained in the valley of the Danube and on the plains of Piedmont.

But before this could come to pass a more important event occurred. In the declining days of 1799, the ruling power in France was confided to a soldier of brilliant fame, to a genius in military and political matters, to a man the equal to whom the world had, perhaps, never seen. This was Bonaparte, the conqueror of Italy. He appealed to the people; he asked for money, iron, and soldiers, and in return promised them victory.

History records how well his promise was fulfilled in the first year of his rule.

The French army, returning from the siege of Saint Jean d'Acre, reached Cairo on the 14th of June, 1799, after a painful march. In the following months, rumours of fresh movements amongst the Mameluke Beys began to circulate. They, in fact, were making fresh efforts with the object of occupying the attention of the French, and to keep them away from the locality which the Turks had selected for the landing of their army. Elphi Osman and Mourad Bey were up in arms, but were defeated before long by La Grange and Murat.

Whilst Bonaparte was promenading in the neighbourhood of the Great Pyramids with Bourrienne on the evening of the 15th of July, he descried the approach of an Arab, who was riding in hot haste. It was a messenger Marmont had sent from Alexandria; the despatch he handed over to the general announced the arrival of a large Turkish army in Aboukir Bay on the 11th. This army, it appeared, had reached the shores of Egypt under the escort and protection of English ships of war.

It was the Turkish army which had arrived at Acre too late; the same that Bonaparte, the conqueror at the battle of the Pyramids,* boasted of having destroyed under the walls of that city.

On the 25th of July, 1799, Bonaparte defeated the army which, under the command of Mustapha Pasha, had landed at Aboukir. The conqueror was never loth to amplify his own performances. He much exaggerated this victory. His relation of the event, in point of numbers, at any rate, was not in strict conformity with the facts.† The number of Turks was not

---

* The battle of the Pyramids, in a certain sense, resembled the battle of Omdurman. The enemy in both instances dashed on recklessly and braved death, resorting to tactics which really proved the most favourable to their opponents. At the battle of the Pyramids the Mamelukes lost more than 2000 men; the French not quite 30, of whom about two-thirds fell victims to the cross-fire of their own squares. The Mamelukes dashed at the French squares, and were literally swept away by the fire of the defenders. The French spent nearly three days in dragging drowned Mamelukes out of the Nile for the sake of the booty to be found on them.

† In strict morality, as Carlyle puts it, no man is at liberty to tell lies. But if we accept the saying, "All is fair in love and war," an exception must be made in favour of the latter, when the end, to deceive the adversary, one of the greatest secrets of the art of war, is good. A falsehood should likewise be condoned when we aim to raise the *morale* of our troops.

quite 8000, but to give greater *éclat* to the victory it was magnified into 17,000.*

Kléber, writing to the Directory, states: "He (Bonaparte) cut to pieces, it is true, nearly 9000 Turks who had landed there (at Aboukir)." In point of fact, these troops were only the advanced guard of the Turkish army. Their main body consisted of 20,000 Janizaries and regular troops, with 25,000 irregulars, which reached Gaza only at the end of October.

From his earliest days Bonaparte gave proofs of a special talent in the elaboration of his bulletins and accounts of his military operations. These accounts were not simply dry details of military events; their style was pompous and studied, and calculated to rouse general admiration. In fact, they were written for a purpose. Even the writing of bulletins requires deep skill. The art lies in so wording them as to make people believe what you want them to believe. In this Bonaparte excelled.

However much the real value of history may suffer from intentional misstatements of this kind, it must be confessed that, in this instance, Bonaparte's exaggeration proved of infinite advantage to his own interests. The importance attached to this victory and to the previous one of Mount Tabor, of which the news reached France at the same time, added very much to the reputation he had previously acquired as a general. It also made up, in some way, for the mortifying check he had recently sustained under the ramparts of St. Jean d'Acre, from which he had to retire after an investment of 60 days' duration —the only check he experienced in his career until his troops crossed the Pyrenees.

Our indisputed dominion of the Mediterranean, and the annihilation of the French flag in that sea, rendered all correspondence with France a matter of extreme difficulty, almost an impossibility. All letters were captured by British cruisers or by the Turks, and sent to Constantinople. The French were as completely secluded from the rest of the world as they could well be.

The story is told that, after the defeat of the Turks at the battle of Aboukir, 400 or 500 wounded Turks were captured by the French, and that Bonaparte thought it desirable to send

* Lieutenant-Colonel Robert Thomas Wilson, "British Expedition to Egypt," p. 29.

them back to Patrona Bey, vice-admiral of the Turkish squadron.   With this object, and under pretext of an exchange of prisoners, Descorches-Sainte-Croix, a naval officer, and Merlin, Bonaparte's aide-de-camp, visited the Turkish admiral under cover of a flag of truce.* On this becoming known to Sir Sidney Smith, he had the two officers sent on board his ship.   Some trifling presents were exchanged, and, possibly with a formed intention of disheartening the French army, Sir Sidney gave the French officers a bundle of newspapers, and amongst others a copy of the issue of the *Gazette Française de Francfort* of the 10th of June, 1799.

We can well picture to ourselves how eagerly Bonaparte perused its pages, and with what poignant grief he learnt that all the fruit of his brilliant achievements in Italy was lost.   In a rapid series of battles all the states he had conquered, with others acquired since, had been wrested from France.   It is related that on learning all this he became much agitated ; and exclaimed, brandishing the papers which he had received from Sir Sidney Smith, " Italy is lost !   All the fruit of our victories has vanished.   It is imperative for me to be off ! "

On handing the newspapers to Descorches, Sidney Smith is said to have told him that, aware of the instructions from the Directory sent to Bonaparte ordering him to return to Europe, he desired to dissuade him from taking such a step, inasmuch as he had strict orders to prevent it.

Are we to credit this story ?   It certainly appears strange in the face of it that in a month's time Sidney Smith should have allowed his vigilance to relax to such an extent as to permit two French frigates, with Bonaparte on one of them, and two smaller ships, to slip out of Alexandria unobserved.   The excuse alleged for Sidney Smith is that when he went to Cyprus for water he never dreamt that a general would abandon his army, nor that the French ships would brave the adverse winds of that season.

There is no doubt that the blockade was occasionally raised ; for in writing to the minister of marine, Le Roy used the words, " during those periods when the blockade is accidentally raised." †

All the time that he was in Egypt, Bonaparte did not cease

* Marmont, " Mémoires," tom. 1–2, livre iv. p. 3.
† See " Copies of Intercepted Correspondence," p. 26.

to keep an eye on France. James states, in his "Naval History," that on the 3rd of July Gantheaume arrived in Alexandria from Cairo with orders to prepare for sea the *Muiron* and *Carrère*, in which Bonaparte intended to return to France at the first opportunity. This resolution the general had taken in view of the critical state of France, and in compliance with the desire of the Directory expressed in a letter dated the 29th of May, which reached him shortly after his return to Cairo from the Syrian expedition.

Had Bonaparte been *ordered* back to France, the simple truth would have been soon told; but there is no direct evidence to this effect. Bourrienne states that the idea of quitting Egypt was not conceived until after the battle of Aboukir. Messrs. Amédée Jaubert and Eugène Merlin, the former secretary-interpreter, the latter aide-de-camp to Bonaparte, who were always by his side, and embarked with him for Europe, agree that it was the intelligence contained in the English newspapers about the reverses suffered by the French armies, that induced Bonaparte to leave Egypt. This is repeated in the "Mémorial de Sainte Hélène." To Kléber Bonaparte sent the English and Francfort papers up to the 10th of June. But he makes not the least mention of an order of recall, which he would not have omitted as a justification for his departure, had he received one.

What Smith told Descorches, and James's statement regarding the letter Bonaparte received from the Directory, under date of the 29th of May, remain still unexplained.

After the destruction of the French fleet in the Bay of Aboukir on the 1st of August, 1798, the English had the entire command of the Mediterranean, and Bonaparte knew too well that it was impossible for the Directory to send him troops for the purpose of effecting more conquests in Africa. It was in the following words that he explained to Marmont the ground for the resolution he had taken :—

"Marmont," he said, "I have decided to leave and to return to France. The state of affairs in Europe compels me to take this serious step. Misfortunes overwhelm our armies; and God only knows up to what point the enemy has penetrated. Italy is lost, and the price of such great efforts, of so much blood spilt, passes away from us. In such a situation what can the incapable people placed at the head of affairs do?

"With them all is ignorance, folly or corruption. I alone have borne the burden, and by a series of successes have infused some consistency into this Government, which, without me, could never have risen and maintained itself. I being absent, all had to totter. Let us not delay, therefore, until the destruction is complete, when the evil will be without remedy.

"The voyage back to France may be doubtful, difficult, risky; nevertheless, it will be less so than it was in coming here; and fortune, which has befriended me up to the present, will not forsake me at this moment. They shall hear in France almost at the same time of the destruction of the Turkish army at Aboukir and of my arrival. My presence, by rousing their spirits, will give the army the confidence which it needs, and the good citizens the hope of a better future. There will be a commotion in the mind all beneficial to France. We must strive to reach France, and we shall reach it."

It was on fortune that Bonaparte always placed such implicit trust, fortune which failed him only when he began abusing its favours.

The dream of the Eastern empire was broken before the crumbling ramparts of Acre. There were no laurels to be gathered in Egypt. In France alone lay the real opportunity.

During Bonaparte's sojourn in Egypt, the members of his family were very uneasy about him, and not a few of his friends considered him entirely lost. So completely did the battle of the Nile cut off the communications of the French army with the mother country, that the general received news from France with the greatest difficulty. The English kept a strict watch over the coast.

The blunders made by the Government, the reverses which had overtaken the French armies in many fields, and the civil war rampant in the west and south of the country, all combined to disturb Joseph Bonaparte. The very unsatisfactory state of affairs, the hopeless incapacity and absence of all political ability in the body of the Directory, made him anxious to communicate with his brother, and in this he succeeded. To accomplish his object he employed a Greek sailor, Santer Bourbaki by name, who undertook to bear despatches to the general advising his immediate return to France. Bourbaki succeeded in his dangerous mission. Quitting Marseilles in a small vessel flying a neutral flag, nominally bound for Beyrout, he reached the coast of Syria, and sailing along in sight of land, so as to be able to fly to the nearest shelter in case of danger, contrived to reach Alexandria in safety.

Miot asserts that Bonaparte received this letter from Joseph Bonaparte through the agency of this Greek named Bourbaki. Other writers, amongst them Bourrienne, deny the story about the letter. Nevertheless the fact is recorded in the "Mémoires de Joseph Bonaparte." Alison corroborates Miot's assertion, and declares that both Lucien and Joseph Bonaparte had caused to be conveyed to their brother full intelligence of the disastrous state of the Republic, and had advised his return to France.*

Bonaparte wrote: "It was by way of Tunis that I received news of my family and of the events in Europe." M. Beaussier, French Consul at Tripoli, and M. Devoize at Tunis, appear to have facilitated the correspondence.

Popular opinion in France most thoroughly regarded Bonaparte as a victim of the Government, and believed that the Directory had exiled him to Egypt to get him out of the country. In France the expedition to Egypt had become extremely unpopular, and a head of accusation against the Directory, the majority persisting in attributing that undertaking to them.

We may well entertain some doubt whether any sincere desire existed on the part of the Directory for Bonaparte's return from Egypt. They regarded him in the light of a dangerous rival, and it is more natural to believe that they must have infinitely preferred to keep him away and to have him forgotten. That such a feeling prevailed may be gathered from the fact that, when Barras proposed to recall him and to give him the command of the Army of Italy, his colleagues unanimously silenced him.† They said, "Have we not already enough generals desirous to usurp the supreme authority without having need of that one? General Bonaparte is well where he is, and it is our dearest interest to leave him there." Nevertheless, in the spring of 1799, the Directory equipped a large fleet with the avowed object of bringing the troops back from Egypt,

---

* Alison, "History of Europe," chap. xxix. p. 193. See "Jung Lucien Bonaparte et ses Mémoires," vol. i. p. 270.

† Barras had first come across Bonaparte at the siege of Toulon. He had taken a great fancy to him, as he averred, on account of his great resemblance to Marat, with whom he had been on intimate terms.

or of retrieving the destruction of their naval power in the
Mediterranean caused by the loss of the battle of the Nile.

After Jourdan's defeat at Stokach, Bruix, then minister of
marine, fitted out a powerful fleet at Brest. Fortune favoured
him, for at the end of April severe weather had blown Lord
Bridport and the Channel fleet away from the coast. Taking
advantage of this propitious moment, Bruix issued from Brest
with twenty-five ships of the line, and appeared before Cadiz
on the 4th of May, but failed in making an intended junction
with the Spanish squadron. He then entered the Mediterranean
on the 5th and steered for Toulon, which he reached on the
14th of May. After a short stay, he sailed from that port on
the 26th.

Lords St. Vincent and Keith followed the French with
sixteen ships. Cadiz being left unguarded, a Spanish fleet of
seventeen ships of the line issued forth, entered the Mediterranean, and dropped anchor in Cartagena.

Bruix apparently did nothing beyond placing himself in
communication with Moreau, and thus, to a certain extent,
raising the flagging spirits of the Army of Italy. After a while
he sailed back to Brest.

This cruise, fruitless as it was, nevertheless marks the commencement of the friction between Nelson and Lord Keith.

In June, 1799, Lord St. Vincent resigned all his command.
His departure considerably irritated Nelson, for it led to Lord
Keith assuming the chief command in the Mediterranean. Under
Lord St. Vincent Nelson had been practically independent; that
experienced commander trusted him so implicitly that he can
be said to have entirely had his own way. He now conceived
a singular antipathy for Keith, and eventually deliberately
thwarted and defied his combinations. Possibly the British
fleet might have rendered a good account of the French, had
the two admirals worked thoroughly in unison; but Lord Keith
was for several weeks ignorant of the locality of Bruix's squadron,
and cruised about without any good result; whilst Nelson persisted in declaring that the presence of his squadron was indispensable in Southern Italy.

It is impossible to account for Nelson's conduct at that
period, when he had, according to his own statement, received
full powers from the King of the Two Sicilies to act as his
representative.

Led by an idea that the appearance of Bruix's fleet in the bay of Naples was a near possibility, and having but inadequate means for the subjection of the insurgents, Cardinal Ruffo and Captain Foote of the *Seahorse*, the Russian (Keroindy) and Turkish representatives, had concluded an armistice with the French troops and Neapolitan insurgents who held the castles of Nuovo, Dell Uovo, and Saint Elmo. These castles were, under this armistice, to be evacuated as soon as transports could be found and got ready to carry their garrisons to Toulon. The treaty received the last of the contracting parties' signature on the 23rd of June, and, as an indication that hostilities had ceased, flags of truce were flying from the forts and the *Seahorse*. The following day Nelson, in the *Foudroyant*, arrived at Naples and immediately annulled the treaty.

Mahan thinks that Nelson acted within his right in disallowing the capitulation, but no argument, however ingenious, can ever demonstrate that he had any right to do so; that the arrival of adequate reinforcements—a fleet of eighteen sail— could put an end to a solemn engagement entered into by parties which, before his casting anchor before Naples, represented the various powers. No one can gainsay Alison's words : "The capitulation of the vanquished should ever be held sacred in civilized warfare."

Whether the treaty was infamous or not lies entirely outside the question; though Captain Foote, an honourable gentleman, seeing the circumstances under which it had been contracted, bitterly resented the use of the word. Cardinal Ruffo of the princes della Motta—the individual who gave back to Ferdinand his kingdom—in a warm discussion he had with Nelson on board the flagship, would not admit for an instant the correctness of Nelson's argument, that the treaty and armistice were virtually at an end by the arrival of the fleet.

The admiral, on his own authority, took out of the Polacks the most notorious chiefs of the rebellion, and had them secured on board British men-of-war. His arrival at Naples was not as fortunate for some of the insurgents as he vaunted, and by his action he connived at the execution of men who had come out of the castles in good faith. Nelson showed a very vindictive spirit, hoping that all those who were false to their king and country would be hanged.

An excuse was held to lie in the words " evacuation " and

"embarkation"—a worthless quibble. Really at this period Nelson was labouring under a reproachful infatuation, and with all his talent was unable to look at things in a perfectly reasonable light.

His admirers can find little fault in any of his deeds. Mahan writes : "Despite his fearlessness of responsibility, he was always careful not to overpass the legal limits of his authority, except when able to justify his actions by what at least appeared to himself adequate reasons." These reasons, however, in this case, did not satisfy many right-thinking persons, and Nelson was severely blamed.

He has been censured for his share in the abrupt execution of Prince Francis Caracciolo, and on good grounds. His most ardent defenders cannot deny that he was saturated with the prevailing Neapolitan court feeling, and immensely under the influence of the queen and Lady Hamilton. The name of the latter is unfortunately intimately associated with his. She was a dangerously fascinating, ambitious, and artful woman, who did much to tarnish the glory of our greatest sea-warrior.

A court-martial on Commodore Caracciolo, a subject of the King of the Two Sicilies, was ordered to assemble on board Nelson's flagship, the *Foudroyant*. Nelson himself had worded the charges. The court assembled at 10 a.m. on the 29th of June. Caracciolo was found guilty, and hanged at the foreyard-arm of the *Minerva* the same afternoon.

In the reaction which took place Nelson did not bring his influence to bear against the cruel executions carried out by order of that most feeble monarch, Ferdinand IV. Lord Keith had written to him, after having become acquainted with the details of Caracciolo's execution, "Advise the Neapolitans not to be so sanguinary." Whether this counsel was given or not no evidence exists. The dignity of virtue, the charm of beauty, and the power of knowledge seem to have been alike lost upon the Government. Men and women to the number of 99 were put to death, and of these unfortunates many were of noble birth, others renowned for their learning, and some even exemplary members of the Church.*

* In 1793, Naples had declared war against France, though its own interests did not in any way call for such a step. In 1798, King Ferdinand IV. conceived the Quixotic idea of reinstating the Italian sovereigns. With a badly organized army, not at all seasoned to war, he took the field in the winter, without waiting for Austria, which began operations only in the spring of 1799. He occupied Rome on

With regard to the difference between the two British admirals we borrow Mahan's words: " Friction between these two began at once. . . . Nelson, exasperated at the mere fact of the other's succession to command, speedily conceived for him an antipathy which Keith would have been more than mortal not to return; but it is to the honour of the latter's self-command that, while insisting upon obedience from his brilliant junior, he bore his refractoriness with dignified patience." *

Nelson's disobedience of orders was not overlooked at home. Keith, who had gone to England, was ordered back to the Mediterranean as commander-in-chief, and on this point

the 27th of November, and his forces which entered the city that day quitted it on the 8th of December. They had succeeded during those eleven days in making themselves thoroughly detested. Mack, who persisted in the system of dividing his forces, was beaten by the French on every side, and compelled to make a hasty retreat to Capua. The king, in a state of great fright, embarked on board Nelson's flagship on the 23rd of December, and fled to Sicily.

On the 23rd of January, after three days' hard fighting, the French found themselves established in Naples, and soon proclaimed the Parthenopean Republic. When Macdonald, in consequence of the defeats in Northern Italy, had to quit Naples, Cardinal Ruffo, by the aid of the *lazzaroni*, recovered the capital. Ferdinand then distinguished himself by his ferocity, which only equalled his cowardice.

" The executions commenced; and killing by order of the tribunals was accompanied by murders at the hands of anarchists. Neither age, sex, nor rank were spared. Great was the slaughter in the capital, but none less that in the provinces. The official records of the *Giunta di Stato* show 99 individuals condemned to death and executed; 222 condemned to imprisonment for life; 322 condemned to imprisonment for shorter periods; and 355 exiled. Heading the list of the executed is Francesco Caracciolo, commander-in-chief of the Republican navy, who was hanged and cast into the sea on the 29th of June, 1799, in consequence of a trial, and possibly condemnation, demanded by Nelson; and this sombre page of history closes on the 23rd of April, 1800, with the execution of Luisa Sanfelice, described as young, handsome, of noble blood, and mother of three children. Near the head of the same list, as an honourable distinction, comes as second Mario Pagano, a benign philosopher and a benevolent philanthropist, whom the entire generation regarded with love and respect. Then follow Domenico Cirillo, a distinguished doctor and naturalist; Francis Conforti, a priest certainly second to none for his learning in parochial and canonical lore, and possibly the first of all; Vincenzo Russo, an exemplary youth remarkable for his elevation of mind, eloquence, and humanity, one of the soundest leaders of the Republic; Gabriele Manthoné, minister of war and captain-general of the Republic; Eleonora Fonesca Pimentel, a woman renowned for her literary abilities, and still more for her virtue; then a score or two of illustrious bishops, priests, and professional men. Such a hecatomb is not to be found in the history of modern Italy; it can only be compared to the slaughters ordered by the Revolutionists in France in 1793."—Tullio Fontana, " La battaglia di Marengo del 14 Giugno, 1800, Raccontata al popolo," p. 81.

* Mahan, " The Life of Nelson," vol. i. p. 425.

Mahan writes : " Whether moved only by routine considerations of rank, as afterwards at Copenhagen, or whether his relations at the Sicilian Court, his conduct of affairs at Naples, and his collisions with Keith had excited doubt of the normal balance of his mind, the Admiralty decided to send Keith back." *

Men of pre-eminence, who set full value on their own worth, are, as a rule, impatient of control. However, it is difficult to distinguish up to what point non-compliance with orders is admissible, and may be condoned. What would be considered a breach of discipline in a moderately gifted individual might come to be looked upon as a stroke of genius in a very able man.

Nelson was superior to Lord Keith in military sagacity and insight ; indeed, Lord St. Vincent held that there was but one Nelson ; still there is such a thing as the accident of seniority to which the greatest genius has to submit.

Complying with the instructions he had received, Gantheaume had prepared for sea two Venetian frigates, *La Muiron* of 28 guns, bearing his flag,† and *La Carrère* of 28 guns, captain De la Rue. With these were two small advice-boats of 4 guns, *La Revanche*, ensign Picard, and *L'Indépendant*, ensign Gastaud, with provisions for 400 or 500 men for two months.

On being informed by Marmont that the coast was clear, as the blockading ships had gone to Cyprus for water, or as some say for provisions, Bonaparte quitted Alexandria with the pick of the officers of his army and a few hundred men. Bernadotte, when minister of war, later on, reproached him for not having brought back all his soldiers from Egypt. Always jealous of Bonaparte, Bernadotte spoke at random, and possibly was trying to make excuses for the ill success which had attended the French armies elsewhere in 1799.

Bonaparte and his suite embarked on board a few fishing-boats which lay concealed in a secluded part of the beach, and

---

* Mahan, " The Life of Nelson," vol. ii. p. 3.

† The ship *Muiron* had been named so after one of Bonaparte's aides-de-camp who was killed in the Italian campaign. Muiron, whose gallantry at Toulon had been noticed by Bonaparte, was serving as his aide-de-camp at Arcole. Seeing a bomb about to explode, he threw himself between it and his general, and thus saved his general's life by the sacrifice of his own. When at Saint Helena, the ex-emperor wished to assume the name of Colonel Muiron, such esteem had he for the memory of that brave officer.

were towed to the frigates then riding at anchor about a league from the shore. All told, officers and troops embarking amounted to something between 400 and 500 men. The horses of the regiment of guides, of the generals and of the staff, which had been left to run loose about the beach, went galloping back to Alexandria, whither their natural instinct led them. This created some alarm in the town, which was dissipated only by the arrival of the Turkish groom who led Bonaparte's charger back to Alexandria.

In August, the winds which almost constantly prevail in the Mediterranean make the voyage to France in sailing-ships extremely tedious. The winds were blowing continuously from the north-west, which obliged the ships to steer a north-easterly course along the coast of Africa. So adverse was the weather that they only made 100 leagues in twenty days. However, this long navigation was free from any danger of falling in with the enemy's cruisers, for the French frigates kept between the 32nd and 33rd degree of latitude, hugging the African coast. They were, consequently, sailing in unknown waters, or at least in waters little frequented by mariners, and too far from the route ordinarily followed by ships sailing from Egypt to Europe.

The voyage back to Europe was of long duration ; adverse winds kept the two frigates for three and twenty days on the coast of Africa, ere a favourable south-easterly breeze enabled them to steer for the western coast of Sardinia. The ships sailed close to the shore the whole way, in order that they might be run aground, if necessary, and so escape falling into the hands of the enemy. It proved a weary voyage, in which the dread of being overtaken or stopped by the British cruisers overpowered every other thought. "Should the English approach," said Bonaparte, "I will run ashore upon the sands, march, with the handful of brave fellows and the few pieces of artillery we have with us, to Tunis or Oran, and there find means to re-embark."

A violent west wind, springing up on the 1st of October, drove the ships on the coast of Corsica, and compelled Gantheaume to seek refuge in the harbour of Ajaccio. The *Revanche* had been sent forward to gain information as to the fate of the island, for there was some uncertainty if it still remained French.

Bonaparte was detained in Corsica some days, impatiently

awaiting until favourable winds would allow him to sail out of the bay of Ajaccio. He was fretting to be gone; even his native town and the attention of his citizens having no attraction for him. It was during his stay there that he first heard of the loss of the battle of Novi on the 15th of August, and of Joubert's death; news which naturally added to his impatience.

Lissoni states that Bonaparte received some of the first details of the disasters of Cassano, the Trebbia, and Novi, from two officers of the Cisalpine cavalry, Sessa of Milan, and Lucki of Monza, after his landing in France.

One night the municipality were giving a ball in his honour, when Gantheaume sent one of his officers to intimate that the wind having veered to the south, not a moment was to be lost, and that advantage ought to be taken of this propitious circumstance. Thereupon all hastened on board, sails were set, and the ships steered in the direction of Toulon. This short stay in Corsica proved to be the last visit Bonaparte made to the island where he first saw light.*

After a voyage of fifty days' duration, having only by sheer good fortune escaped between Corsica and France from falling into the hands of a British fleet,† Bonaparte arrived at Fréjus on the 9th of October, 1799. At the moment of his landing the great majority of the French were far from expecting to hear of his return. As the signals had been changed since the departure of the expedition to Egypt, *La Muiron*, not being able to reply to those made by the garrison, was fired upon by the shore batteries.

The spirit of the nation was reflected in the reply the people gave when warned to keep at a distance from *La Muiron*, for the ship had not complied with the laws of quarantine.

---

* In 1793, Bonaparte having quarrelled with Paoli, the latter sent to have him arrested as a traitor to the Corsican cause. In the floor of young Bonaparte's room there was a trap-door which communicated with the cellar; by this trap-door Bonaparte made his escape, and was able to make his way to a vessel lying in port. Had he been captured he would in all probability have been shot, and the history of Europe for the following quarter of a century would have been far different from what it was.

† The fourteen British battle-ships were only sighted at sunset on the 8th of October, and, as the French frigates were steering in their direction, Gantheaume's ships were believed to have belonged to the admiral's squadron. Others assert that the French vessels, being of Venetian build, were believed to be Italian store-ships.

The people fully ignored the risks they incurred, and loudly protested, " We prefer the plague to the Austrians ! "

Egypt was subdued ;* the care of keeping it could not satisfy the ambition of the conqueror ; greater destinies he conceived called him to other lands. The moment was supreme ; France was in a dire situation ; her armies were routed. How sadly changed for the worse had the state of affairs in France become during Bonaparte's absence from Europe !

Defeat had followed defeat in Italy. The Archduke Charles had compelled Jourdan to recross the Rhine, whilst an Austro-Russian army was advancing towards the frontiers of Switzerland, ready to take possession of that country, and thence find a passage into the heart of France. Holland was generally disaffected, and partial insurrections had taken place in Belgium. Little was wanting to bring about a return of the sanguinary days of 1793. The French troops, disgusted, badly paid, insufficiently cared for, were ready to rebel, leaving the eastern and northern frontiers badly defended. In France itself, every province was a prey to anarchy and to the peculation of the constituted authorities. The Royalist bands of Bretagne, the Chouans, had risen afresh, and were organizing themselves to light the flames of civil warfare throughout the country. Disorganization was everywhere perceptible; the highways were infested by robbers, and the whole nation denounced the Government as incapable, and destitute of power, justice, and morality. France was threatened with invasion, and the restoration of the Bourbons seemed inevitable.

What Bonaparte thought of the sad change which had come over the country in such a brief space of time can be learnt by his words to Boutot, who was Barras's secretary. " What have you done," he said, " with the country I left so flourishing ? I left you in peace, and I have found you in war ; I left you victory, and I have found defeat ; I left you conquest, and the enemy are passing our frontiers ; I left you the treasures of Italy, and I find nothing but oppression and poverty. Where are the 100,000 heroes, my companions in arms, whom I left covered with glory ? What has become of them ? Alas ! they are no more. This state of things cannot continue ; in three

---

* Napoleon at Saint Helena declared that from the moment of Nelson's victory at Aboukir, the expedition was doomed ; since an army which cannot have its waste made good can only melt away and end by laying down its arms.

years it will end in despotism; but we will have a Republic founded on the basis of civil liberty, equality, and political toleration."

No wonder, then, that " a change was ardently desired by all classes," and all were looking for a man possessing public confidence, and capable of restoring tranquillity and order by concentrating the supreme power, and giving scope for the development of those institutions, hitherto free in name only, which had been purchased by France at enormous sacrifices.*

Orders had been sent by the Directory for Bonaparte's return from Egypt, but he had crossed them on the voyage, and the messenger sent never landed in Egypt. After his arrival in France his brother Joseph informed him of this fact, and made Fain show him the original drafts. He, however, much preferred to let this circumstance remain unknown, so as to give a more extraordinary semblance to his return.

Nothing caused more intense surprise than Bonaparte's unexpected arrival. While Barras was at dinner on the 9th of October, 1799 (17th Vendémiaire), the following telegraphic despatch was handed to him: "General Bonaparte has landed at Fréjus, followed by generals Berthier, Lannes, Marmont, and Andreossy; he is preparing to set out for Paris."

It was on the 21st Vendémiaire that the citizens of Paris were startled as if by a clap of thunder by the cries, "Bonaparte is in France! He has landed at Fréjus! He arrives!" That same night the news was proclaimed in all the theatres, and received with loud acclamation. The following day the columns of the *Moniteur* contained these short paragraphs—

" 1st.—General Bonaparte arrived on the 17th of this month at Fréjus (birthplace of Siéyès). He was received by an immense multitude, who cried, ' Vive la République!' etc.

" 2nd.—General Moreau has arrived in Paris."

The Directory was at first astonished by the news, and when communicating it to the Councils tried clumsily to tone it down by placing Berthier's name before that of Bonaparte.

Bonaparte's return to France caused Nelson the deepest mortification. He had been baffled in his determination that not a single Frenchman should be suffered to find his way back from Egypt. He certainly took comfort in considering that no blame could attach to himself. Still, as he was at the time

* George Moir Bussey, "History of Napoleon," vol. i. p. 227.

commander-in-chief in the Mediterranean, he cannot be held quite blameless for such supineness.   As the guarding of the coast had been left to a commodore with one ship of the line and two frigates, there could have been no very great difficulty in evading such a small number of ships.

It is difficult to agree with Monsieur Durdent, who states that " when Bonaparte was nothing more than a commander-in-chief, without authority from his Government, he abandoned the army which he had led to Egypt to certain destruction." * He certainly abandoned an army which he had launched on a perilous enterprise, but there was no one in France who would have rescued this army in Egypt. There is pretty good evidence that Bonaparte tried his best in this respect, but he was badly seconded by the French navy. Gantheaume made several attempts, one from Brest in January, 1801, one from Toulon on the 19th of March, and another from the same port on the 27th of April.

Bonaparte declared to Gohier that he left his army to come and share the national perils, so alarmed had he been in Egypt by the dangers which threatened the Republic.

His desertion of his army caused considerable indignation amongst the troops. Michelet, Lanfrey, Walter Scott, and other writers blame Bonaparte for having quitted his army in Egypt. Alphonse de Beauchamp states that, suddenly deserting his army in Egypt, he hastened to France to seize the supreme power which he knew to be up at auction. We may, however, conclude that a nation knows better than any historian of what it is in need. At Fréjus France rushed forward to welcome the daring islander whom she already instinctively recognized as her master; in whom all classes appeared to discern the destined saviour of the country.

The French, in fact, far from reproaching him for his desertion, hailed Bonaparte's return with rapture. His presence was a pledge of safety, a presage of a return of the past glories; it aroused the enthusiasm of the entire population. His voyage from the sunny Riviera to Paris, amidst the ecstasy of the people, resembled a triumphal march. As he went from Fréjus to Lyons he was received with ringing of bells, illuminations and fireworks. At Lyons a brilliant reception awaited him.

* Durdent, "Campagne de Moscou," p. 80, 5th ed.

c

No sooner had the news spread that Bonaparte was on French soil, than a general joy filled all hearts, coupled with a forgetfulness of past misfortunes and present dangers. All voices were ready to cry hail to the mighty warrior, who hardly made a step in his journey from Fréjus to Paris without his ears being pleasingly struck by applause and festive welcomes. From every quarter the French rushed in crowds to behold him, to bow to him, and to proclaim him victorious even before he fought. The healthy, the young, the old, the women, all went, even the sick who could not walk bade their friends carry them where he was about to pass, and in seeing him found a solace for their ailments. France knew that a great man had appeared, and could admire his strength and his power.

The battles of the Pyramids and of Aboukir, the capture of Alexandria and Cairo, the French flag waving over the cataracts and the crumbling ruins of Memphis, were sufficient facts to dazzle the imagination of the French people.* The nation, under the charm of his victories, extolled his abilities, and from the moment he set his foot on French soil confided into his hands all the elements of moral and material power. The French, who had sadly missed his military genius, were grateful for his being again in their midst. Peace was the general aspiration of the country, and the French believed that it was Bonaparte alone who was capable of giving them the peace and rest of which they were so much in need.

This idea was not quite new, for in 1798, before he left for Egypt, a party composed of deputies possessing a certain influence in the two Councils, finding the Directory extremely unpopular, had urged Bonaparte to place himself at the head of the Republic. This, however, he had refused to do, as his good sense told him that he was not strong enough then to stand alone.

On the 16th of October, Bonaparte arrived in Paris, and when, two hours later, he waited on the Directory, the soldiers at the gate recognized their former general and raised loud cries of *Vive Bonaparte!* By the time of his arrival at the capital it was impossible for Bonaparte to make a mistake about the situation. It was only too evident that France was at his feet.

---

* The check before the walls of Saint Jean d'Acre, on the confines of Africa and Asia, Carrion Nisas calls a slight spot, soon obliterated by his return and by his last triumphs.

It is generally believed that up to that moment he had conceived no idea of seizing the reins of government. The acclamations by which he was welcomed on his arrival in Paris, however, put a term to all irresolution. This showed him that he possessed the unbounded popularity without which his daring enterprise could not succeed, and how very easy it would be to assume the supreme authority.

The utmost discontent and dissatisfaction existed. The ten years of revolution had made the people weary of strife and bloodshed. The unbounded distress and anarchy which had followed in the wake of the Revolution had given rise to an intense longing for some sort of orderly control. The impossibility of continuing the government of France for any length of time under the Republican form had come to be recognized by all alike.

The year VII. of the Republic had ended in a sad way for France. The Anglo-Russians in Holland and the Austro-Russians in Italy had proved too much for the French commanders. Every day France was saddened by the reports of fresh reverses, and the people, accusing the Directory as their cause, threatened to overthrow it. Only the battle of Berghen, Massena's victory at Zurich, and Bonaparte's at Aboukir, had managed to prop up the Government.

During her husband's absence in Egypt, Madame Bonaparte had opened her house to a choice and seclusive society; her *salon* was frequented by a number of the ablest men of the time. Of these, the greatest part were devoted to Bonaparte's interests, so that she built a strong party which had come to look upon Bonaparte as the only possible saviour of France. Josephine's conduct may not have been irreproachable, but although she gave cause for jealousy, she made some powerful friends for him at home ; and these he needed.*

Nevertheless, on his return to Paris he refused to see his wife, for he had had suspicions of her honour. After three days, urged by Bourrienne, who made him understand how likely a conjugal quarrel was to interfere with his ambitious plans, he consented to a reconciliation.

* No one can be blind to the fortunate influence which Josephine exercised on Bonaparte's glory and happiness. When, thirteen years later, Napoleon cast away the wedding-ring which bound the two together, his star grew dim and the murmur of the distant thunder commenced to resound in his ears, as if that little ring had been the talisman which had sufficed to stave off all reverses.

Bonaparte attached a good deal of importance to babbling and scandalous tittle-tattle. It more frequently than not furnished him with false reports, and it was this that irritated him against his friends, his courtiers, and his own wife.

In the capital he did not find a vigorous opposition. The men against whom he had to contend were so insignificant that they are not worth mentioning. Indeed, everything was ready for a great change. Barras and his colleagues were at a discount, and for the space of two years had produced nothing but disasters. The majority had no aptitude for governing. The Government, in fact, was composed of incapable men. Siéyès was the least so, and, though a cool, shrewd calculator, possessed of considerable political resources, he was not a man of transcendent talent.

The Directory was tottering; it was absolutely necessary to substitute for it something really imposing, and what, after all, can be more imposing than military glory? As long as the world has existed, how many empires have owed their origin to the irresistible power and renown of a conqueror?

Many weighty motives existed for effecting a change at this critical period ; but the greatest of all was the feebleness of the Government. This was composed of two democratic Chambers, one-third of which was renewed every year, and an elective quinquevirate.

Before the events of the 18th Brumaire, Bonaparte, by his own words, felt thoroughly convinced that France could not exist except under a monarchical form of government ; but at that moment he felt that the country was not yet ripe for so great a change.

Perhaps nothing could afford a better proof of the nullity of the Directory than their inertness, for by making good use of the power which the Constitution gave them they could have easily thwarted the conspiracy for overthrowing the Government. But they were not even of one accord.

Many men who had made their mark during the Revolution had proposed to Moreau that he should place himself at the head of affairs ; but Moreau would not hear of it. He desired them to address themselves to Bonaparte, who, as he said, understood perfectly the art of making war in the streets of Paris. The general stated that he believed himself made to command armies, and had not the least ambition to command the Republic. If Bonaparte became the statesman of the impending revolution, Moreau reasoned that he himself would become the general of the new Government—fine ambition, well worthy of the man. Soldiering, in short, held out more attraction for him than governing. Of the other generals, Augereau, Jourdan, and Bernadotte were openly hostile to Bonaparte. The three were leading members of the Jacobin Club.

Bernadotte was the only one who flatly refused to listen to Bonaparte's arguments. Surrounded by a brilliant crowd of officers, Bonaparte saw him quitting his house in a furious temper, carrying in his breast his revelations, avowing himself his adversary, if not his denunciator. Segur states: " That same night, a meeting, formed of ten deputies of the Council of the Five Hundred, was held in S——'s house. Bernadotte attended it. It was then arranged that at nine o'clock on the morrow the sitting of the Council would open, but that only such as were of their way of thinking would be warned ; that in order to imitate the wisdom shown by the Council of the Ancients in naming Bonaparte general of their guard, the Council of the Five Hundred would choose Bernadotte to command theirs ; and he, fully armed, would remain ready to attend the first call."

Very little trust could be put on any one at that period. Self-interest seems to have overridden every other consideration. The above scheme had been concocted in Salicetti's house, and it was this very Salicetti who hastened to reveal it to Bonaparte. A simple menace sufficed to restrain these conspirators, not one of whom dared to attend the Council.

The majority of the nation seemed to agree that it was high time that some military leader of commanding talent should seize the helm; but of the most noted none possessed the courage and the moral resolution necessary for such a task. Bonaparte had returned, and from the moment he was back all eyes were fixed on him, for he was essentially the man for the emergency. He had the gift, so rare in men, of being able to rule others.

Siéyès spoke plainly enough. " We must have done with declaimers," he said; " what we want is a head and a sword." He expressed nothing more than the vote of the country when he told Bonaparte, " The sole hope of the Republic is in you ; " for Bonaparte was the only man the nation judged able enough to restore peace to desolate France, the only individual who had the genius and the strength necessary for governing the country.

By a blow equally illegal, but equally necessary, he assumed the government of the state. It may be questioned if the necessity, the good of France, did not, after all, sanction the step. Most people might feel inclined to think it did.

Considering how important were the consequences which followed, the revolution of the 18th Brumaire was a mean affair. It must be admitted that in this Bonaparte hardly showed himself equal to the occasion. His measures were extremely feeble, and but for the energy displayed by his brother Lucien he might have scored a failure. Lucien's share in it was still more contemptible. His statement, intended to seduce the soldiers, that a factious band, armed with stilettoes, besieged the tribune and interdicted all freedom of deliberation, was an unblushing falsehood.

The victory of the 18th Brumaire was in point of fact due to Lucien, for there was a moment when the issue was very doubtful, when the soldiers hesitated, as if overcome by some scruple in acting against the Corps Législatif. Lucien saved the situation by declaring that body to be tyrannized over by representatives armed with poignards, by brigands paid with English gold; by solemnly declaring that should his brother ever dare to menace the liberty of Frenchmen he would himself plunge his sword in his breast. It was his fiery address which raised the enthusiasm of the soldiers. After it, all hesitation was at an end, the grenadiers were too willing to invade the hall.

Rœderer was directed to write a letter of resignation for Barras to sign, which was presented to him by Talleyrand and Bruix. This letter contained a remarkable passage, the only instance in which Bonaparte ever paid a tribute of gratitude to Barras for having brought him to the front on the 13th Vendémiaire. Barras was made to declare in this letter that all the perils of liberty having been overcome, thanks to the return of the illustrious warrior to whom he had the good fortune to open the road to glory, he reverted with pleasure to the rank of simple citizen.

Still, the country was much in need of a new man, and necessity, dire necessity, could well afford to overlook any inadequacy in the arrangements. The plot succeeded, and the Directory was overturned. On the 24th of December, 1799, the new constitution was proclaimed, and by this overthrow, which received the name of *la victoire sans larmes*—"victory without tears"—Bonaparte became First Consul. With him were associated two others, but of inferior power, inasmuch as they were to enlighten him by their counsel, but could not restrain him by their vote. In fact, all the authority of government was by the constitution vested in the First Consul, to the joy of the people, who cherished the hope of a new and better government founded on principles of justice and humanity.

On the 10th of November, 1799, Bonaparte, Siéyès, and Ducos were elected provisional consuls. The constitution of the year VIII. was published on the 13th of December, and came into operation on the following day. Bonaparte was elected First Consul by a popular vote, or plebiscite, on the 22nd Frimaire, year VIII. (13th of December, 1799). France had adopted him; France had sided with the strong man, with the man of all others who she thought might be able to give her what she needed so much, peace.

On the 18th Brumaire France saw at its head a warlike chief surrounded with the halo of victory and all the paraphernalia of invincible power. This chief, with his broad and vivid imagination, with the restless energy of his character, was predestined to be amongst the band of those who do and dare, who achieve great deeds. Bonaparte was not made for a quiet life; opportunities undoubtedly helped him to a prominent place in history, but he would have made his mark in the world even without them.

Looking at the sad condition into which the Republic had drifted for want of an able direction, it was not merely a general that France needed. What she required at that time was a thoroughly able statesman. The new head of the state had exceptional endowments. Not only was he remarkable at the head of armies, but he could acquit himself with distinction of the various functions of government. His genius was pre-eminent, and his grasp of knowledge was not limited to one single subject. He soon proved to France and to Europe that he was as conspicuously successful in the cabinet as in the field. As a writer well puts it, he united in his own person the various talents of the sword, the gown, and the finances.*

* It was remarked of the Emperor Napoleon how, even at the period of his greatest prosperity, he never lost the habit of inquiring into the price of articles, so as to ascertain if what was demanded was just.

In ingenuity of plan, audacity, and above all celerity of movement, he had outshone all the competitors he had yet met. Amongst the higher officers of the army there was not one of equal ability and weight; Moreau and Bernadotte in breadth of knowledge and in capacity could not be compared to Bonaparte. He possessed the moral courage without which no man can be truly great. To his natural impetuosity he united a remarkable decision of character. His was an iron will incapable of enduring opposition or contradiction, a quality of great help at that supreme moment.

He had unbounded confidence in himself, but though he appeared to trust overmuch in his good fortune, nevertheless he never neglected any precaution which it was possible to adopt. He never missed examining diligently all the facts and circumstances of a case; he always considered things under every imaginable point of view, and prepared beforehand for any failure or mischance. Let the after-result be what it would, he was consequently never taken unprepared.

It was his breadth of knowledge that had captivated the mind of the people. His disposition was also marked by an incredible degree of pertinacity, and by a scornful contempt for the feebleness of human nature.

Not only was he an able organizer and a thorough master of detail, he was more, he was a deep thinker and a man of great circumspection. No one, like him, could hold in his mind the threads of a multitude of different combinations.

Alert, masterful, skilful, and a thorough believer in his destiny, Bonaparte was created to guide the destinies of a mighty nation. Now and then, only at very rare intervals, like meteors, men of this stamp are born. Of him Johnston wrote:

" A frame of adamant, a soul of fire,
No danger fright him, and no labour tire."

His influence over all around him seemed equally electric and irresistible. All who approached him were captivated by the versatility of his gifts, the keenness of his intellect, and the seductive charm of his speech.* Penetrating as his glance was, he possessed the power of banishing all expression from his face

---

* Of the personal fascination he exercised there is the well-known story of Lord Keith, who, after an interview with the ex-emperor, blurted out, " Damn the fellow, if he had obtained an interview with His Royal Highness (the Prince Regent), in half an hour they would have been the best friends in England."

at will. His visage told nothing of what was actually passing in his mind. The fascination this extraordinary man exercised upon all who heard him was so potent as to inspire the greatest confidence.

With regard to his universal supremacy, Count Balmain, the Russian Commissioner at Saint Helena, wrote many years after : " What is most astonishing is the ascendency that this man, dethroned, a prisoner, surrounded by guards and keepers, exercises over all who come near him. Everything at Saint Helena bears the impress of his superiority. The French tremble at his aspect, and think themselves too happy to serve him. . . . The English no longer approach him but with awe. Even his guardians seek anxiously for a word or a look from him. No one dares to treat him as an equal."

Never was a master so adored, and even privations and dire sufferings were incapable of lessening the devotion with which he was served by his soldiers.

Fitchett says of Bonaparte that, visionary as his character was, "it was marked by the hard-headed common sense, the grasp of practical details, the cool vision of realities such as we associate with the intellect of a Lowland Scot and of a Dutch burgomaster." *

"Nothing," wrote Meneval, " is more likely to strike the imagination than the prestige exercised by a man who has probably no equal in history, and in whose person Providence was pleased to unite an incomparable genius, fortune without limits, and an excess of adversity. To this imposing memory are attached imperishable souvenirs of glory and at the same time of sorrow."

Taking an impartial view of this great man, of his brilliant genius, of his remarkable deeds, it is impossible to deny that he was a great success.

Having now become the First Magistrate of the Republic, Bonaparte enjoyed, as he very well deserved, the entire confidence of the nation. The general wish had been to see him at the head of the Government, and he was nothing loth to take up the reins. The selection of capable coadjutors is always the mark of a great man, and in nothing does he show his ability more than in his choice of his colleagues. Bonaparte at once selected capable ministers, men who enjoyed a good reputation.

---

* Fitchett, "How England saved Europe," vol. i. p. 337.

Monsieur Gaudin received the portfolio of the finances; Talleyrand had that of foreign affairs; Berthier, of war.

On Talleyrand's advice, Bonaparte retained the direction of all that pertains to politics—namely, the Home, Foreign, and Police departments. Besides these he controlled the War and Marine—in all a pretty laborious task for any one man. But his was a master mind, and the complication of affairs and interests he attended to never once clouded his perception.

The First Consul not only conquered the enemies of his country, but he grappled with the chaos of the French Revolution, and reduced it to order. He had hardly been in office one month ere all the men of ability he had gathered round him, and whose opinions he had solicited, testified to the quickness of his apprehensions and the correctness of his views. All who had worked with him declared that he was a thorough administrator and politician. But what made Bonaparte more than anything else acceptable to the French nation was that the world also recognized in him civil and military talents of the highest order.

The First Consul was soon governing by himself, without paying much regard to the other consuls or to the two legislative commissions. Even before the constitution of the year VIII. had been accepted and had become law, he had repealed the law of hostages, recalled the proscribed prisoners from the Isle of Oléron and from Sinnamari, most of them transported on the 18th Fructidor, had reformed the ministry, and distributed the chief commands in the army.

Nature had endowed him with that rare ascendency which is given only to a few men, of leading and coercing the rest. No one will ever contest that he possessed in a pre-eminent degree the instinct of governing. His steering of the bark of state was very remarkable in a man who up to that moment had not made his apprenticeship in the art of governing.

Siéyès comprised the whole of his gifts in one short sentence, '*Il sait tout, il peut tout, il fait tout.*" With good reason in Bonaparte was epitomized the saying, *Knowledge is power.* On all matters he took in hand he left the imprint of his practical mind.

Nearly all were reconciled to Bonaparte's leading, and submitted in silence to an authority which they felt they could not resist. The army, that great power in the state, was dazzled by his brilliant exploits; most of it had rallied to his standards, and it was his heart and soul. When he returned from his first Italian campaign, it was observed that the troops made him the subject of their songs, in which they lauded him to the skies. Their verses expressed a wish that the lawyers should be turned out and the general made king. On the 18th Brumaire the very guards of the Directory sided with Bonaparte. When enjoined to receive no orders but such as emanated from him, who by a decree of the Council of the Ancients had been appointed to command the troops, their startled commanding officer consulted his soldiers, and they answered with shouts of joy. The same occurred when he addressed the grenadiers from the Council of the Ancients.

There were signs on every side that at last a strong hand had seized the reins of public affairs. A general improvement was soon seen; a brighter future loomed in view. Domestic tranquillity was being gradually re-established throughout the country. Churches were reopened for public worship, religion was freely practised. Emigrants were wending their way back, and recent misfortunes and terrible scenes of violence were being forgotten.

Alison writes : " There is nothing more striking in European history than the sudden resurrection of France under the government of this great man." Indeed, what he was able to do in such a short space of time seems miraculous. Called to power at a period when things in France were at a very low ebb, he completely pacified the Vendée, revived public credit, and placed 250,000 men on a war-footing, with a reserve of 100,000 more.

The five years in which Bonaparte governed France as First Consul were undoubtedly his best. That was the period of his greatest and most enduring renown. It was during the Consulate, in a number of interviews which he had with erudite and practical men, that he acquired the science of finance, of industry, of commerce, of administration and of foreign affairs. He retained all their lore; he forgot nothing of what he heard.

He never disdained to seek the advice of any who were willing to let him, so as to judge if their counsel was in any way preferable to his own thoughts. Nor would he be intentionally deceived, if the deception was attempted with the sole object of pleasing him.

There remained to stamp out the Jacobins, who were agitating in their clubs and papers, and at the same time to check the Royalists in their machinations in the west and south-west of France. He proved equal to the occasion, accomplished this, and laid hands on the low revolutionists who had grovelled in the mud since the 18th Fructidor. Some of them he deported, some he confined in La Rochelle. In this manner he took a first step towards repressing a bloody anarchy with a strong hand.

One of his first thoughts also on coming into power was the army, and naturally enough, considering that the hostility of the European powers had not abated in the very least. It was no secret that they still persisted in their determination of subduing and humiliating France.

As a soldier and conqueror, and that is the light in which he should be examined in this study, he had no equal. His genius for war has never been questioned. His exploits were greater than those of Hannibal and Cæsar. The tactics he followed were singularly his own. Surprise, despatch, and promptitude were their prominent features. His conceptions and their execution commonly followed each other as quick as thunder succeeds the lightning. He was conquered, but only by a very powerful combination of all the sovereigns of Europe.

What must have been the working of the master mind where germinated and grew the most original and daring conceptions! Bonaparte had the capacity of supervising operations down to the most minute details; nothing ever escaped his eye. He was not content with planning, he went further. He examined the difficulties and how to overcome them, sketched out the manner in which his plans were to be carried out, how the impediments were to be thrust aside, and devised the means. He was a strict disciplinarian; from his youth he had been accustomed to acknowledge no master and to command; once at the head of the nation, he obeyed no laws but those of his own creation. As emperor, he used to be greatly irritated by any opposition or resistance to his will; nevertheless, no man could, as Alison says, better appreciate dignified and honourable conduct in an adversary.

Bonaparte worked regularly from twelve to fifteen hours a day. A few years after Marengo, in 1803, Rapp, who was one of his aides-de-camp, speaking of the duties the officers in attendance on him were called to perform, gives us an idea of his restless activity. " One would absolutely require to be made of iron to support it. The First Consul lives in the saddle and in his carriage. He has no sooner alighted from the latter, than away he goes on horseback for ten or twelve hours together. He talks with the men, and examines and looks into everything himself."

CHAPTER II.

BONAPARTE'S PROPOSALS FOR PEACE.

Bonaparte proposes peace to the King of England—Reply from Lord Grenville—
His lordship urges the restoration of the Bourbons—Pitt believes in the exhaustion of France—Does not think there was sufficient guarantee for a durable
peace—The advantages would be all for France—Bonaparte was sincere in his
wish for peace—Nothing was ready for war—Austria not likely to conclude
peace on the basis of the Campo Formio Treaty—Was already busy calling on
the auxiliary states to arm—France needed and desired peace—The national
pride hurt by England's refusal—Bonaparte sets to pacify the Vendée—France
declares in his favour, and helps him to prepare for war—Volney's forecast of
Bonaparte.

FOLLOWING great calamities and distress, rest and security come
to be looked upon as the greatest godsends. After nearly eight
years of war, it was but natural that the great majority of the
French people should be longing for peace. The French Revolution had commenced with hunger, and the many years of
struggle which ensued were not conducive to prosperity. Peace
was, in fact, necessary to complete public felicity. How, in fact,
but through peace, could commerce, industry, and public credit
be restored?

From the moment that Bonaparte had become First Consul,
and the destinies of France had been placed in his hands, he
showed the greatest desire to let his country enjoy an honourable peace. He had promised peace to the Republic, and the
first step he took, after seizing the reins of government, was to
make proposals of peace to the King of England and to the
Emperor of Germany. As the head of the French nation, he
directly addressed the former of these monarchs on the 25th of
December, 1799, barely six weeks after a revolution had placed
him in power, so neglecting the customary channel of diplomatic
intercourse.

He wrote with unostentatious simplicity, announcing his

accession to power, and suggesting a cessation of hostilities which had for the last eight years injured commerce, impaired national well-being, and destroyed domestic happiness. His words were, " Called by the wishes of the French nation to occupy the first station in the Republic, I think it proper, on entering into office, to make a direct communication to your Majesty. Must the war, which has for eight years ravaged the four quarters of the globe, be eternal? Are there no means of coming to an understanding? * How can the two most en-lightened nations of Europe, powerful and strong beyond what their independence and safety require, sacrifice to ideas of vain greatness the benefits of commerce, internal prosperity, and domestic happiness? How has it happened that they do not feel that peace is of the first necessity, as well as the truest glory? These sentiments cannot be foreign to the heart of your Majesty, who reigns over a free nation with the sole view of rendering it happy. You will see in this overture only the effect of a sincere desire to contribute efficaciously, for the second time, to a general pacification, by a step' speedy, implying confidence, and disengaged from those forms which, however necessary to disguise the dependence of feeble states, prove only in those which are strong a mutual desire of deceiving each other. France and England may, by the abuse of their strength, continue for a time, to the misfortune of nations, to retard the period of their being exhausted; but I will venture to say, the fate of all civilized nations is attached to the ter-mination of a war which involves the whole world."

Lord Grenville, the English minister of foreign affairs, sent, on the 4th of January, a brusque letter to Talleyrand, refusing all negotiation with a Government the stability of which was not assured. "The king," he wrote, "has given frequent proofs of his sincere desire for the re-establishment of secure and permanent tranquillity in Europe. He neither is, nor has been, engaged in any contest for a vain or false glory. He has had no other view than that of maintaining against all aggression the rights and happiness of his subjects. For these he has contended against an unprovoked attack; and for the same objects he is still obliged to contend. Nor can he hope

---

* This brings to mind one of Bonaparte's letters to the Grand Vizier, which commences with, "Alas! why are the Sublime Porte and the French nation, after having been friends for so many years, now at war with each other?"

that this necessity could be removed by entering at the present
moment into negotiation with those whom a fresh revolution
has so recently placed in the exercise of power in France ; since
no real advantage can arise from such negotiation to the great
and desirable object of a general peace, until it shall distinctly
appear that those causes have ceased to operate which originally
produced the war, and by which it has been since protracted,
and in more than one instance renewed. The same system, to
the prevalence of which France justly ascribes all her present
miseries, is that which has also involved the rest of Europe in a
long and destructive warfare, of a nature long since unknown to
the practice of civilized nations. For the extension of this
system, and for the extermination of all established Governments, the resources of France have, from year to year, and in
the midst of the most unparalleled distress, been lavished and
exhausted. To this indiscriminate spirit of destruction, the
Netherlands, the United Provinces, the Swiss Cantons, his
Majesty's ancient allies, have successively been sacrificed.
Germany has been ravaged ; Italy, though now rescued from
its invaders, has been made the scene of unbounded rapine and
anarchy. His Majesty has himself been compelled to maintain
an arduous and burdensome contest for the independence and
existence of his kingdom.

  "While such a system continues to prevail, and while the
blood and treasure of a numerous and powerful nation can be
lavished in its support, experience has shown that no defence
but that of open and steady hostility can be availing. The
most solemn treaties have only prepared the way for fresh
aggressions ; and it is to a determined resistance alone that is
now due whatever remains in Europe of security for property,
personal liberty, social order, or religious freedom. For the
security, therefore, of these essential objects, his Majesty cannot
place his reliance on the mere renewal of general professions of
pacific dispositions. Such dispositions have been repeatedly
held out by all those who have successively directed the resources of France to the destruction of Europe, and whom the
present rulers have declared to have been, from the beginning
and uniformly, incapable of maintaining the relations of peace
and amity. Greatly, indeed, will his Majesty rejoice whenever
it shall appear that the dangers to which his dominions and
those of his allies have so long been exposed have really

ceased; * whenever he shall be satisfied that the necessity for resistance is at an end; that, after the experience of so many years of crimes and miseries, better principles have ultimately prevailed in France; and that all the gigantic projects of ambition, and all the restless schemes of destruction, which have endangered the very existence of civil society, have at length been finally relinquished: but the conviction of such a change, however agreeable to his Majesty's wishes, can result only from experience and the evidence of facts.

"The best and most natural pledge of its reality and permanence would be the restoration of that line of princes, which for so many centuries maintained the French nation in prosperity at home and consideration and respect abroad. Such an event would at once have removed, and will at any time remove, all obstacles in the way of negotiation or peace. It would confirm to France the unmolested enjoyment of its ancient territory; and it would give to all the other nations in Europe, in tranquillity and peace, that security which they are now compelled to seek by other means. But, desirable as such an event must be, both to France and the world, it is not to this mode exclusively that his Majesty limits the possibility of secure and solid pacification. His Majesty makes no claim to prescribe to France what shall be the form of her government, or in whose hands she shall vest the authority necessary for conducting the affairs of a great and powerful nation. He looks only to the security of his own dominions and those of his allies, and to the general safety of Europe. Whenever he shall judge that such security can in any manner be attained, as resulting either from the internal situation of that country, from whose internal situation the danger has arisen, or from such other circumstances, of whatever nature, as may produce the same end, his Majesty will eagerly embrace the opportunity to concert with his allies the means of a general pacification. Unhappily, no such security hitherto exists; no sufficient evidence of the principles by which the new Government will be directed; no reasonable ground by which to judge of its stability."

The British Cabinet had no desire to conclude peace. Lord

---

* With regard to the dangers which threatened his own dominions, his Majesty was right enough. But his ally, Austria, was not so disinterested. Austria did not fight so much for a principle as for an expansion of her territories.

Grenville's despatch was clearly not couched in that sense ;
it gave no hope. It reproached France, and justly too, for all
that had passed during the last twelve years, but it gave no
promise of suspending hostilities to judge " of the principles by
which the new Government would be directed." The main condition would seem plainly enough to be contained in the last
paragraph, the restoration of the ancient line of kings. This
was a stipulation which any statesman might have at once seen
to have been tantamount to an abrupt rejection of the First
Consul's advances. It also ignores the fact that it was the
weakness and irresolution of one of these same kings that had
indirectly brought about the Revolution.

Bonaparte had disappointed the hopes which not a few of the
Royalists had formed of him. A fraction of the party had persisted in regarding him as a probable restorer of the royal family
of the Bourbons. He might certainly have accepted the *rôle* of
a Monck, and by reinstating the Bourbons have restored peace
to France. But what prospect, after all, did such a *rôle* offer to
an officer who was young, who had tasted victory, who was
devoured by endless ambition, and who had unbounded faith in
his star and a firm confidence in the future ? It is very doubtful, moreover, if the people would have countenanced the return
of the Bourbons ; for the insistence that Europe had the greatest
interest in the restoration of the Bourbons had great effect in
making the old dynasty more than ever unpopular in France.
As events proved, an entirely new dynasty was much more
acceptable.

Had the answering of Bonaparte's letter rested with Pitt, the
reply would probably not have wounded the French half as
much, for Grenville, as will be seen, sent to the foreign minister
at Paris a supercilious and overbearing note,* which in effect
was nothing more nor less than a fresh declaration of war. He
told Talleyrand that his Majesty could not place any reliance in
the mere renewal of general professions of pacific dispositions.
He demanded more tangible guarantees, the chief of which
appeared to be the restoration of the Bourbon dynasty. Even
King George did not like the tone of the reply, and it is stated
that he wrote on the margin of the dispatch, "In my opinion
much too strong, but I suppose it must go."

* This answer the Opposition styled as lofty, imperious, declamatory, and
insulting.

Grenville tried to dictate terms to a soldier on whom fortune had been singularly smiling, and one, consequently, not likely to submit to anything couched in terms so authoritative.

Whilst Lord Grenville was inditing this letter to the First Consul, Pitt, who had decided on the continuation of the war before Bonaparte even wrote to the king, was arranging with the enemies of France the subsidies they were to receive to keep their armies in the field. When Bonaparte returned to France, France was much exhausted by the long continuous wars, but by no means yet in a desperate state. Pitt committed the mistake of believing that France was completely exhausted, foreign emissaries being eager to make the world believe that France was reduced to a miserable condition. This might possibly have been not far from the truth had the destinies of the country rested in the hands of an incompetent and corrupt Directory. But with the First Consul, who knew how to call forth fresh resources, at the head of affairs, the case was different. Pitt's refusal to come to terms and to bring the war to an end gave Bonaparte Marengo and the empire.

It was not a blind hatred of France, but the true interests of England, which made Pitt refuse the peace proposed by Bonaparte. According to him there was no sufficient guarantee of such peace as was desirable so long as France continued to hold Belgium and could dispose of the maritime resources of Holland, which constituted a menacing condition against England. According to Pitt's opinion, all the victories of 1799 did not make up for this.

A point which was fully debated in the House of Commons was whether the amount of confidence which might be accorded to Bonaparte was sufficient to guarantee entering into negotiations with him. Dundas, who led the debate, asked whether it were possible to place any trust in a man who whilst in Egypt had abjured his own God when he deemed this to be useful to his designs. That in treating with the former Government, the treating was carried on with the French nation, whereas now it would be with Bonaparte alone, because Bonaparte was everything in France. To accept his overtures would be to recognize him, to consolidate him, to become the instrument of his will.

That France must have constantly fresh stimulants has often been said. Pitt thought that the seizure of the consular throne by Bonaparte made France more dangerous on account of his restless and insatiable spirit, consequently he deemed it unwise to sheathe the sword.*

Yet Pitt was eager enough for a cessation of warfare. Only, being a far-seeing statesman, he discerned that the actual state of the situation in France did not hold out any lasting security for peace. If he advocated the prosecution of the struggle— which he had named "a social war"—it was because he could foresee that a peace under the existing conditions would only prove a momentary truce, to the advantage of the French, who would await more propitious circumstances to renew hostilities. He believed that by persevering a few more months the coalition would impose a more advantageous and durable peace.

Pitt argued thus : "France would now derive great advantages from a general peace. Her commerce would revive, her seamen be renewed, her sailors acquire experience, and the power which hitherto had been so victorious on land, would speedily become formidable on another element. What benefit could that bring to Great Britain ? Are our harbours blockaded, our commerce interrupted, our dockyards empty ? Have we not, on the contrary, during the war acquired an irresistible preponderance on the seas; and is not the trade of the world rapidly passing into the hands of our merchants ? Bonaparte would acquire immense popularity by being the means of bringing about an accommodation with this country ; if we wish to establish his power, and permanently enlist the energy of the Revolution under the banners of a military chieftain, we have only to fall into the snare which he has so artfully prepared. In turbulent republics it has ever been an axiom to maintain internal tranquillity by external action. It was on that principle that the war was commenced by Brissot and continued by Robespierre, and it is not likely to be forgotten by the military chief who has now succeeded to the helm of affairs." †

In Parliament he said, "It is because I love peace sincerely that I cannot content myself with vain words ; it is because I love peace sincerely that I cannot sacrifice it by seeing the shadow when the reality is not within my reach. *Cur igitur*

---

* " William Pitt the younger was born at Hayes in 1759, in the full splendour of his father's famous ministry ; in the year that saw Quebec fall before the dying Wolfe ; that saw the glorious but inconclusive victory of Minden ; that saw Hawke in November storm and crush the French fleet—the year that produced Burns and Wilberforce."—Rosebery, " Life of Pitt."

† Alison, "History of Europe," chap. xxx. p. 256.

pacem nolo! quia infida est, quia periculosa, quia esse non potest." *

In Parliament the question of peace was fully discussed. Fox reflected the mistrust of the Government when he said that they wished to keep Bonaparte some time longer at war as a state of probation. Nevertheless, the desire for peace was very general, and a proof of this was given by the transports of joy and enthusiasm with which Lauriston, the French envoy, bearing the terms of the treaty, was received in London in the autumn of 1801.†

For a man like the First Consul, who had only just assumed the reins of government, in a country in which public affairs had been so grossly mismanaged, nothing would appear more natural than that he should really desire peace. Bold indeed would have been the man who would have voted for war at a time when the armies were defeated and discouraged, the treasury exhausted, and the people disunited.

Peace was necessary because nothing was ready for war. It was necessary to gain time, and at that moment war was very unpopular in France.

When Bonaparte landed at Fréjus, France was not only without an army, but without the resources necessary for raising one. The department of war had shared in the general mismanagement. After the 18th Brumaire, when Bonaparte assumed the presidency of the Consulate, Dubois de Crancé was the minister at war. No one could have been more ignorant of his duties. He was unable to furnish a single report on the state of the army. Many corps had been formed in the provinces, of which even the very existence was unknown to the minister. When asked for an account of the pay, he simply replied, " We don't pay the army." When called upon to furnish the returns of the victualling office, he declared that it was quite out of his province. "What, then, about the clothing?" "We do not clothe the troops." All this had to be thoroughly rearranged before any one could think of going to war; for none knew better than Bonaparte that energy in a campaign cannot atone for the neglect of previous preparations.

Many writers hold that all Bonaparte desired to do was to create a great effect, that he neither hoped nor desired peace,

---

* Words borrowed from Cicero.

† The Treaty of Amiens was not definitely signed till the 27th of March, 1802.

but simply wished the French people to believe that he had done all in his power to obtain it.

The great desire for peace was not a fiction or a political make-believe, it was Bonaparte's prevailing thought as being imperative to secure the safety of France. It was said that he was insincere; that the desire for peace he paraded was not to be trusted; that the dealings of the French with other nations, even when in progress of treating, did not inspire confidence. But the First Consul must have yearned for peace more than the people. Peace he needed, for his position was anything but well established. Still, the peace he wanted for his country was not to be a cringing peace, but one adorned with laurels.

Lanfrey tells how elated Bonaparte was at England and Austria having rejected his pacific proposals. He had attained his object, which was to pose as a moderate and pacific chief. He believes that no one more ardently desired war. His letters to England and Austria were apparently written more to irritate than to convince foreign rulers. Now, however, he could throw the responsibility of the war on the coalesced powers.

Madame de Staël has written : " Nothing was more contrary to Bonaparte's nature or his interest than to have made peace in 1800." These words were evidently written after the event, and it is notorious how that woman of genius detested the emperor.* The pacification of the Vendée, which occupied the First Consul's attention at that moment, would tend to show that the desire for peace was not strange to his mind.

Such has been the habit of attributing ulterior motives to all Napoleon's actions, that he is never given credit for having acted in good faith. We are fully convinced, however, that in this instance he would have welcomed peace, more especially as it was most convenient for him. Surrounded as he was

---

* From the very first she distrusted Bonaparte's designs, and her *salon* was the head-quarters of the anti-Bonapartist faction. She used to call Napoleon Robespierre on horseback (*c'est Robespierre à cheval*), and thought it great wit. But Napoleon was a genius, a master of the art of war. Of the two, one raised an empire, was and shall ever be the glory of France ; the other was a monster, the evil genius of the Reign of Terror, who caused streams of innocent blood to flow through every part of the country.

To Madame de Staël's honour, she bravely sought to save the life of Marie Antoinette by writing a pamphlet, " Reflexions sur le procès de la Reine, par une Femme," urging the impolicy and injustice of further severity against the royal family, and appealing to the women of France to defend the queen by the arms which Nature had given them.

with perils, at the head of an uncertain Government, menaced by a powerful coalition of which England was the head, compelled to press heavily upon the resources of an impoverished people, it was surely in his interest to seek a peaceful arrangement. To declare that he was acting a part, that the sole object he had in view when he wrote to the King of England and to the Emperor of Austria was to prove to the people his anxiety to put an end to the scourges of war, and that the proposals for peace were simply a mask to veil aggressive intentions, cannot be true. Nor can we tax him with bad faith, had he, under cover of this peace, laboured to perfect his army, as was supposed to have been his intention.

When he was emperor it was another thing. Then it was said, and with truth, that no one could count on peace from one month to another.

Europe had combined to crush France and place her without the pale of social community. The British Cabinet had steadily followed that policy. Peace was only to be made with that country when it had been thoroughly humiliated. Pitt did not relish seeing Malta and Egypt remain in the hands of the French if the proposed peace was concluded. Even more he desired the restitution of Belgium and the renunciation of the influence the French Republic exercised over Holland. Nothing short of this would be accepted as a basis of an arrangement. This, however, the Consuls were not likely to concede; there was scarcely any hope of their going back from the Treaty of Campo Formio, little inclination towards giving and taking.*

Mathieu Dumas pertinently remarks that peace could not have been made without some concessions by the French; that Bonaparte could not endanger his popularity at the very commencement of his administration by concluding an humiliating treaty.

Our belief is that when Bonaparte proposed peace he was seriously disposed to come to some amicable arrangement,† but

---

* When, at a later date, Pitt, through Lord Minto, who was at the time the British Ambassador at Vienna, made overtures for peace, the French tried to take advantage of this amicable disposition, and stipulated that they should be allowed, while the negotiations were pending, to send supplies to their army in Egypt and likewise to their garrison at Malta, which place was then blockaded by a British fleet. These were terms beyond what was reasonable, no doubt, but recent success had emboldened the French to make such demands.

† Sir Walter Scott adduces as a proof of the sincerity of Bonaparte's desire for

that when treating was denied to him he at once saw what political capital he could make of the summary rejection of his overtures.

Very probably no lasting peace was practicable, and nothing more than a truce the ulterior object of Bonaparte's overtures to the British Government, nevertheless it cannot be denied that it was the hatred of all his neighbours that thrust war upon him. They refused to recognize in him a new order of things, political as well as military, and would not give him a chance. Rosebery acknowledges that "in the first period of the Consulate, Bonaparte was almost an ideal ruler," and an ideal ruler is not one who seeks to plunge his nation into war simply to satisfy his own personal ambition. No more can any one be described as such who provokes a flat refusal, simply for the purpose of putting himself in a good light with his subjects. The emperor certainly admits in his own memoirs that when he made proposals to Pitt he had no serious intention to conclude peace, but on this point, as on many others, it is doubtful what amount of credence can be placed on these memoirs. Bonaparte could, at any rate, well declare that he had proposed peace to the Cabinet of St. James's and of Vienna, and that his amicable overtures had been rejected.

In replying to Lord Grenville, he denounced England as the author of the war which had raged since 1792 and was about to be resumed. He reminded the king at the same time that he himself, as First Consul, ruled by the consent of the people. In one sense he had a right to complain, for it was Great Britain that was the mainspring of the coalition; and the majority of the Parliament were most decidedly in favour of a continuance of the war.

Peace did not suit the Austrians, who deemed it inadvisable to stop short in their career of success. It was nothing more than could be expected that they would refuse to treat when the basis laid down by the First Consul was the Treaty of Campo Formio. How could Austria consent to this whilst still in possession of Lombardy, Piedmont, and a portion of the Papal States? She consequently replied that she could not treat except in conjunction with her allies. Consequently, nothing remained but to fight.

peace his moderation after the signal victories of Marengo and Hohenlinden, when the conditions imposed were not more advantageous to France than those of Campo Formio.

On the 4th of December—three weeks before the First Consul addressed himself to the rulers of Austria and Great Britain in the interests of peace—the Archduke Charles issued circulars to the several states of the German empire to urge them to raise fresh levies. He went on to show the futility of hoping for a durable peace with a country in such a state of revolutionary excitement as France, adding that France was not likely to be less formidable or more pacific now that all the power of government had been concentrated in the hands of a successful chief.

It seems particularly strange that, in the face of this urgent appeal, Archduke Charles should have strongly advised his Government not to fight. This counsel was pressed very strongly on the grounds that Russia was withdrawn on one hand and Bonaparte was added on the other. The Archduke was removed from his command, having lost confidence in the issue of the approaching contest.

The First Consul must not be accused of insincerity for having, early in the month of January, with the other consuls, decreed the formation of an Army of Reserve. What other Government, however much it might have desired peace, would have neglected to make preparations when the enemy threatened two of its frontiers?

There can be no question that it was peace, and not war, that the French nation so ardently desired; nevertheless, it must have been evident to all that, according to the Latin saying, *Si vis pacem, para bellum*, the best guarantee for peace was speedy preparation for war and the creation of an army which would impose respect. Bonaparte fully comprehended the aspirations of the people, and intended that the French should be thoroughly persuaded not only that the new chief magistrate was inclined to bring about a general peace, but also that he would give it to them the moment he could do so with honour.

The coalesced powers, as we have seen, were not to be conciliated. Nothing seemed likely to satisfy them short of the restoration of the royal family of France, and the punishment of the Republicans. With the exception of the Czar of Russia, who had commanded his troops to withdraw behind the confines of his dominions, the other powers took every possible measure for insuring the success of the next campaign. Austria, it had been agreed, would furnish the men, Great Britain the funds.

Pitt rendered Bonaparte an immense service. Till then public opinion in France had been all in favour of peace. The disdainful rejection of the peace proposals deeply wounded the national pride, and the people became exasperated with England. The consequence was that all parties soon became convinced that to obtain peace it was absolutely necessary to conquer; that peace could only be the reward of victory. The entire nation promptly stepped forward ready to make any sacrifice. France was prepared to grant to the First Consul all that he wanted. War, in short, became very popular. The nation had not forgotten the brilliancy of his early Italian campaigns, and how utterly indifferent he had shown himself to any consideration beyond those which tended to advance the interests of France.

The French nation had by this time undergone a change. The fanaticism entertained for liberty had passed into a craving for dominion, for glory; an ambition had taken possession of every one to carry the French name very far. Of the French people a goodly number were casting longing looks to the other side of the Alps, thinking of the smiling Italian provinces which the incapacity of the Directory had lost. Bonaparte promised them victory. "Frenchmen!" he said, "we have conquered liberty. But it still remains for us to conquer peace, which we have in our power to do. I will lead you in person, and in the fullest confidence conduct you to victory." He had become the idol of the Parisians, and from him alone they expected everything.

Still, Bonaparte spoke to all of peace, of humanity, of the termination of the existing evils, of an age of prosperity about to commence for the general happiness of the human race. He was a master of the art of seduction, and his plausible words raised great hopes in many breasts. At one period he professed himself willing to sacrifice his life if peace could only be obtained.

Meanwhile he devoted himself to putting down internal troubles. Hoche, by his prudence and firmness and the employment of a number of movable columns, had made an end of the civil war; but this was not long in breaking out afresh. Its original ennobling character had disappeared. It was no longer a people in arms for the defence of its religion, of its traditions, or of its allegiance. The Vendeans were absolutely tired of war; they no longer looked upon the Republican troops with dread; they prayed only for peace and quiet. The strife in Brittany and Normandy had degenerated. It was carried on by feeble bands of vagabonds and rolling stones, allured by the love of pillage, the stopping of diligences and the abduction of public revenues. The Directory had closed their eyes on these disorders, which were the natural outcome of the general sad state of affairs, and the Royalist party had taken advantage of their neglect. The resistance of the insurgents was encouraged by the British Cabinet and by the promises of help, in which it was profuse.

Bonaparte took decisive measures for bringing this state of things to an end. He sent Brune from Holland to the banks of the Loire with 20,000 men. These troops swept all parts of the Vendée, separated the various bands, and pursued them in every direction. Georges, conquered at Grand-Champ, laid down his arms. Luzannet, Bourmont, La Prevelay, beaten in every encounter and deserted by their soldiers, had to submit. The last in arms in Brittany and in Normandy, overpowered by the numerical superiority of the forces brought against them, were compelled to capitulate. Count Frotté was betrayed, tried, and shot.

Frotté had irritated the First Consul by holding him up to ridicule, so that Bonaparte conceived a bitter animosity against him. Writing to Gardanne, he placed a price on his head, 1000 louis were to be the reward for whoever should capture or kill him. Frotté demanded to treat, but in reply was told to surrender and trust to the generosity of the Government. He acted accordingly, but was tried on the 17th of February, condemned, and shot on the following day.*

---

* Bonaparte was opposed to executions for political offences. He granted a suspension of the capital sentence passed on Frotté, but unfortunately the reprieve reached its destination too late. Some will have it that this was done intentionally.

He neglected no measure for pacifying the Vendée. He made use of the former parish priest of St. Laud, the Abbé Bernier, and also appealed to the priests who were at that time returning from all parts of the provinces. He desired immensely to have an interview with Georges Cadoudal, and this took place on the 5th of March, 1800. Comparing his size with that of Bonaparte, Cadoudal stated that, had he wished it, he could have crushed him in his arms. Nothing was spared to induce him to quit the cause of the Bourbons, but even Bonaparte's irresistible

All armed opposition being overcome, the insurrection ceased to torment those regions. Bonaparte succeeded in tranquillizing La Vendée rather by lenient than coercive measures.

To insure the continuance of tranquillity, he proclaimed a general amnesty, he also declared the principle of religious tolerance, suppressed the conscription, and remitted some of the taxes. In this manner he brought back calm to the population. Everywhere regularity succeeded to trouble and disorder. Canclaux looked after the administration with a vigilant and severe police to back him.

But Bonaparte knew far too well that his destiny would have been nothing without the strength and splendour of battles. Once shorn of his victories, what remained to his name ? War was his element; his most dazzling and effective triumphs were those of the battlefield. It was war that was to electrify public opinion with bulletins of victories gained, of trophies captured. The day when he could no longer dominate the people of France by this means, his power would be compromised. He was inconsolable for the loss of Italy; a feeling which can be easily appreciated when we look at the immortal renown he had acquired in 1796 by his striking strategy in his first campaign. Now the nation had declared in his favour, and was ready to back him, no difficulty was too great to prevent his recovering the fruit of his early victories. He was not only resolved to hasten to renew the glories of his first Italian campaigns, but also to wipe out the defeats which had shorn the French armies of their well-merited laurels.

It was, then, for these reasons that Bonaparte embarked on his own enterprise and laid the foundations of his victory at Marengo. Marengo, the name of a very insignificant little Italian hamlet, was to be rendered famous hereafter in history, for by the reputation gained there Bonaparte eventually placed the crown of France on his head. Marengo gave the name to the gold coinage of the Republic.

The campaign of Marengo was a most important event, inasmuch as it decided the fate of Europe, consolidated the French

---

seductions failed. " Rather death," he was wont to say, " than to betray my oath." *Potius mori quam fœdari*, and he clung to this resolution to the very last. One of his biographists has written of him, " Georges Cadoudal was a genius of his own kind, he fought without ambition for the simple principle of royalty, and all his actions are marked by the very greatest disinterestedness."

Revolution, and proved the audacity, the good fortune and the glory of Bonaparte. To such as taunted him with being the Corsican usurper, he could well say, "The crown of France was lying upon the ground, and I lifted it upon my sword-point."

Marengo recalls the finest days of this famous soldier's career and the commencement of his dominion. The name alone—Marengo—awakens in every mind an echo. Whatever faults Bonaparte may have committed in later years, when he had attained supreme power and had become a despotic ruler; however unscrupulous he may have been in his dealings; however insatiable in his love of power,—we must all admit that in 1800 we find in Bonaparte more of the soldier bent in using his brilliant talents as a means for humbling the enemies of his country and endeavouring to restore peace and tranquillity to France, than of the absolute monarch consumed by a craving for subduing all nations and imposing his will on the vanquished, careless of the blood he spilt and the misery he caused.

At that time Bonaparte was thirty-one years of age, in full vigour of mind and body, and in robust health. Of his career the earliest years were unquestionably the best and the most brilliant. The prediction of Dugommier to the Committee of Public Safety was, " Reward and promote that young man ; for if you are ungrateful towards him, he will raise himself alone." *
Both in Italy and in Egypt this prediction had been fulfilled. Up till then circumstances had not caused Bonaparte to resort to measures which have since called down on him the opprobrium of the entire civilized world.†

* Barras took part in the defence of Pondichéry, and soon after quitted the service with the rank of captain. He was commissary of the Convention at the siege of Toulon, and it was there he detected the great military qualities of young Bonaparte. When on the 12th Vendémiaire France needed a general of great nerve and skill, Barras proposed him to the Convention.

† The celebrated traveller and academician, Volney, disgusted by the excesses committed in France, crossed over to the United States. When he told Washington's old comrades that a young man of twenty-six had been appointed to the supreme command of the Army of Italy, they became persuaded that the French had gone mad. But when Volney predicted and explained to them in minute detail all that this young man was about to accomplish, they thought that it was the narrator who had lost his head.

Volney had known Bonaparte in Corsica, and, on landing at Nice, one of the first persons he came across was Bonaparte, who was then doing ordinary duty on the coast of Provence. At a dinner at which Volney, a commissioner of the Convention, and two or three other functionaries were present, Bonaparte denounced the inaction of the army to which he was attached, which became later on the Army

The general order Bonaparte issued after assuming the reins of government at once satisfied the soldiers that, though elected first magistrate of the Republic, he would himself direct their future operations; and that the distress, mismanagement and disorganization which the crass negligence of the Directory had brought about, would speedily disappear. " Soldiers ! " he said, " in promising peace to the French people, I have been merely your organ. I know your valour. You are the same men who conquered Holland, the Rhine, Italy, and gave peace under the walls of astonished Vienna. Soldiers ! the defence of your frontiers must no longer limit your desires. The states of our enemies remain to be subdued. There is not one among you who, having made a campaign, is ignorant that the most essential quality of a soldier is to endure privations with constancy. Many years of maladministration cannot be repaired in a day. As First Magistrate of the Republic, it will be grateful to me to declare to the whole nation what troops deserve, by their discipline and valour, to be proclaimed the best supporters of their country. Soldiers ! when the proper time arrives, I will be in the midst of you, and awe-struck Europe shall confess that you are of the race of the brave ! "

of Italy. Warming on his subject, he explained his conception of crossing the Alps and carrying the war into Italy.

The following day, before the same individuals, whose interest and curiosity had been aroused, he developed his plan of campaign, map in hand, with the greatest wealth of detail. All had been marked down, all had been foreseen.

When in after-time the newspapers from Europe reached the United States, this plan, which at one time had appeared so fabulous, or at least so extraordinarily daring to the American warriors, developed itself point by point.

CHAPTER III.

MOREAU.

Moreau sides with the Revolution—Captures the Danish fleet when ice-bound—
Suspected of having favoured Pichegru—Operations in Northern Italy under
Schérer—Defeat of the French at Magnano—Moreau replaces Schérer—
Macdonald's defeat at the Trebbia—Moreau replaced by Joubert in command
of the Army of Italy—Battle of Novi, Joubert killed, and Moreau resumes
command — Appointed to command the Army of the Rhine — The 18th
Brumaire, Moreau aids Bonaparte—Strength of the Austrian forces in
Germany—French Army of the Rhine—Bonaparte's plan for the campaign in
Germany—Moreau objects—Dessoles goes to Paris to explain Moreau's plan—
The Army of the Rhine not very favourable to Bonaparte—Moreau delays,
Bonaparte urges him to commence operations—Bonaparte stipulates for a
portion of the army to pass into Italy—Moreau crosses the Rhine in three
places—Battles of Stokach, Engen, Mösskirch, and Memmingen—The
Austrians lose their magazines—Carnot goes to Moreau to get the troops for
Italy—Moncey sets out for the Saint Gothard.

THE officer who after Bonaparte played the most important *rôle*
in the great events of 1799 and 1800 was General Moreau.

Jean Victor Moreau was born at Morlaix, in Brittany, on the
11th of August, 1763. The Revolution found him a law student
at Rennes, where he exercised considerable influence on his
fellow-scholars. The political events altered the whole course of
his life; Moreau embraced the side of the Revolution, resigned
the law, and gave his attention entirely to military matters. He
was selected to command the battalion of volunteers d'Ille-et-
Vilaine, and his advancement, as often occurred in those
turbulent times, was rapid. He displayed such military talents
under Dumouriez, that in 1794 he was promoted general of
division.

Moreau's devotion to the new order of things received a rude
shock when his father, an honest advocate, was put to death by
the guillotine during the Reign of Terror. In Morlaix, Moreau's
father had, by his probity, charity, and humanity gained th
honoured name of " Father of the poor." Virtue, learning

generosity, however, were not respected by the bloodthirsty Jacobins, and an exhibition of leniency towards some emigrants in administering their affairs supplied an excuse for sending him to the scaffold.

Distracted by this terrible event, Moreau wished to retire from France, but his friends' sage advice and his own patriotism prevailed. His first grief over, he came to recognize the fact that his services were only too necessary to his country.

He himself but just escaped a fate similar to that of his father. The Convention had sent forth a barbarous decree, ordering that no quarter was to be given to British soldiers. Moreau, in the face of such an order, allowed the garrison of Nieuport, composed entirely of Hanoverians, to go free. This step had been approved by the commissioner Lacombe Saint Michel, who was at that time attached to the army of the north. Moreau's conduct, nevertheless, was denounced to the Convention on the 8th Thermidor, and Robespierre demanded his head.* A deputy observed that Moreau's clemency towards the British soldiers had probably been instrumental in saving 5000 or 6000 soldiers to the Republic, as they might have been shot by the English by way of reprisal. The tyrant replied, " And what are 6000 men to me when it is a matter of principle ? " It would most certainly have gone hard with Moreau had not Providence intervened, for on the following day, 9th Thermidor (27th of July, 1794), Robespierre himself was denounced, arrested, and soon after executed with twenty-two of his partisans.

The tyrant's reply reminds one of an incidert related of young Bonaparte. One day while he was speaking of Turenne with considerable warmth, a lady observed " he was a great man, but I should have liked him better had he not ravaged the Palatinate."

" What does that signify," replied Bonaparte, briskly, " if this burning was necessary to his views ? "

Moreau was a soldier of great abilities. Amongst other qualities, he excelled in keeping his plans from the enemy, who is almost always beaten when surprised.

He commanded on the occasion of that marvellous seizure of the Danish fleet on the 18th of January, 1795, when it was

---

* The bloodthirsty canaille that crowded round the terrible guillotine was within an ace of seeing the heads of some of the most gifted soldiers of France roll 'he basket.

overcome by the frost in entering the straits between West-Frise and the island of Texel. Moreau, perceiving the precarious position of the vessels arrested by the ice, battered them with cannon, and sent cavalry to secure them.

In 1796, Pichegru fell under suspicion of treachery, and the Directory conferred on Moreau the chief command of the Army of the Rhine and Moselle. The campaign against the Archduke Charles, and, above all, Moreau's able retreat to the Rhine, added greatly to his military reputation. Nevertheless, a suspicion that he had connived in Pichegru's plots cost him his command.

It all rested on the fact that Moreau had shown a certain degree of forbearance towards his old colleague at the time when the waggon belonging to General de Klinglin was seized. This fostered the idea that a political intrigue was at the bottom of the delay which Moreau allowed to occur before inform- ing the Directory of the seizure of Pichegru's compromising correspondence.

This correspondence, found in General de Klinglin's waggon, by means of which Pichegru's treason became revealed, was in cypher, but in this case was made out without any difficulty.*

After Bonaparte's departure for Egypt matters for the French in Italy had gone from bad to worse. The invasion of Switzerland had offended the Austrian emperor, Francis II., and the occupation of Malta had irritated the Czar, Paul I.

The news of the battle of the Nile and of Nelson's destruc- tion of the French fleet in the Bay of Aboukir re-echoed from one end of Europe to the other in the month of September, 1798. The so-much-dreaded Bonaparte and his invincible army were settled in Egypt, and unable to return to Europe. What more propitious moment could the enemies of France desire for resuming hostilities ?

So the news acted like an electric spark, and caused a con- flagration which soon enveloped the entire Continent. The King of Naples welcomed Nelson, and received him in triumph. Turkey declared war against the Republic, and at the close of

---

* Little use appears to have been made of secret correspondence during the wars of the Revolution and the Empire. Possibly this may be attributed to the fact that there exists no system of secret correspondence which the expert will not soon be able to unravel.

the year, England, Austria, Russia, and the Two Sicilies, found themselves united in a second coalition.

About the same period the Czar Paul, with all the characteristic impetuosity of his disposition, entered into the alliance against France, and laboured to cement a league between all the sovereigns of Europe for the overthrow of the French Revolutionary power, and for the restoration of all the interests which had been subverted by the French arms. He went further, for he contemplated the settling of all religious controversies, and the union of all followers of Christ, to whatever denomination they might belong, under the banners of one Catholic Church.

Suwarroff,* the conqueror of Ismail, a general of the very highest order, was appointed to command the Russian auxiliary army which was to co-operate with the Austrians in Italy.

The Austrians and Russians together numbered about 225,000 men. The Archduke Charles commanded the army in Germany, Suwarroff being appointed general-in-chief of the allied armies in Italy.

It was only on the 12th of March, 1799, that the Republic, looking on the passage of the Russian troops across the territory of Austria as a *casus belli*, declared war. Hostilities commenced in Germany. Massena invaded the Grisons, and drove the Austrians out of it, defeating them afterwards, on the 25th of March, at Taufers. He thus opened a direct communication with the Army of Italy then posted on the Adige.

In Italy hostilities commenced somewhat later. Schérer only reached Milan on the 11th of March, and at that time Melas had not quite completed the concentration of his army.

Early in the year 1799, the contending forces in Germany and in Italy were disposed as follows : Jourdan was chief commander of a French army of 45,000 men in Germany. He had 30,000 men under Massena in Switzerland, and a corps of observation under Bernadotte on the Rhine. In Lombardy, Joubert, incensed by the manner in which the Directory had treated Championnet, had resigned.† His resignation had been

---

* Suwarroff had naturally a weak constitution, but rendered it almost invulnerable by exercise, strict temperance, and the regular use of cold baths. His mode of life was of Spartan simplicity.

† For attempting to arrest the exactions of the French commissaries, Championnet was removed from his command and indicted for disobedience.

accepted, and Schérer, who had been minister of war, replaced him. Schérer had on the Adige 57,000 French, 10,000 more were in Lombardy, another 10,000 in Piedmont, and 5000 in Liguria. Macdonald, who had replaced Championnet in Southern Italy, had 34,000 men, mostly at Rome and Naples. The Directory had thus scattered one-half of the troops along the Peninsula from Piedmont to Calabria.

In the plan of operations sketched out for the Army of Italy, Schérer was to push his left forwards towards Trent, whilst the right, crossing the Adige by Verona and Legnago, would drive the enemy beyond the Brenta and the Piave.

In Germany, Jourdan was beaten by the Austrians at Stokach, and compelled to recross the Rhine. Jourdan and Bernadotte thereupon quitted the army, the command of which was conferred on Massena. Massena prudently retired into Switzerland.

In Italy the contending armies were, in the latter part of March, face to face in the neighbourhood of the Adige on the line Verona-Legnago. Kray, an officer who was only surpassed in ability by the Archduke Charles, had assumed temporary command, as Melas at that time was absent through indisposition. With great foresight, the Austrians had been strengthening their position on the Adige. On the 25th of March, the French made preparations for crossing the river the following day. In the battle which raged on the 26th their left was routed with the loss of all its artillery. On the 30th, Serrurier's division was defeated above Verona; and on the 5th of April, the French suffered a still greater defeat on the plains of Magnano. The French force amounted to 34,000 infantry, with 7000 cavalry; the Austrians had nearly 45,000, of whom 5000 were cavalry. The success was dubious until Kray, having called up the garrison of Verona, was able to separate and envelope the two French divisions of the right.

The victory was decisive; nevertheless the Austrians, fearing they might tarnish their success by a too precipitate advance, moved very slowly after the beaten army.

Undoubtedly Magnano was a dire defeat for the French. Still, covered by the Mincio, and resting on Mantua and Peschiera, Schérer could have offered a vigorous resistance, and might to some extent have regained the superiority and prestige which the French arms had lost. It was hopeless, however, to expect great things from him, for he had entirely lost his head. Forming an exaggerated conception of the danger of his situation, he placed 10,000 men within the walls of Mantua, and with the remainder of his army fell back behind the Adda.

On the 11th of April, Kray handed over the command of the Austrian forces to Melas, who had by that time recovered. On the 14th, arrived Suwarroff with the advanced guard of the Russian contingent, and at once assumed the supreme command of the allied armies. Schérer, who had lost by the defeat at Magnano, and by the confusion of the retreat, the little confidence and consideration remaining to him amongst his officers and soldiers, was replaced by Moreau in the command of the Army of Italy. This had been sadly reduced in numbers by sickness and the sword.

The Archduke Charles and Suwarroff had planned the entire separation of the French armies of Italy and of Switzerland, with a view to combining the movements of the Russian and Austrian armies in the conquest of the Italian Alps, Lombardy, and Piedmont, to penetrate afterwards into France through its most defenceless side by the Vosges mountains and the defiles of the Jura.

Suwarroff, having detached 20,000 men under Kray to besiege Peschiera and blockade Mantua, took steps for forcing the line of the Adda.

Moreau strove to hold that line, but his predecessor had imprudently scattered his troops along the course of the river. The French position extended for more than twenty leagues between Lecco and Pizzighettone. The allies coming from Brivio and Vaprio defeated Moreau at Cassano on the 27th of April, forced the passage, and inflicted an immense loss on the French.

They had lost above 11,000 men, and could hardly muster in their retreat 20,000 with whom to make head against the 60,000 of the allies. Milan had to be abandoned, and the Republican army, having left a garrison of 2000 men in the castle, was withdrawn behind the Ticino into Piedmont.

On the 29th, Suwarroff entered Milan in triumph. The multitude, always fickle, received him with the same enthusiasm they evinced when Bonaparte first came amongst them. A reaction had set in, and a religious fanaticism now replaced the love of liberty.

Moreau retired on Alessandria and Turin. The army was divided into two columns; he himself took the road to Turin, his column forming the escort for the artillery parks, the military chest, and the baggage. The other column, composed of Victor's and Laboissière's divisions, moved towards Alessandria, with a view to occupying the defiles of the Bocchetta and the approaches to Genova. Suwarroff followed him very slowly.

By his tardiness he missed on this occasion the opportunity of destroying the French army in its retreat. Suwarroff's slowness of movement is difficult to explain, for he hated all manœuvring, and all his military principles could be expressed in these few words, *Stoupaï i bi* ("Forward and strike"). His skill as a general has often been questioned, and it certainly failed him on this occasion. Incalculable results are sometimes attained by vigorous enterprise; but Suwarroff frequently relaxed his efforts when victory had been gained, and abstained from reaping from his victories the full fruit which might have attended them.

On one occasion General Chastelar, chief of the staff of the Austrian army in Italy, proposed to Suwarroff to make a reconnaissance. The marshal promptly replied : "Reconnaissance! I am for none of them; they are of no use but to the timid, and to inform the enemy that you are approaching. It is never difficult to find your opponent when you really wish it. Form column; charge bayonet; plunge into the midst of the enemy; these are my reconnaissances."

Suwarroff sent Vukassevich * by Novara, and Ivrea towards Turin by the left of the Po. He himself crossed that river at Piacenza and Pavia, advanced on Tortona, and took the town under the fire of the fort. His design was to interpose between Macdonald's and Moreau's armies, and to threaten Moreau's communications with Genova. Macdonald remained too long in Tuscany, and thus unwittingly enabled Suwarroff to repair the mistake he had made.

After the retreat of the French forces into Piedmont, they were destined to meet with humiliating defeats in two severely contested battles, those of the Trebbia and of Novi.

As the fortune of war had manifestly declared itself against the French, General Macdonald was called up from Naples with the object of reinforcing Moreau's army. Macdonald's march,

* According to Alison, Wukassowich.

however, was delayed by an insurrection which broke out in
Tuscany and kept him twelve days in Florence. Rejecting the
most direct route leading to Genova by the Corniche, which
was reputed impracticable for artillery, he descended from the
Apennines in the provinces of Bologna and Modena. He defeated
the Austrians at Saint Giovanni, near Bologna, on the 11th
of June, and again close to Modena on the 12th. After
these minor engagements, Macdonald continued his march,
reaching Piacenza on the 16th, but he was unable to prevent
Suwarroff from placing himself athwart him and Moreau.
Victor's division alone, which had marched by way of Sarzana,
succeeded in joining the latter.

On the 17th, 18th, and 19th of June a most sanguinary
battle was fought on the Trebbia, in which Suwarroff inflicted a
complete defeat on his adversary. A combined plan of action
had been settled between Moreau and Macdonald. Moreau was
to advance on Tortona, and Lapoype's corps was to come down
the valley of the Trebbia to Bobbio to keep up the communication between the two armies, to flank Macdonald's left, and if
necessary to make a powerful diversion in his favour. On the
19th the issue was yet uncertain, though both sides had lost
very heavily. Suwarroff could bring up reinforcements, Macdonald was without resources; nor was there any news of
Moreau and of Lapoype. The reappearance of Hohenzollern
and of Klenau at Parma and Modena decided Macdonald to
declare himself beaten and to retire.[*]

On the 16th of June, Moreau advanced in two columns
against Tortona at the head of 14,000 men. Bellegarde was in
front of Tortona with four brigades, but deeming his force not
sufficiently strong to arrest Moreau's progress, he retired to a
defensive position near Alessandria. Moreau speedily raised
the blockade of Tortona, after which he turned his immensely
superior force against Bellegarde, and defeated him with a loss
of 1500 prisoners and five guns. Moreau was advancing towards
Piacenza when news reached him of Suwarroff's victory over
Macdonald at the Trebbia and the fall of the citadel of Turin.

When Suwarroff, at that moment on the Larda, heard of
Bellegarde's defeat and of Moreau's advance, he marched to
meet the French general. Moreau, however, after having

---

[*] Macdonald was recalled by the Directory; and his division generals, Montrichard and Lapoype, were disgraced.

revictualled Tortona, fell back rapidly by Novi and Gavi to his former position in the Apennines. Suwarroff had received positive orders from the Aulic Council not to attempt any operations beyond the Apennines till the fortresses of Lombardy had been reduced. This injunction checked his movements, and gave time to Moreau and Macdonald to join forces. The month's suspension of hostilities which ensued gave Moreau an opportunity of reorganizing his army.

The Russians made their entry into Turin on the 26th of May; but the citadel was not captured till the 22nd of June, after a bombardment which lasted six days. Alessandria surrendered on the 31st of July.

However able may have been Moreau's conduct of the war, the Directory reposed little faith in him, and did not confirm him in the chief command of the Army of Italy. This was conferred on Joubert. On the same day, the 18th of July, Moreau was appointed to the command of the Army of the Rhine.

The previous year Joubert had found himself compelled to submit his resignation, and he was at the time idling about Paris. A party hostile to the Directory undertook to draw him again into activity as a reproach to the Government. Joubert was first given the command of the 17th Legion, stationed in Paris, and subsequently the command of what still remained of Moreau's and Macdonald's troops in Italy, with the injunction to drive the Austro-Russian forces out of that country.

Joubert had just married Mademoiselle Montholon, and wasted a precious month and more over his honeymoon ; a fatal delay which enabled the allies to concentrate their troops.

On quitting his bride, Joubert told her : " You will behold me again dead or a conqueror ; " an excusable boast for a youthful general—for he was barely thirty years old—about to assume the chief command of an army. The first of Joubert's predictions came true, for he found a soldier's grave at Novi.

When he joined the army he stipulated that the formal handing over of the command should not take place until after the battle which he was about to fight against Suwarroff. Moreau complied with Joubert's wish, remained with the army, and aided that young general to the utmost of his power.

On the 21st and 30th of July, the citadel of Alessandria

and fortress of Mantua had fallen into the hands of the allies,[*] and Kray, at the head of 20,000 men, set out to join Suwarroff. This raised the Austro-Russian army to 62,000 men; the French had barely 40,000.

When Joubert found himself in a position to take the field, he moved his army from the Riviera di Genova, with the intention of relieving Tortona and Mantua, and on the 9th of August made for Novi. Some rumours already announced the fall of Mantua, and of this the French soon had ocular proof, for they found Kray's corps deploying in front of their left.

On thus learning that Mantua had fallen, Joubert was undecided whether to retire or not, and naturally enough, seeing that the principal motive for assuming the offensive no longer existed. He now felt sure that he would have to contend with very considerable forces. On the morning of the 15th of August, before he had begun to withdraw his troops, he was vigorously attacked by Suwarroff, and was killed in the first onset.

In the terrible battle that ensued the allies were at first repulsed. For eight hours victory remained in suspense. Suwarroff's impetuosity had brought on an attack before all his troops were at hand. The Russians were a league from the battlefield when the first attack was delivered, and Melas did not reach it before four o'clock in the afternoon. Moreau took advantage of Suwarroff's thoughtlessness to repair to the threatened point and make dispositions for a fresh charge. The French, irritated by the death of their general, attacked the Austrians with fury, and drove them back into the plain.

At four in the afternoon Melas arrived on the field with his column, turned the French right first, and then their entire position, which was far too extended.

No one can contest the fact that Melas made a fine flank attack. It was a most dexterous and decisive movement, and he had every right to claim a large share in the results of the battle.

At Novi the allies outnumbered the French, who, with 36,000 men, fought 45,000. The battle was one of the most

---

[*] Mantua, which has never yet yielded to direct assault, had sometimes succumbed to famine and capitulation. In 1796, Bonaparte invested it on the 4th of June; it surrendered, starved out, on the 2nd of February, 1797, after eight months' blockade. In 1799, with a garrison of 13,000 men, it capitulated, after a vigorous siege of eleven days!

bloody and obstinately contested that had yet occurred in the war, but without commensurate results.

Moreau continued to hold his position on the Apennines, and an attempt made by Klenau to capture Genova was defeated by Moreau's right wing. Moreau and Macdonald had had to contend against Suwarroff, who was, in the beginning of October, overcome by great difficulties in Switzerland. This occurred almost at the very moment that the news of Bonaparte's return restored hope in every breast.

Suwarroff turned his back on Italy on the 11th of September to go to the assistance of the allies in Switzerland. He arrived there two days after the battle of Zurich had been fought. His troops were to replace a number of Austrians which had been moved to the Lower Rhine. One of the effects of Massena's victory was that Suwarroff found himself isolated from the friends he expected to meet; and the forces with him being insufficient in number, he had to think first of placing his army in safety. This he was able to accomplish only after his men had endured untold hardships and made superhuman efforts, which extended over a period of ten days. On the 9th of October, he reached a place of safety at Ilanz.

After the battle of Novi, Moreau, having reconducted the army to the mountain passes above Genova, departed to assume the command of the Army of the Rhine. It was in Paris, on his way through, that he was sounded with regard to assuming the government of the country; but he refused, not thinking himself equal to the task at a time when France was so divided into parties.

Championnet succeeded Moreau in the command of the Armies of the Alps and of Italy. Coni was captured on the 4th of December, when the French armies in Italy reverted to positions nearly identical to those which they had occupied when Bonaparte was appointed to their command in 1796.

Thus in a short time the French lost all that they had conquered. They might have fared even worse but for the misunderstandings which arose amongst their enemies; those alone saved them from still greater humiliations.

Bonaparte and Moreau did not meet until the return of the former from Egypt. When chance threw them together for the first time, they contemplated each other for a while before speaking. Bonaparte spoke first, and expressed to Moreau the desire which he had long felt to be personally acquainted with him. Moreau replied : " You arrive from Egypt victorious, and I from Italy after a signal defeat. Had Joubert determined to profit by the first enthusiasm which his presence would have caused in the army, and joined it the moment he was appointed to be its chief, it is beyond doubt that the Russians and Austrians, with the troops that they had at that moment, would have been unable to withstand Joubert's impetuous attack. But the month he remained in Paris for his marriage had given them time to collect all their forces, and the premature surrender of Mantua added to the rest 15,000 men, who arrived on the very eve of the battle. It was impossible for our brave army not to be overwhelmed by so many forces united. It is always the greater number that beats the less."

Moreau, like many other intelligent men, deplored the incompetence of the Directory, and threw himself with little scruple into the scheme for displacing the incapable men then ruling the Republic. He was amongst the officers who rallied round Bonaparte on the 18th Brumaire, and was given the command of the troops at the Luxembourg, the residence of the executive, so that indirectly he had the custody of those Directors who had not resigned.

Sloane thinks that Moreau helped Bonaparte only to forward his own personal ambitious views, inasmuch as once the young general had become a civilian there should be no military rival to oppose him. Moreau, however, at no time showed such cunning foresight, nor had Bonaparte, by becoming a statesman, cast all military ambition to the winds. It would have been indeed strange if, once having tasted the sweets of conquest and renown, his ears tingling with the uproarious acclamations of the multitude, he could forego such gratification for ever, even to be the Chief Magistrate of the Republic.

On the 18th Brumaire, Moreau was detailed to guard the Luxembourg, and 500 men of the 86th Regiment were placed under his orders for the purpose. But the troops refused to obey. They evidently had no confidence in Moreau, who was not, they said, a true patriot. The suspicion which had fallen on him had not yet been effaced. Bonaparte found himself compelled to address the troops, and to assure them that they could depend on Moreau acting uprightly.

The friendship between Bonaparte and Moreau at first

appeared sincere, as their correspondence shows. It was after Moreau's marriage that this feeling cooled down, and in the course of 1801 it gave place to bitter animosity. A jealous influence on the part of Madame Moreau is generally supposed to have brought this about; nevertheless there are very good grounds for believing that it was due to professional jealousy, which had its origin in 1800, in the contentions regarding the plan of campaign in Germany.*

Moreau's independent disposition being somewhat difficult to overcome, Bonaparte began by writing him a flattering letter; and, though it was said that the First Consul was very jealous of him, he placed under his orders the finest and strongest army the Republic had at the close of the century.

Meanwhile the Cabinet of Vienna, led by Thugut, who was animated by an inflexible hostility to republican principles, disdaining the wise counsel of the Archduke Charles, and fully persuaded that France was at the end of her resources, determined on prosecuting the war.

The Austrians, who had brought together a very considerable army—about 228,000 men in all—had resolved on resuming the offensive vigorously in Italy, whilst remaining purely on the defensive in Germany. The First Consul had likewise decided to assume the offensive, but he had determined to employ the principal forces of the Republic in the valley of the Danube, so that the danger which threatened their capital might have the effect of staying the march of the Austrian army in Italy. With singular ignorance of the art of war, the Aulic Council had made operations in their own country secondary in importance, and dreamt of conquests on the Var and in Provence. When hostilities recommenced, the Austrian forces were already in the neighbourhood of Genova.

Their army of Germany was 92,000 strong, of which 18,000 were splendid cavalry, with 400 guns. To these numbers should be added 20,000 more belonging to Bavaria and other minor states. What, however, told so greatly against the Austrians was that their forces in Germany were spread over a very large front from the Maine to the Tyrol, for which reason they could not bring a large number of men together at any one point.

* It stood to Moreau's credit that, when compelled, in 1796, by the admirable skill of the Archduke Charles to retire, knowing Bonaparte to be hard pressed by Alvinzi in Italy, setting aside all ignoble rivalries, he generously detached a corps from his own army to march across the Tyrolese Alps to reinforce him.

The centre, under Kray, who had succeeded the Archduke Charles in the command of the army, comprised 40,000 men, and was behind the Black Forest near Villingen and Donaue-schingen. Its advanced posts observed the Rhine from the lake of Constance to Kehl. Kray's headquarters were at Donaue-schingen, and his principal magazines at Stokach, Engen, Mösskirch, and Biberach.

His army was divided into four corps, including his own. Kienmayer guarded the passes from Renchen and the valley of Hell with 15,000 men. A brigade watched Vieux-Brisach. The right wing, about 16,000 strong, guarded the course of the Rhine from Renchen to the Maine. The left wing, commanded by the Prince of Reuss, numbering 28,000 regular troops and from 8000 to 10,000 Tyrolese militia, was almost an independent body, and only connected with the rest of the army by an armed flotilla on the lake of Constance. It occupied the Vorarlberg and the Grisons.

Three advance-guards were thrown out in front of the army to screen it; that of the Archduke Ferdinand was to observe Bâle and the course of the Rhine as far as Schaffhausen, where it connected with those of the Prince of Lorraine and of General Sporck, which extended as far as the lake of Constance.

The Republic in the coming struggle with Austria assembled a powerful army on the eastern frontier. Everything in the way of men and materials was sent to this "Army of the Rhine," the most imposing that France could produce. The corps were composed of old soldiers, of men who had borne arms under the most famous leaders the Republic had brought forth—Pichegru, Hoche, Kléber, and Moreau. Of conscripts there were few, just enough to infuse youth in the mass. Thiers says in their praise: "They were wise, sober, disciplined, instructed and intrepid. The chiefs were worthy of these soldiers." Lecourbe, Riche-panse, Saint Cyr, Ney were secondary leaders of the highest order.

This brave army was led by Moreau, a chief broken to war, whose martial spirit seemed to increase every day amongst the trials of active service. Practice had sharpened his military insight, and by his experience, his habit of commanding, and his high renown, he was at that period the only man, after Bonaparte, who was reputed capable of handling an army of over a hundred thousand combatants. To skill in war, Moreau added prudence and circumspection. He trusted nothing to chance. Gifted with rare sagacity and imperturbable coolness in presence of danger, he could judge to a nicety the right condition of a contest. In the midst of brilliant successes he was unpretentious, and when overcome by reverses he met them with admirable fortitude.

If at times he was undecided, once face to face with the enemy his indecision invariably gave way to wise and firm resolutions. Moreau trusted for victory to skilful combinations and methodical arrangements, rather than to those master strokes which, though attended with peril, frequently turn out successfully.

Of the two frontiers threatened by the Austrian armies that of the Rhine was the most important for both France and Austria alike, for to either of these powers a battle gained or lost on the Danube or on the Rhine would involve the gravest consequences. A victory in the Riviera di Genova or elsewhere in Italy was not likely to have the same effect. Melas risked much by taking up a position so far from the Austrian territory and his natural base, for, should a defeat have overtaken Kray, coming to his aid was quite out of the question. It was here that Bonaparte showed his skill. He made Moreau's army strong, and did little or nothing to strengthen that of Massena. In doing this he acted in keeping with his declaration that, "the commanding frontier is that of the Rhine, for in Germany alone could he look for decisive results." Moreau asked too much, for before he knew to what purpose Bonaparte intended to employ the Army of Reserve, he urged time after time that it should be sent to Switzerland to act as a support to the Army of the Rhine.

The Austrians left the French in undisputed possession of Switzerland. That advanced position, so valuable for offensive operations both in Germany and Italy, remained to the French. Their opponents evidently feared to assail Switzerland after the disastrous results of their operations in the previous year.

The configuration of that country was very favourable to Bonaparte's designs, for Switzerland jutted out like an enormous wedge between the two Austrian armies. He could consequently use the country, which has been aptly called the great central bastion of the European system, as a base of operations for an attack on Kray's army in Germany or on the one which Melas commanded in Italy. The distance between the two Austrian armies already prevented any combined operations, and they were destined to find themselves more and more separated by the interposition of a large part of the Republican forces. Bonaparte's intention was that the Army of the Rhine should drive Kray back from the Alps, and put it out of his power to render any assistance to Melas.

The Austrians were in an embarrassed condition, for not a single alternative open to them presented much prospect of success. The best plan they could have followed in the emergency would have been to increase their army in Swabia at the expense of their army in Italy. But by so doing Italy would have been simply handed back to the French.

Bonaparte had conceived a very brilliant and bold plan for the French armies in 1800. It was a real inspiration of genius. He had recognized the expediency of operating with vigour in Germany, for he, quite as well as Moreau, was aware that it was in that country where the fate of the war was to be decided, and where the bulk of the troops were to be concentrated. All the efforts of the French were to be directed against Kray, while Massena remained strictly on the defensive. Once Kray was defeated, it was possible either to dictate peace at Vienna, or to take Melas's army in reverse and cut off its retreat.

Moreau was to drive Kray back along the valley of the Danube, and separate him from Switzerland and Italy completely. This done, Bonaparte would come into action with the Army of Reserve, gather to himself the troops Lecourbe would be bringing from Germany, and cross into Italy, while Melas's attention was completely fixed on Liguria. What the First Consul did not relish was that all the honour should be reaped by Moreau; he had decided that it should be himself who would deliver the decisive strokes of the war. In place of making the operations in Germany the principal object of the campaign, he made them in his scheme entirely subordinate to the blows he intended to deliver in Italy at the head of the Army of Reserve.

Moreau was to prepare for the advance of that army by deceiving the enemy, crossing the Rhine between Schaffhouse and the lake of Constance on Kray's extreme left, and so turn the defiles of the Black Forest.

Now remains to be related a most remarkable part in this

memorable campaign, how the ideas and dispositions of two talented leaders differed, and how their conflicting opinions were reconciled by the prudent foresight of one of them.

Bonaparte, as we have said, had conceived a skilful plan. All the troops of the Army of the Rhine were to concentrate in Switzerland and cross the Rhine in the vicinity of Schaffhouse. The march of the left wing from left to right was to be concealed by the river, and, all the measures having been carefully taken beforehand, it could be kept totally unknown to the enemy. By collecting in the affluents of the Rhine, and above all in the Aar, a sufficient number of boats, four bridges would be simultaneously thrown over the river in the neighbourhood of Schaffhouse. By the aid of these bridges the entire army could move across the river, and in twenty-four hours would be able to reach Stokach, overpower the enemy's left, and take in rear all the Austrian forces stationed between the right bank of the Rhine and the defiles of the Black Forest. Bonaparte fully believed that if this operation was executed with vigour and suddenness it would promptly end in crushing the Austrian army. Moreau, by gaining two or three marches on Kray, would have been at the point of passage before the Austrians could have gathered sufficient forces to prevent the crossing.

From Constance to Bâle the Rhine flows from east to west. At Bâle it takes a northerly direction, passing by Brisach, Strasbourg, and Mayence. The Black Forest (Schwarzwald), which derives its name from the dark-tinted leaves and immense number of its fir trees, is a wooded mountain chain in Baden and Würtemberg, running from south to north along the western side of Swabia, parallel to the course of the Rhine after its great bend near Bâle. These mountains lie in the angle of the Rhine between the lake of Constance and Strasbourg on the south. They are very steep, rugged, and thickly wooded.

The French army, had Bonaparte's scheme been followed, would have appeared before Ulm six or seven days after the opening of the campaign, and those of the Austrian army who could not get away would have been compelled to fall back on Bohemia. In this plan the first movement of the campaign would have resulted in separating the Austrian army from Ulm, Philippsburg, and Ingolstadt, and in placing Würtemberg, Swabia, and Bavaria in the power of the French. Such a scheme of operations would be calculated to bring about more or less decisive events, conclusive according to the good fortune, the audacity, and rapidity of the movements of the French commander.

Thiers writes : " *Moreau agissait, à la guerre, sans grandeur, mais avec sûreté* " (" Moreau waged war without grandeur, but with security "). Always more remarkable for prudence than for daring, he had not quite the talent necessary for executing or possibly even for comprehending all the import of such a plan of campaign. Its very boldness startled him. Not accustomed to such venturous conceptions, he dreaded most that Kray, having penetrated his intentions, might concentrate rapidly before the spot selected for crossing the Rhine, present himself in strength at the point of passage, contest the crossing and render it impossible. These fears furnished some reason for not accepting Bonaparte's plan. Moreau, however, gave to the Austrians credit for effecting their concentration with more ease and speed than the event proved to be within their power. The alternative plan he set forth met with full success.

Bonaparte on the 1st of March wrote to Berthier, then minister of war, a long letter of instructions for Moreau. One of the paragraphs runs as follows : " You will let General Moreau know that I desire that his chief of the staff should proceed as speedily as possible to Paris, with a plan of the organization of the army in conformity with the above. This chief on his return will take with him the plan of the first operations of the campaign, combined with those of the other armies." In compliance with this order, Dessoles quitted Moreau and went to Paris, arriving there on the 13th of March.

Bonaparte, glad to have to deal with a man of judgment and penetration, endowed with tact and a conciliatory disposition, explained to him all his ideas, and made him understand and even prefer them to Moreau's. Nevertheless, Dessoles pleaded in favour of Moreau's plan. Thiers reports the conversation that ensued, which, he states, he heard from the mouth of General Dessoles himself. " But General Dessoles did not persist any the less in advising the First Consul to adopt Moreau's plan, because, according to him, it was fitting to leave the general who operates to act according to his ideas and his character, given that he is a man worthy of the command which has been entrusted to him. Your plan," he said to the First Consul, " is grander, more decisive, probably also the most sure; but it is not adapted to the genius of the person who has to carry it into effect. You have a way of making war which is superior to all others. Moreau has his, which doubtlessly is inferior to yours, though, nevertheless, excellent. Let him act. He will do well, possibly slowly, but surely; and he will procure you as many results as you require for the success of your general combinations. If, on the other hand, you try to impose your ideas on him, you will vex him, you may even offend him, and in consequence of having wanted too much you will get nothing from him." The First Consul, who had a great knowledge of human nature, appreciated the wisdom of Dessoles' words and yielded. "You are right," he said to the general; "Moreau is not capable of grasping and executing the plan I have conceived. Let him do as he likes, provided he beats Marshal Kray back on Ulm and Ratisbonne, and that afterwards he sends back in good time his right wing to Switzerland. The plan which he does not understand, which he dares not execute, I am going to carry out, on another part of the theatre of war. What he hesitates to do on the Rhine, I am going to do on the Alps. He may regret in the time to come the glory which he hands over to me."

The plan which Moreau's chief of the staff was enjoined to set forth did not depart greatly from the strategy of the campaigns of 1796 and 1797. Moreau proposed crossing the Rhine at three points—at Mayence, Strasbourg, and Bâle, in place of at one. But this missed the principal end of Bonaparte's plan, which was to cast the entire French army on Kray's left flank, and thus sever him at once from Bavaria.

Bonaparte felt that he was not strongly enough seated in the Consular chair to alienate so influential a rival as Moreau, and that it behoved him to treat him with tact. It was therefore wiser to leave him all the honour of the conception of his plan of campaign, and to furnish him with all that was needed to carry it out. Much of what has been set down as the jealousy of a rival on the part of Bonaparte may possibly be more correctly accounted for as under-estimation of Moreau's abilities by a general of a very different stamp, who judged things in a different way.

Though Moreau's reserve and simplicity of manner were against him, and did not make him popular in the ordinary acceptation of the term, his character was held in high esteem.

F

At the end of the eighteenth century he was more popular with the army than Bonaparte. The latter's brilliant campaign in Italy, the humbling of Austria by the Treaty of Campo Formio, and the marvellous expedition to Egypt, had not been sufficient to gain for him an exclusive ascendant. Besides which, the nation had not quite forgotten that what had first brought him to notice was his cannonading the sections on the 13th Vendémiaire. Though Bonaparte had eclipsed all competitors by his talents and fortune, at that moment Moreau was better known, and possessed the affection of the soldiers to a greater degree. He had fought with distinction in Holland, in Germany, and in Italy, in the last of which theatres of war his spirited retreat before Suwarroff had gained him immense consideration.

The Army of the Rhine may have nourished some feeling of jealousy towards Bonaparte and his Army of Italy for their brilliant success in 1796, and for the rich harvest of glory they had reaped in Northern Italy.

Lanfrey states that the Army of the Rhine was the seat of discontent. The officers were better instructed than those of the Army of Italy, entertained more liberal ideas, and were deeply attached to Republican institutions. They consequently witnessed their fall with silent sullenness.

Historians aver that Bonaparte designed the expedition to San Domingo with the intention of getting rid of that army. The land forces for the expedition were almost all composed of the conquerors of Hohenlinden. These he sent to a distance, knowing full well at the time the dangerous climate and the difficulties to be encountered, points on which he had been thoroughly instructed by Colonel Vincent. It seems strange, if he had any dark designs on these troops, that he should have sent his favourite sister * and his brother-in-law out with them. But it is said that he did so purposely as a proof to show how entirely he disbelieved the reports as to the insalubrious nature of the climate.

Fouché writes on this subject : † " The First Consul ardently seized the happy opportunity of sending away a great number

---

* Pauline Leclerk, Bonaparte's lovely sister, who for her silliness was nick-named la Princesse Folette, so resisted being sent to San Domingo that force had to be employed in putting her on board.

† Fouché, " Mémoires," p. 148

of regiments and general officers formed in the school of Moreau, whose reputations caused him anxiety, and whose influence over the army, if not quite a subject of alarm, was at least one of restraint and inquietude. He likewise comprised in the expedition the generals whom he judged not to be sufficiently devoted to his person and interests, or who were considered as still attached to republican institutions." * Bourrienne, who wrote the instructions for Leclerk, is silent on this point.

For the important expedition to San Domingo Bonaparte naturally selected his best soldiers, and none more than those of the Army of the Rhine were so inured to war. What others were there to compare with them? In this he followed his custom ; when he went to Egypt he did not hesitate to take the choicest battalions of the Army of Italy.

Moreau's plan consisted in turning to account the three bridges on the Rhine at Strasbourg, Brisach, and Bâle, and in moving in several columns over to the right bank of the river. He hoped by so doing to mislead the Austrians, and draw their forces to the defiles of the Black Forest corresponding to the bridges of Strasbourg and Brisach. Then his own forces were to steal away, skirt the Rhine, and take up a position in front of Schaffhausen, so as to cover the remainder of his army.

Moreau, generally admitted to have been one of the best generals of the time in Europe, lacked the dash and audacity necessary for doing what the First Consul would have done, and what he did afterwards in 1805 when he had become emperor. On that occasion, uniting a considerable army on the Rhine, and leaving a small force in Italy, Napoleon marched like lightning on Vienna, without troubling himself about his flanks or rear, relying for safety on the dashing blows he dealt to his principal enemy.

With his habitual prudence, Moreau delayed commencing operations. His assumption of the offensive was the indispensable condition for the advance of the Army of Reserve across the Alps, for Kray had it in his power to attack its left wing or rear.

---

* San Domingo was, with the exception of Cuba, the largest and most flourishing of the West India islands. Its prosperity had increased in a most extraordinary degree, and it seems quite natural that when Bonaparte had leisure he should turn his eyes in that direction and try to stamp out the revolution and reassert French dominion in the island.

Time was everything—looking at Massena's critical position at Genova—nevertheless, Bonaparte had to await the arrival of favourable news from the army in Germany. The reason was plain enough, as only if the operations there took a favourable turn, and Kray was entirely separated from Melas, could he feel justified in demanding that Moreau should place a portion of his troops at his disposal.

Such was his annoyance at the delay that at one moment Bonaparte even contemplated placing himself at the head of the army. He calculated that he could be under the walls of Vienna before the Austrians could penetrate as far as Nice. Nothing but the agitation still rife in the interior of the Republic restrained him. It was not prudent for him, the chief officer of the state, to absent himself from the capital for so long a period. Moreau also had shown too plainly that he had no intention whatever of serving under his orders.

On the success of the first operations of the Army of the Rhine depended that of the Army of Reserve. Moreau alone could open a passage into Italy for the latter, by driving the Austrians away from those outlets through which they might have cut the communications of the Army of Reserve with France.

Again and again did Bonaparte urge Moreau to commence operations, for time was precious; but the general, cautious and slow by nature, could not grasp the necessity for all this despatch. What appeared to him of much greater consequence was not to cross the frontier and advance into the enemy's territory until his army had been supplied with everything necessary to render its fighting power complete.

In one of his letters we find the First Consul writing: "Hasten, hasten by your success to accelerate the arrival of the moment when Massena can be extricated. That general is in need of provisions. For fifteen days he has been enduring with his debilitated soldiers a struggle of despair. Your patriotism is entreated, your self-interest; for should Massena be compelled to capitulate, it will be necessary to take from you a part of your forces, for the purpose of hurrying down the Rhine, in order to assist the departments of the south."

But there was another reason to explain Bonaparte's impatience, inasmuch as it had been arranged with Moreau that as soon as he had scored a victory over Kray, he would detach a body of 25,000 men to strengthen the army which the First Consul was passing into Italy.

This was a delicate matter ; delicate because no commander relishes, after he has once entered into a campaign, consenting to a diminution of his forces. In his letter to Berthier of the 1st of March, to which reference has already been made, Bonaparte directs that Moreau's 100,000 men shall be divided into four corps. "This fourth corps," he adds, "will bear the name of Reserve Corps, and shall be commanded by General Lecourbe. In reality it is destined to serve as a corps of reserve to the other three, to hold Switzerland, and to combine its operations with those of the Army of Italy."

To insure compliance with his demand in future, Bonaparte compelled Moreau to sign a stipulation with General Berthier, under the terms of which he bound himself, when once he had succeeded in driving Kray back from the lake of Constance, to detach from his army some 20,000 or 25,000 men to send to Italy under Lecourbe. Berthier and his chief of the staff, Dupont, proceeded to Bâle, where an informal conference was held to settle the effective strength of the troops which were to remain in Switzerland, and those which Moreau would detach for operating in Italy.

It appears strange that a convention should have been thought necessary to bind Moreau. This shows how independent the military chiefs could be, and that the head of the state could not make sure of their faithfully carrying out his orders.

Besides the troops to be withdrawn from Moreau's command, Bonaparte longed to have Lieutenant-General Lecourbe placed at his disposal. Lecourbe was known as an able, energetic officer, well versed in mountain warfare. His abilities had been clearly demonstrated in the previous campaign. Moreau, who reposed unbounded confidence in him, distinctly refused to part with him, and nothing availed to make him change his mind on this point. In order to harmonize with him, Bonaparte yielded, and it was decided that General Moncey should go to Italy in Lecourbe's place. Moreau complained to the minister of war and to Bonaparte (29th of December, 1799, and 2nd of January, 1800) that Massena had taken away the best divisional generals from the Army of the Rhine. Writing to the former, he states that he was impatient for the arrival of General Saint Cyr. On the 15th of December, 1799, Saint Cyr, by his brilliant combat of Montefascio, had brought to an end the series of fine operations by which he secured possession of the Riviera di Genova. He was loth to quit the Army of Italy, and protested against his removal; however, Massena, who was not on the best terms with him, insisted on his leaving, and taking up his post with the Army of the Rhine.

In all justice to Moreau, it must be noted that what delayed the commencement of his operations was the deficiency of horses for the artillery and cavalry, the scarcity of means, and the want of a pontoon-train, tools, and camp equipment. His letters to the First Consul, to the minister of finances and of war, show most clearly how badly found his army was in all essentials. Such had been the mismanagement of the war department in Paris during the year 1799 that the force at his command was not properly supplied with any single requisite. Alsace and Switzerland, utterly exhausted, were unable to furnish the amount of transport which his movements demanded; and he was simply unable to commence operations until a month after the time arranged.

Moreau's plan, as has been already stated, was to employ the bridges at Strasbourg, Brisach, and Bâle, and then to reascend the Rhine to Schaffhausen. The execution of this commenced on the 25th of April. Three imposing columns crossed the Rhine simultaneously by the above-named bridges. Sainte Suzanne, on the left, crossed by the bridge of Kehl at the head of his three divisions, and advanced on the road of Rastadt and Appenweier, chasing before him Kienmayer's light troops. Having, after a brisk fight, got possession of Griesheim, he established his left at Linx, and his right beyond the Kintzig. Saint Cyr the same day issued from Vieux-Brisach and marched on Fribourg. Ney, who commanded his first division, pushed in the direction of Burkheim and of Eichstetten, as if desirous to connect with Sainte Suzanne. Richepanse, Delmas, and Leclerk, with the reserve, crossed the Rhine at Bâle.

The enemy was led to believe that Sainte Suzanne intended to approach the Danube by the Black Forest, advancing by the valley of the Kintzig, and that Saint Cyr was bent on operating in the Val d'Enfer (Höllenthal); that being the most direct route for an army intending to reach the Danube from the Rhine.

On the 26th, Sainte Suzanne and Saint Cyr did not stir, and

most of the 27th was occupied by the French in misleading the enemy with regard to the direction about to be followed by their columns. But at nightfall Sainte Suzanne withdrew quickly on Kehl, recrossed the Rhine with his corps, and marched by the left bank of the river for Neuf-Brisach.

Saint Cyr had quitted Fribourg, and was marching up the Rhine by the right, or German bank, by way of Saint Hubert, Neuhof, Todnau, and Saint Blaise. Unfortunately, the French staff had been led to believe in the existence of certain roads which in reality were not to be found. Saint Cyr was compelled to cross a frightful country, always in close proximity to the enemy, and without his artillery.

Moreau marched up the right bank with the reserve. On the 29th, the centre under Saint Cyr and the reserve under Moreau were in line on the Alb, from the Abbey of Saint Blaise up to the junction of the Alb and Rhine. Sainte Suzanne, at Neuf-Brisach, followed the left bank of the river, Lecourbe was concentrating between Diesenhofen and Schaffhausen.

On the 30th, Sainte Suzanne recrossed the Rhine and showed himself in the Val d'Enfer ; Saint Cyr remained in the vicinity of Saint Blaise. Moreau moved on the Wutach. On the 1st of May, Sainte Suzanne came across Kienmayer in retreat, and followed him step by step. Saint Cyr continued to march side by side with the corps of the Archduke Ferdinand, and drove him out from Bettmaringen to Stühlingen on the Wutach, which stream Moreau's troops crossed without experiencing any resistance.

Lecourbe, having early in the morning placed a large battery of artillery (thirty-four guns) in position on the heights on the left bank of the Rhine, to sweep the approaches to the village of Reichlingen, moved a bridge, which had been prepared on the Aar, into position on the Rhine. This was firmly established in an hour and a half, and then Vandamme led a large part of Lecourbe's troops over the river.

By the evening of the 1st of May, the French army, from 75,000 to 80,000 strong, was across the Rhine. It extended along its right bank from Bondorf Stühlingen, Schaffhausen Radolfzell, to the lake of Constance. Lecourbe's troops were on the roads leading to Engen and Stokach, menacing at the same time the enemy's magazines and line of retreat.

The manœuvre had been completed in six days and in a very

fortunate manner. As Moreau's plan met with success it was judged accordingly, but if Bonaparte's was objected to by Moreau as being too bold, what must be said of his own, which was full of risks? Saint Cyr and himself for several days marched between the mountains and the Rhine, presenting a flank to the enemy, whilst Sainte Suzanne proceeded all alone in the Val d'Enfer. The dangers of these movements were very great. Had it only occurred to Kray to attack either of these columns, its defeat would have rendered a retreat of the whole French army unavoidable.

Bonaparte relied on being able to surprise the Austrians by keeping his flank march concealed from their knowledge by the waters of the Rhine, and by concluding it with crossing the Rhine with overwhelming forces, against which the unprepared Austrian left would have had no chance of making head. Moreau's object was to attain the same end by misleading the enemy whilst the flank march was being carried out, by riveting his attention to the principal issues of the Black Forest. Whereas in Bonaparte's scheme the Austrians would have remained unaware of the storm till it was on the point of bursting, till the French army had concentrated at Schaffhausen and was crossing the Rhine; according to Moreau's they were put on their guard from the first day of the French movement, and they could accordingly take the necessary precautions. There can be no doubt in which plan the balance of advantages rested.

Kray, who, by drawing Reuss and Starray to himself by forced marches, might have rendered the happy issue of the French plan highly problematical, did next to nothing. However, in this Kray was overruled by the Aulic Council, which had given him peremptory orders for his left to remain in the Vorarlberg. Uncertainty had full sway at his headquarters, and, as invariably happens, this gave rise to many unnecessary and contradictory directions. Kray imagined the French columns to be pressing forward by all the roads, and in place of employing light troops to gain timely notice of the enemy's advance, only issued tardy and powerless orders.

Soon a series of engagements took place, at Stokach, at Engen, at Mösskirch, at Memmingen, the result of all being that Kray before long found himself cast back on Ulm.

Acting in conformity with his instructions, Lecourbe arrived before Stokach on the 3rd of May, beating and pursuing the

Prince of Lorraine and Generals Sporck and Kospoth. Stokach contained immense magazines, and on account of its communications was a position of the very highest importance for either side. The Austrians were determined to defend it; but Lecourbe had sent in the morning Vandamme's division to Wahlnnes and Seruadingen round their left flank. This precaution, and a vigorous attack delivered by Montrichard and Nansouty, ultimately gained the day. The principal result of this victory was that henceforth a junction between Reuss and the rest of the army was almost hopeless.

Moreau beat Kray's army at Engen on the same day, and again at Mösskirch on the 5th. On the 9th, the two armies were once more face to face.* The Austrians were placed in a wrong position on the heights of Mittel-Biberach. They only made a show of resistance, and soon went pell-mell into the valley of the Riss.† Kray, by advancing powerful reinforcements, came to their help. Nevertheless, a general retreat ensued, the Austrians being seriously pressed by the two divisions of Saint Cyr. On the 11th of May, Kray found safety for his army in Ulm, and after that for a certain period neither the French nor the Austrians performed anything of much importance.

The Austrians had collected in magazines at Stokach quite close to the lake of Constance and at Donaueschingen immense quantities of supplies. As all know, the localized accumulation of stores acts as a drag on military operations; they shackle to a great extent the movements of an army, and so it proved in this instance. To this must be added the fact that the magazines had been established far too close to the frontier. If we look at the action at Biberach we shall see that it was evidently fought with the hope of saving what remained of the magazines. But Kray lost a very large amount of provisions, and got beaten as well. The French army revelled in abundance, for

* In these battles of Engen and Mösskirch it has been remarked that the French erred in bringing up their divisions in succession, and that this accounted for their being so long contested. The first divisions that came up were greatly wearied when the others arrived, and the latter had to re-establish the balance in the contest before thinking of striving for victory.

† After his proscription, Pichegru had taken refuge in Germany. As the French entered Biberach he hastily left the town. Moreau's rapid march had surprised him there. Here was a strange accident. Pichegru, the conqueror of Holland, afraid of falling into the hands of French soldiers; a general flying before Moreau, his pupil in the art of war!

not only was the country rich, but it had captured the greater portion of the magazines which the Austrians had formed with such pains. To the latter the loss was double; for, as the French did not establish magazines of any like magnitude, the capture not only deprived the Austrian troops of the stores accumulated in them, but these went to meet the wants of their adversaries, and to nourish the victorious troops.

After the first successes of the Army of the Rhine, Bonaparte awaited Moreau's compliance with the stipulation entered into at Bâle.

The demand made on the Army of the Rhine was not acceptable to Moreau, and he was considerably annoyed when it was reiterated. Some critics accuse the First Consul of having taken from Moreau one quarter of his troops, and of having in that manner crippled his army. A careful examination of the operations will show this criticism to have been hardly fair. Not only had the first battles much reduced his opponent's forces, but Moreau was far from crippled, and strong enough to contend against Kray, as was seen in the operations which culminated in the victory at Hochstett.

To smooth the way, Carnot, who had been appointed minister of war in the place of Berthier when the latter was appointed to the command of the Army of Reserve, was sent to Moreau's headquarters to insist that the troops should be directed to set out forthwith. Being a determined man, Carnot succeeded in his mission, and persuaded Moreau into compliance. He had left Paris on the 6th of May, was at Bâle on the 8th, and travelling day and night, was at Moreau's headquarters by 9 a.m. on the 10th. He was the bearer of an order from the Consuls for a corps of 25,000 men to be detached from the Army of the Rhine, and sent by the way of the Saint Gothard into Italy. Having accomplished his mission, Carnot quitted the Army of the Rhine, and reached Lausanne on the night of the 13th of May. According to Thiers, he left for Paris immediately after having witnessed the start of the troops intended to descend into Italy by way of the Saint Gothard.

Carnot related the circumstances of his mission in a letter he wrote to Lacuée, who was at that time acting for him.

"I could well expect that I should cause a good deal of pain to the general-in-chief, coming, so to say, to stay him in the course of the most brilliant victories by a demand for a

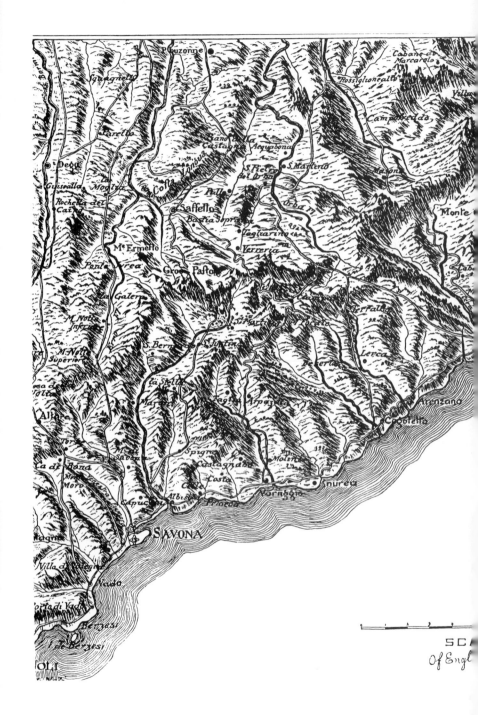

MILES

considerable portion of his forces for another army. He has been really affected by it. But, as he is at the same time a good citizen as well as an able general, he has complied, after having explained to me the inconveniences that might affect the Army of the Rhine, which only fights with success against the enemy through its superiority in bravery and by extraordinary efforts. He fears he will not be any longer able to maintain an offensive attitude, and then will find himself incapable of holding his advanced position. He will be obliged to fall back, and abandon the resources which the locality furnishes. Discouragement would then seize hold of the minds of his soldiers, and the enemy would become more bold. These reasons have not, however, prevented his complying with the First Consul's orders."

From Gouvion Saint Cyr we learn his opinion of Carnot's visit. Very probably his views were shared by other officers of the Army of the Rhine.*

"The mission of the minister of war at a moment when he must have had so much work to attend to at the headquarters of his ministry, and for the purpose of enforcing the execution of an order (a thing which might have been done just as well by an ordinary officer employed as a message-bearer); the employment, I say, of so high a functionary must have furnished plenty of matter for conjecture. The most likely supposition was that the chief of the state, entertaining no doubt of Moreau's ambition, and attributing to him a character which was never his, considered it quite possible that Moreau would refuse to allow so considerable a section of his army to quit him, lest its departure should in any way lessen his personal influence or even put a period to his successes. As Carnot had for a long time been on friendly terms with him, it was hoped that he would exercise sufficient influence on him to overcome his repugnance. Those who understood Moreau's character best, who knew him so timid in political affairs, imagined that he would have obeyed the most simple order without the least hesitation; and believed that Carnot's mission would only serve to heighten his importance, by showing him with what delicacy the First Consul acted towards him."

Carnot was the bearer of a letter from Moreau to Bonaparte, written from Biberach. The general expresses himself thus:

* Gouvion Saint Cyr, " Mémoires," tom. ii. p. 235.

" The detachment which you demand upsets our arrangements, nevertheless, we shall do our best. . . . I am going to concentrate in Switzerland and as speedily as possible 20 battalions, 20 squadrons, and the guns which the minister has demanded from us. These troops will be placed at the disposal of General Moncey."

Carnot was at the same time furnished with a return showing what troops were about to be transferred from the Army of the Rhine to the Army of Reserve, in all 18,714 infantry and 2803 cavalry. Moncey, nevertheless, writes to Bonaparte from Lucerne on the 24th of May, and says he has not more than 11,000 men in all. His totals, in a return which accompanies his letter, are—

Cavalry ...	...	...	...	...	2160 men.
Infantry	...	...	...	...	9350 ,,

11,510

Bonaparte evidently was not entirely satisfied with the arrangements proposed by Moreau. In a letter written on the 14th of May, he remonstrates, pointing out the distance some of the corps were from Switzerland, which would make their arrival in Italy far too late. He concluded by urging that a good corps might be given to Moncey, and that it might be so arranged for him as to be in a position to issue from the Saint Gothard during the first decade of the month Prairial. He strengthens this recommendation by showing the unfortunate results which would follow the capture of Genova and a defeat of the Army of Reserve.

It was Carnot's personal influence that succeeded in making Moreau accede to Bonaparte's wishes, for the general a short time before had entertained quite different views. This is shown by the two letters sent by Berthier on the 2nd of May to the First Consul, in both of which mention is made of a letter from General Dessoles which proved that not only Moreau had no intention of sending reinforcements to the Army of Reserve, but that he contemplated calling up Moncey with all the troops he had under him, and making the Army of Reserve undertake the protection of Switzerland.

On the 11th or 12th of May, Moncey * set out for Italy with

---

* Moncey, as senior marshal, was ordered to preside over the council of war which was to try the unfortunate Marshal Ney. He declined, and for so doing was sentenced to three months' imprisonment, and was deprived of his rank.

the troops Bonaparte had demanded from the Army of the
Rhine. To conceal from the enemy the diminution of his
forces, Moreau had drafted men from every corps to make up
the contingent for Italy. It was left to Moncey to undertake
the organization of this corps on the march. Marmont states
that it co nsisted of two divisions, under Lorge and Lapoype, and
that it was about 12,000 strong.

Evidently in numbers it fell below what was expected.
Bonaparte complained to the minister of war that where he
expected at least two-thirds of the troops shown in the return
delivered to him on the 13th of May, Moncey arrived in
Lomb ardy with only one-third, and of that third one-half were
unreliable men.

The idea of a diversion by the Saint Gothard appears to have
been entertained by Massena, Berthier, and other officers.
Writing to the First Consul from Chalons, Berthier says : "But
I believe, as I have already thought, and Massena is of the
same opinion, that the enemy is lost should a corps of 12,000 or
15,000 men show on the Saint Gothard at the moment when we
shall enter into Italy by the Saint Bernard. This is the only
measure for destroying the enemy."

In Massena Bonaparte had a stubborn officer, one who
would in all probability find plenty of occupation for Melas in
Liguria, and was likely to keep him there the time necessary
for giving the Army of Reserve full development. For all that
Massena was left without any help ; he was accorded no reinforcements, no stores, no materials. His army might struggle
to the utmost, and then succumb, so that the armies in the other
fields might have time to issue out victorious.

To Moreau, on the contrary, was given the very best army,
and, though the First Consul has been accused of having been
jealous of him, all the men and materials available were sent to
him. He had a fine body of artillery, and sufficient means for
crossing the Rhine.

Of the three armies of operation, Moreau was to have about
130,000 men, Bonaparte 40,000, and Massena 36,000. Bonaparte's genius had nevertheless recognized the importance of
driving Kray back on Ulm and Ratisbonne as being vital for
the success of all the operations. This could not be done without employing a force about equal to his own.

CHAPTER IV.

AUSTRIAN PLANS.

The Aulic Council—Thugut overrides the advice of the Archduke Charles to negotiate—The Archduke removed from his command—Discourtesy of the Russian generals—The Czar Paul approaches the First Consul—Withdraws from the coalition—Austrian preparations—Prussia promises to remain neutral —The Austrian army in Italy to assume the initiative—The Aulic Council believes that France is quite exhausted—Kray ordered to remain on the defensive in Germany—The Austrians are blind to the danger which menaces them in the valley of the Danube—Melas appointed to command the Austrian army in Italy—He scatters his troops—The Aulic Council obstinately disbelieves the existence of an Army of Reserve—Melas does so likewise, and fails to concentrate his army betimes.

THE events in Northern Italy have been described in Chapter III. The coalition in which Austria, Russia, England, and the Two Sicilies were represented had in the year 1799 chased the French literally out of the country. Coni, the last place they held in Italy, had been captured, and when that fell all that was left to the French in Italy was a narrow strip of littoral bound by the sea on one side and by lofty hills on the other. All Germany had been evacuated, and on that side the French were on the defensive, occupying the strong places on the left bank of the Rhine.

At that period a vicious system obtained in Austria of intrusting the best interests of the country to the consideration of the Aulic Council. This was a council of high officers at Vienna, with whom rested the direction of the military concerns of the empire. This method of sending from Vienna, far from the seat of operations, plans of campaign cut and dried was an eminently vicious system. Instructions prepared far away from the theatre of war necessarily labour under many serious inconveniences. To the meddling of the Aulic Council with the designs of the various Austrian commanders during the Napoleonic wars, and to its forcing upon them instructions regarding the conduct of their operations, may be attributed many of the disastrous results of the various campaigns both in Germany and in Italy.

Austria, badly advised by Baron de Thugut and the Cabinet of Vienna, had committed a great error in not profiting by the favourable situation which the victories of Suwarroff had gained for her to enter into negotiations with France. Furthermore, Austria did even worse, for it took away from the Archduke Charles—the best general the nation possessed, the only one who could direct the war with some hope of success—the command of the army, and this for no other reason than because he was opposed to the continuance of the war.*

This distinguished officer had in his wisdom and experience foreseen the dangers which threatened his country, should Austria continue at war with the Republic. He argued that now, when the coalition would no longer have to contend against an incapable Directory, and when Russia, on one hand, had withdrawn her army, and such a distinguished antagonist as Bonaparte had been added on the other, it would be prudent to take advantage of the successes of the last campaign, and endeavour to come to terms with the French.

The Archduke's treatment—for, under pretence of being appointed Governor of Bohemia, he was removed from his command—caused intense displeasure in Germany, for his achievements in the campaign of 1796 had gained him a well-deserved reputation in his country. His removal from the command, moreover, shook the confidence of the soldiers, who simply adored him.

Thus at the very time when Bonaparte was appointing Moreau to command the Army of the Rhine and Massena to lead the Army of Italy on account of their personal acquaintance with Germany and Italy, the Cabinet of Vienna was removing from the command of their army an officer who not only possessed the full confidence of the soldiers, but was quite familiar with the probable theatre of operations.

At the close of the past year a disagreement between the Archduke Charles and Suwarroff regarding the conduct of the

---

* In 1804, General Duka, Quartermaster-General of the Austrian army, supported the Archduke Charles in his remonstrances against a fresh war with France. He was at once named commander of the district of Temeswar, the most distant quarter of the empire!

war, the jealousy of the two states, and the exhausted condition of the Russian treasury were causes which combined to lead to a rupture. The Russian troops withdrew, and took no further part in the war.

When the Czar Paul joined the coalition, in a very disinterested spirit he had laid down the principle of restoring to all belligerents what territory they had lost, and Suwarroff in his conversation made no secret of this intention of his master. Austria, nevertheless, was very grasping, and while keen to make the Russian victories the means of strengthening the hold she had on the territory of Northern Italy, she became very uneasy regarding her possession of Venice. Chevalier de Cavour asserts that the very apple of discord between the Russians and Austrians was the occupation of Ancona by the latter. The only plausible reason the Austrians could adduce for placing there a garrison of 6000 men was that such a measure would prevent the French from occupying that city.

The behaviour of the Russians towards their allies seems to have been somewhat strange, and, to say the least, very discourteous. Alison quotes two instances, which are as follows: "The presumption and arrogance of Korsakoff were carried to such a pitch, that in a conference with the Archduke Charles, shortly before the battle (of Zurich), when that great general was pointing out the positions which should in an especial manner be guarded, and said, pointing to the map, 'Here you should place a battalion.'—'A company, you mean,' said Korsakoff.— 'No,' replied the Archduke, 'a battalion.'—'I understand you,' rejoined the other; 'an Austrian battalion, or a Russian company.'"[*]

Later, in October of the same year, not quite approving of a plan Suwarroff had proposed, to abandon the Grisons, advance with all his forces to Winterthur, form a junction with Korsakoff and attack the French in concert with the Austrians, the Archduke suggested an alternative one not quite so difficult and perilous. But Suwarroff, who still smarted under the irritation caused by the defeat of the Russians at Zurich, replied in angry terms. Hart relates that Suwarroff's letter terminated with the following expressions: "I am field-marshal as well as you; commander, as well as you, of an imperial army; old, while you are young; it is for you to come and seek me."

---

[*] Alison, "History of Europe," vol. v. p. 124.

Alison * quotes from Hard part of a letter from a Russian officer on Suwarroff's staff to Count Rostopchin at St. Petersburg : " Our glorious operations are thwarted by those very persons who are most interested in their success. Far from applauding the brilliant triumphs of our arms, the cursed Cabinet of Vienna seeks only to retard their march. It insists that our great Suwarroff should divide his army, and direct it at once on several points, which will save Moreau from total destruction. That Cabinet, which fears a too rapid conquest of Italy, from designs which it dares not avow, as it knows well those of our magnanimous emperor, has, by the Aulic Council, forced the Archduke Charles into a state of inactivity, and enjoined our incomparable chief to secure his conquests rather than extend them ; that the army is to waste its time and strength in the siege of fortresses which would fall of themselves if the French army were destroyed. What terrifies them even more than the rapidity of our conquests, is the generous project, openly announced, of restoring to every one what he has lost. Deceived by his ministers, the Emperor Francis has, with his own hand, written to our illustrious general to pause in a career of conquest of which the very rapidity fills him with alarm."†

In the summer of 1799, by insisting that no operations were to be undertaken against the Army of Italy until Mantua and other places were reduced, the Aulic Council had thwarted Suwarroff's scheme for completing Moreau's overthrow. The Russian commander-in-chief's plan consisted in blockading, and nothing more, the principal fortresses the French still held in Italy, so as to be able to follow with overwhelming forces the army of the Republic, at that moment in retreat, and to drive it over the Maritime Alps. Austria was evidently jealous of having to share the conquest of Italy with a powerful ally, whilst the pride of the Russians was hurt at beholding their most renowned commander held subject to the orders of the Aulic Council, a body which was all in favour of a slow and methodical system of warfare.

---

* Alison, "History of Europe," vol. v. p. 63.

† An essential requirement in war is singleness of direction ; alliances generally lead to friction. The idea that a common interest binds the two nations is illusory. Differences of opinion soon crop up, and are apt to mar concerted operations. The *entente cordiale* is not lasting, it is a myth. The desire to obtain the lead in the command, jealousy, national prejudices, etc., are all against it.

Looking at this conflicting state of ideas, how was a cordial co-operation of the allied troops possible? Things went from bad to worse, until there was a separation of the Russian from the Austrian forces, both in Italy and in Switzerland. In point of fact, their mortifying defeat at Zurich had greatly irritated the Russians. Suwarroff abruptly stopped all further discussion by declaring angrily that his troops were unfitted for mountain warfare, and much in need of rest. He would not listen to the Archduke's representations, and churlishly rejected all proposals for a personal interview.

Bonaparte possibly had become aware of this unsatisfactory state of things, and foresaw how very advantageous it would be for France if he could succeed in detaching Russia from Austria, and put an end to their dangerous alliance. He devised means for conciliating the Czar, and to pave the way sent back to Russia 5000 or 6000 Russian prisoners who had been captured at Zurich and in Holland; and not only did he forbear to demand an exchange, but he had the Russians freshly equipped.* This act of generosity, added to the misunderstanding existing between Suwarroff and the Austrian generals, had the result of making the Czar hold aloof from the coalition.

He was much exasperated with George III. for various reasons. One was that the Russian soldiers included in the capitulation of Alkmaar were coolly received when conveyed to England, and afterwards as good as imprisoned in the island of Guernsey. Another was that the king would not comply with his whimsical demand for the surrender of Malta, and his own recognition as Grand Master of the Order of Malta. The English, besides, had laid siege to the place, and this caused him great offence. He was ready to accuse England of treachery.†

The Emperor Francis furnished other causes of complaint. Not only was he fully determined to retain all Northern Italy,

---

* When returning from Marengo, the First Consul passed through Sens, where a large number of Russian prisoners were confined. These unfortunates were in a pitiable state. Bonaparte had a sum of money distributed amongst them, and promised that their lot would speedily change. In this he kept his word.

† The Czar had been elected Grand Master of the Order of Malta in October, 1798, but Nelson held that the King of Naples was the legitimate sovereign of the island. England, in any case, did not like Malta to pass into the hands of either the French or the Russians, considering it very necessary for her communications with India.

but he was against the re-establishment of the House of Savoy and the reinstatement of Charles Emanuel IV.*

What annoyed the Czar greatly were the sufferings of his army whilst transferred from Italy to Switzerland in the latter part of the previous year, the utter want of preparation which led to one long disaster, and to Suwarroff's retreat into Bavaria. Again, when Ancona fell before the attack of the combined Austrian, Russian, and Turkish forces, the Russian standard had been hauled down, and only the Austrian left flying.

The Czar Paul, in short, had become dissatisfied with the politics of Austria and England. The flower of his army had perished in Italy, fighting under Suwarroff, in Switzerland under Korsakoff, and in Holland under Hermann. The old and new pretensions of England regarding the navigation of neutrals had day by day added to his discontent. He now imagined that he detected a new era in the measures introduced by the French Government since the 18th Brumaire. His hatred of the Revolution abated; and, added to all this, a certain personal admiration for the character of the First Consul led to his ordering his armies to recross the Vistula.†

The Archduke Charles makes some sound observations on the hapless result of coalitions. He says: "The alliance between Austria and Russia came to be broken, as occurs with

---

* Charles Emanuel IV. came to the throne at an evil moment in October, 1796. His predecessor, who had obstinately entrusted his armies to the care of very aged officers, had lost all Savoy and the county of Nice. Embued with great hatred for the French Revolutionists, Charles Emanuel contracted a very close alliance with Austria. To keep a portion of his territory, he had been compelled in 1797 to make a treaty with France. Notwithstanding this treaty, the French instigated the Republican party in Piedmont. Joubert, on the plea that the king had not furnished the contingent of 9000 men he was bound to provide by virtue of this offensive and defensive treaty with France, and on account of his refusal to give up the arsenal, seized all the principal towns of the kingdom. It was then that Charles Emanuel IV. retired with his family to Cagliari.

When Suwarroff took possession of Turin, one of his first acts was to send Count di Gifflenga to Cagliari to induce the king to return to Piedmont; but the king made no move. Had it not been for Russia and England, Austria would have taken possession of Piedmont, but she was forced to moderate her views, limiting her ambition to the possession of Tortona and Alessandria, which in past times had been wrested from the Milanese by the sovereigns of Savoy, and which she claimed had to return to Austria.

† Paul soon lost Suwarroff, that commander who had the reputation of being invincible. Shortly after his arrival at St. Petersburg he fell under the displeasure of the emperor; that and vexation for the loss of his reputation for invincibility hastened his end.

most coalitions founded on the computations of powers equal in forces. The idea of a common advantage, the prestige of a confidence which rests on identical opinions, prepare the way for the first advances; the difference of opinion with regard to the means for attaining the common end sows the seed of misunderstanding, and this perfidious feeling goes on increasing in proportion as the events alter the point of view, disconcert the objects, and deceive the expectations. In the end it breaks out just when the independent armies should be acting together. The very natural desire to obtain pre-eminence in success as well as in glory, rouses the rival passions of the chiefs of nations. Pride, jealousy, tenaciousness, and presumption are born from the contention between ambition and conflicting opinions. Endless contradictions keep irritating more and more, and it is a fortunate accident when a union of this kind is dissolved without the two sides taking up arms against one another."

All these irritating matters led to the Czar withdrawing from the coalition in December, 1799. The discord between the allies can be reckoned as one of the fortunate circumstances which favoured Bonaparte in his campaign. The egoistic and covetous policy of Austria led to it. Rather than restore the lost provinces to the princes who had been driven out, Austria hoisted everywhere the yellow and black flag, and in place of recalling the rightful sovereigns made herself mistress of their states.

Bonaparte had detected his opportunity, and at once commenced by flattering attentions to gain Paul's favour. He lost no chance for cultivating a good understanding with the capricious Czar, and was so adroit in his acts that at length he succeeded in establishing a perfect understanding between the two Governments. Paul, who had been dazzled by the brilliancy of Bonaparte's victories in Italy and in Egypt, remained up to the day of his murder his most ardent admirer. He wrote to him a flattering letter—

"CITIZEN CONSUL,
          "I do not write to you to discuss 'the Rights of Man;' these are the abstractions of your Revolution. I confine myself to a fact, that when a great nation has placed at its head an estimable man, of distinguished merit, it has a Government; and I address myself to you because we can understand each

other, and I can treat with you. I wish to unite with you to put an end to the injustice of England, who violates every article of the law of nations, and has no guide but her egotism and interest."

The friendship of the Czar was flattering to Bonaparte, being the homage of a sovereign ; but, on account of the peculiar characteristics of that monarch, less valuable in a political point of view.

The withdrawal of the Russians from the war was a great disappointment to Austria and to Great Britain, for those two powers had derived very efficient assistance from the Russian troops in the past campaign.*

Notwithstanding the secession of the Russians and the retirement from the army of the Archduke Charles, whose views about the prosecution of the war were not in unison with

---

* On the night between the 23rd and 24th of March, 1801, the Czar, at the age of forty-six, was brutally murdered in the Michael Palace. A conspiracy, numbering sixty members, had been formed to dethrone him, as latterly his actions had been so extravagant as to have given rise to a very general belief that he laboured under a certain degree of insanity. It was said that the intention was simply to dethrone the Czar without depriving him of his life, but the brutality shown in the sequel proved that the conspirators were prepared to go any length. A portion of the conspirators, led by General Benningsen, who took a leading share in the execution of the plot, presented themselves before the door of the Czar's apartments and demanded admittance. A trusty Cossack, who slept there, having refused to let them pass, the conspirators set on the faithful and unfortunate soldier, and after a desperate resistance he was despatched.

Paul, who was in bed, startled by the noise, tried to escape to the empress's apartments, but he had forgotten that by his own orders the door of communication had been closed up. He then concealed himself in a press. The conspirators, having broken the door open and searched everywhere, eventually found him out, and dragged him from his hiding-place. They presented him with a paper containing his abdication, which he first refused to sign. At last he consented to abdicate, if the conspirators would consent to release him, but, fearing a rescue, they seized him, knocked him down, and tried to suffocate him. The Czar was making a desperate resistance, when one of the conspirators despatched him by stamping his heel into his eye, thus beating his brains out, while others held him down. Another version of the murder is that Paul was strangled with an officer's sash after a desperate struggle, but that before this was accomplished his brain had been nearly beaten out with the pommel of a sword.

Paul undid in the evening what he had done in the morning ; raised one and crushed the other, without any one knowing why. He was described in three words, *Order, counter-order, disorder.* Countess Potoka writes of him, " To say the truth, Paul's tyranny and his extravagances, which partook of cruelty in a certain measure, justified those who, having failed to force his abdication, found themselves obliged to take his life." A strange justification for murder, surely, especially

those of Thugut and the English party in Vienna, Austria, proud of the successes gained in the preceding campaign, and relying on its superb army, which numbered 200,000 combatants, resolved to continue the war.

By a treaty signed on the 16th of March, the Elector of Bavaria agreed to put 12,000 men in the pay of England to be employed in the war. The Elector of Mayence and the Duke of Würtemberg each agreed to furnish 6000 men under the same conditions. On the 20th of June of the same year Great Britain and Austria made a very important treaty, binding themselves not to make a separate peace; each power covenanting to obtain the consent of the other. The emperor agreed to raise his forces in Germany and Italy to the greatest possible strength; England engaged to advance a subsidy of two millions sterling, and to augment as much as possible the German and Swiss troops in the British pay in the German campaign.

Notwithstanding the flattering promises Bonaparte made to Prussia, she refused to become his ally. However, she promised to remain neutral, and to induce many of the minor German states to follow her policy.

There were two theatres of war, one in Germany in the countries of the Rhine and Danube, the other in Italy in the valley of the Po. On the first, the Austrians had concentrated under the command of Baron Kray an army of over 112,000 men, with a fine proportion of cavalry and well found in artillery. In Italy, another army was commanded by the veteran Melas, somewhat superior in numbers, and composed of tried soldiers rendered confident by the victories of the previous year. The army in Italy was supported by an English fleet, which was cruising about the gulf of Genova.

murder attended by a ferocity which was hardly to be expected considering the rank of the conspirators.

Bonaparte evidently at [first did not know what was the manner of the Czar's death, for he writes to his brother Joseph—

"Paris, April 11, 1801.

"The Emperor of Russia died on the night of the 24th of a stroke of apoplexy. I am so dreadfully afflicted by the death of a prince whom I highly esteemed that I can enter into no more details. He is succeeded by his eldest son, who has received the oaths of the army and of the capital."

Bonaparte's insinuations that England had connived in the assassination of Paul I. were unworthy of him. Possibly they were prompted by the letter the Emperor Alexander wrote to the King of England, expressing his earnest desire to re-establish the amicable relations of the two countries.

It was at that time open to the Austrian Government to adopt one of the following plans. The Austrians could concentrate their principal forces in Swabia on the Lower Rhine, advance on that river, and, after having scored a first success, combine with a British army landed in Holland or in Belgium. The Austrian forces in Italy would in that case remain peacefully on the Po, ready to meet on the plains a French army which might have arrived with little cavalry and badly horsed artillery.

On the other hand, the Austrian forces might have remained on the defensive in Germany, and operated with their army in Liguria and on the Var. This latter was the plan that was adopted by the Austrians.

The Cabinet of Vienna were by this time nourishing vast and bold designs. The Austrian army under Kray in Germany was intended to maintain a strictly defensive attitude up to the moment when the French, recalled to their southern provinces by Melas's progress, would withdraw from the banks of the Rhine. Kray was then to seize the fortunate moment and carry the war into Switzerland and Alsace, pushing on, possibly, to the valley of the Saône to effect a junction with Melas in the plains of Burgundy. There the terrain was favourable for the development of their numerous cavalry, and their armies could act with much greater energy, as the country presented far less difficulties than were to be encountered in a mountainous region.

But what real prospects were there of these designs meeting with success? Their two armies were already too far from each other to admit of rendering mutual support in the coming operations, and would find themselves driven further asunder by the interposition of the greatest portion of the Republican forces.

Their army in Italy was intended to operate too far from the hereditary states on which it was naturally dependent for aid. Neither could it go to Kray's assistance should he fare badly in the coming conflict.

The initiative in the operations was to be left to their army in Italy, which the previous year's victories, those of the Trebbia and of Novi, had led to the foot of the Apennines. That army, aided by the British fleet, was to blockade and capture Genova, advance on the Var, and march on Toulon. At

Toulon it was not only to be joined by the British fleet, but by a body of British soldiers coming from Mahon,* and also by a number of French emigrants. It was, moreover, thought possible to endeavour to profit from the restlessness of the *Chouannerie,* which was again commencing to make itself felt in the southern provinces of France.

The Austrians were led to assume the offensive in Italy by certain plausible considerations, the principal of which appears to have been the great difference in the numbers of the opposing forces. The 116,000 men the Austrians had in that country could well cope with Massena's army, which was known to be very weak. To this should be added the promised co-operation of the British fleet. The disastrous result of the battles fought the previous year had likewise been taken into account, as being likely to have lowered the self-confidence and *morale* of the French army.

To all this should be added that the Aulic Council steadily derided such a thing as the existence of an Army of Reserve. Even after it had received notice of the destination of the same army, it paid not the least attention to this warning. All the bombast regarding its formation so loudly trumpeted in the *Moniteur* was taken to be nothing beyond a ridiculous invention, originated to frighten Melas and to divert him from his bold designs for an invasion of France. The real formation of this army had been so carefully concealed that for a time even in France no one would believe in its existence. Thugut enjoined Melas not to place the slightest faith in the so-called Army of Reserve, and to consider it a pure fabrication.

The Aulic Council also shared the common belief that the strength of France was exhausted, and that the allies would

---

* A despatch from Downing Street of the 8th of February, 1800, promised the Austrian Government a loan. Also that a body of from 15,000 to 20,000 British troops would be employed in the Mediterranean to act in concert with the Austrians in Upper Italy. It was understood that Sir Charles Stuart was to have commanded this contingent, but these expectations were disappointed by the arrival of intelligence that he had declined accepting the command. The disappointment of the troops on that occasion was considerably lessened by the happy choice as successor to their late commander-in-chief of Sir Ralph Abercromby, who arrived on the 22nd of June, 1800. The delays which occurred in the organization of this army rendered it useless as far as the plan of the allies was concerned. The victory of Marengo quite altered the situation before the British contingent was in a condition to be landed on the Continent. The following year it rendered a good account of itself in Egypt.

only have to engage in a war of invasion, certain that in the ensuing campaign the French would easily be brought to sue for terms.

Moreau's army was large, the Army of Italy was small, so it was possible for the Austrians to remain on the defensive in Germany and to hold the larger French army in check, whilst their superiority in numbers was made to tell in overcoming the French in Italy. Evidently the object of the allies was to compel the First Consul to weaken the Army of the Rhine by drawing off a certain amount of troops to cover the southern provinces of France. This would have enabled Kray to assume the offensive and enter into action. Had this plan been successful, France would have been invaded by two powerful armies, and left to the mercy of the invaders.

The Austrians were deceived by the great success of the former campaign, and little dreamt how great would be the change when a man of genius like Bonaparte assumed the direction of the operations. They had considered many things, but had omitted to take the most important into account. They forgot that the ruler of France was a general of the very first order, a real genius in war, a man who defied and overcame all obstacles.

Bonaparte had to be prepared for either eventuality, but finding the first alternative the more dangerous of the two, he posted an army of 140,000 men on the Rhine, and created an Army of Reserve. It was possible to employ the latter in two ways : it might either be told off to reinforce Moreau, and so enable him to outnumber Kray in Germany ; or, by drafting a contingent from Moreau's army, strengthen with it the Army of Reserve sufficiently to enable it to act alone, cross the Alps, descend into Italy, and operate on Melas's rear.

Fortunately for Bonaparte, the Austrians played into his hands by remaining on the defensive in Germany. By doing this they gave him the opportunity of assuming the offensive and gaining some victories in the valley of the Danube which indirectly favoured the operations of the Army of Reserve in Italy.

Moreau wrote to the First Consul from Strasbourg on the 28th of February, 1800 : " The offensive beyond the Alps leads to nothing particular. The emperor can neither hope for marked success on the Rhine on account of the strong places which line that frontier, nor will he be able to collect an army as strong as ours with all the troops of the empire put together.

" He has caused some troops to pass over from here into Italy, where, in reality, his army was much reduced. But I repeat it, I believe he wants to capture Genova, and, after that, will be ready to make what conditions you like for Germany as long as you will let him enlarge himself in Italy."

Alarmed by the result of the previous campaign, Austria renounced to dispute the possession of Switzerland, of that advanced position so precious for the French. Bulow argues that they should have attacked the French in that country, as the conquest of Genova was not so important by half. But Italy was the sole aim of Austria and the ardently coveted prize of the war.

The greatest error the Cabinet of Vienna committed in 1800 was to suppose that Italy was the quarter in which the decisive attack was to be made. The country about the Apennines and the Var was full of natural obstacles, and consequently easily defended, notwithstanding the numerical superiority of the Austrians. While dreaming of conquests on the Var and in Provence, Austria was quite blind to the danger which really menaced the empire in the valley of the Danube, the true avenue to the Austrian states. The Cabinet once committed to this plan, Bonaparte had the game in his hands, as long, naturally, as he could act with vigour.

Blind to their best interests, the Austrians, who had adopted the second alternative, were compelled to make their army in Italy a strong one, leaving the French numerically superior on the Rhine. Alison gives the Austrians 96,000 men in Piedmont, with 20,000 more in Venice, Lombardy, and Tuscany. In Germany he reckons they had 92,000 men—of which number 18,000 were excellent cavalry—and 400 guns. To this should be added 20,000 men furnished by Bavaria and some of the smaller German states subsidized by England.

Everything considered, it is very evident that it would have paid the Austrians better had they carried hostilities into French soil, and made France support the burden and miseries of the war.

At the head of the Austrian army in Italy was Melas, an officer of considerable experience and ability. But he was old, and little competent to cope with the fiery and enterprising generals of the French Republic. He was also badly seconded.

Melas had commenced his military career during the Seven Years' War, fighting against the Prussians. Like the rest of the Austrian officers, he was strictly tied to traditions; his conceptions were made subordinate to certain rules, from which he never departed. He was systematically slow and without energy. His chief of the staff was Baron de Zach, an able officer, brisk, intelligent, and well versed in administration and tactical details.

In fighting qualities the Austrian troops were not to be at all compared with the French. Nothing, possibly, had demonstrated this point better than the continuous attacks on the outworks round Genova, when the Austrians, contending against a straitened and starving army, always lost more heavily than their adversaries.

When, in the first days of April, 1800, the campaign in Italy opened, the Austrian active troops amounted to 96,000 men. Melas had, however, made a poor disposition of his forces, and wasted his strength by scattering them injudiciously. Consequently, he was not able to put more than 60,000 men in the field. The French had no more than from 25,000 to 30,000, and occupied only Genova and the Littoral, with Oneglia and Nice. In Germany Austria had a numerous army, but the troops were scattered over an immense extent of country, from the sources of the Rhine up to the banks of the Maine. Kray, consequently, could only concentrate 45,000 men about the decisive point—the valley of the Danube. The French, on the other hand, could bring fully 75,000 men to compete with them.

Every salutary lesson which dearly bought experience had taught the Austrian commanders was fated to be wasted. Before the battle of the Trebbia the allies had in the field an army of 100,000 men; nevertheless they could hardly assemble 30,000 at any one point. Their troops were scattered over the plains of Italy, for the Aulic Council insisted in adhering to the old system of establishing a cordon of troops all over the territory which they occupied.

Chevalier Cavour, the great-uncle of Count Camillo Benso di Cavour, the able and faithful minister of King Victor Emanuel —a Piedmontese cavalry officer who was at Alessandria when the battle of Marengo occurred—declares that all the faults committed by the Austrians in the wars in Italy were revived and heaped together in the single campaign of Marengo. " These faults were the outcome of disdainfulness, obstinacy, avidity, and ignorance; and their result the misfortune and desolation of Europe."

Much of the dispersal of the Austrian forces was a consequence of the plan of operations adopted. The intended invasion of France by the line of the Var, carried too far from the base, and exposed in all its length to a flank attack from any French force which might issue from the Alps, was pregnant with risk. The plan might have answered at one time, but certainly not when the destinies of France were in the hands of such a pre-eminent master of the art of war. Possibly, even without Bonaparte being there, such an invasion might have collapsed from want of vigour, for the Austrian reinforcements had a very long march to make to join their army.

Melas is not to be entirely reproached for having disbelieved the existence of an Army of Reserve, after the most positive assurances on this point which he had received from the Aulic Council at Vienna. But he remained incredulous too long.* It was on the 13th of May that the first note of alarm reached him, that he received the first intimation that the Army of Reserve was moving in the direction of the Saint Bernard. He was on the point of crossing the Var and invading France when this news reached him. Still he did not believe it. He laughed when first told of it, and remarked that those who had seen this army must have looked through a magnifying-glass. How was it possible for an army at that early season of the year to cross the mighty Alps with cavalry and artillery? Nevertheless, as a precaution, he sent Generals Haddick and Palfy towards Turin, with orders to watch the issues of the valley of Aosta, if necessary.

News more and more pressing was arriving every day. At last Melas resolved to go back. He left Nice on the 20th, arrived at Cuneo on the 23rd, and continued *viâ* Sevigliano for Turin. He arrived at the last place on the 26th, to hear the unwelcome news of Haddick's defeat at Chiusella.

---

* It is related by Bonaparte himself that, to make sure of his presence with the army in Italy, Melas ordered an officer of his staff, who was personally acquainted with him, to go and confer with the First Consul under a flag of truce.

A general and well-understood principle enjoins, when the enemy manœuvres against your communications, to retaliate at once by manœuvring against his. It is evident that one cannot cause him greater embarrassment and injury than by going where he is not. At one moment, when Bonaparte marched from Ivrea to Milan, his position was critical, for an advance of the Austrians would have severed his communications before he had opened fresh ones by the Saint Gothard.

When surprised by the arrival of the Army of Reserve in Italy, the Austrians had no settled plan, and kept to a strict defensive against an enemy that, badly provided with artillery, weak in cavalry and wanting in munitions and supplies, had ventured into a vast basin studded with fortresses. The Austrian troops were made to march and to countermarch; the plans of to-day were upset on the morrow. Melas allowed himself to be hemmed in; to be deprived of all his communications, until matters got to such a point that he felt bound to venture Austrian supremacy in Italy upon the doubtful issue of a battle.

Melas would have done better had he at once withdrawn all his troops from Piedmont, from the Var, and from Genova, and directed them by forced marches on Piacenza. This could have been done in time had not a moment been lost. After he left Genova, Ott was very near reaching Piacenza before the French. What immense difference a few hours make in military operations! Had Ott complied with Melas's orders on their first arrival he would have been at Piacenza to contest the crossing of the Po on the 6th of June.

The essential point, when the news that the Army of Reserve had entered Piedmont had been received, was to concentrate every possible detachment. To do so at Alessandria was questionable, owing to the distance. The concentration should have been carried out further to the east, at Piacenza, where Vukassevich could have come. What was to be gained by his being left to cover Milan? It could have only brought about small fights in which good soldiers would have been lost to no purpose. Was it not better to gather all the forces, to be strong at some point, ready to deliver a good blow?

CHAPTER V.

MASSENA'S OPERATIONS IN LIGURIA.

Massena's early career—Destitute state of the Army of Italy—Massena reaches
Genova—Insufficient troops, and bad disposition of the Genovese—Orders for the
division commanders to concentrate—Bonaparte recommends not to occupy too
extended a line—How circumstances prevented his doing so—Austrians delay
commencing the operations—Melas attacked on the 6th of April—Separates
Suchet from Massena—Ott expels the French from Monte Faccio—Massena
recovers the position on the 7th—Operates outside Genova to recover communications with Suchet—Operations in the Ligurian hills for two weeks—Soult fails
to gain possession of Ponte Ivrea—French forces retire on Voltri—Melas fails
to cut them off from Genova—Genova blockaded—Ott invests it with 25,000 men
—Serious difficulties of supply—Ott makes a general attack on the 30th of
April—Massena attacks the heights of Coronata, and is driven back with heavy
loss—Attacks Monte Creto, baffled by a storm—Soult wounded and captured—
Internal discontent—Massena's heroic determination—Franceschi's mission to
Bonaparte—Returns and brings back news of the Army of Reserve—False
rumours of the approach of the Army of Reserve—Massena is invited to a
parley—Compelled to lend an ear to the proposal of the allies—Conceives a plan
for cutting his way through—Ott very keen to remain before Genova till Massena
capitulates—Massena accedes to an evacuation of the city.

In the year 1800 the destinies of France rested in the hands of
three of her most able generals, Bonaparte, Moreau, and Massena.
Of the two last, Moreau was eminent above all others for
wisdom and the soundness of his combinations; Massena
possessed incomparable seduction, and inspiration in the heat
of the combat.

Massena was born at Turbia, in the principality of Monaco,
on the 6th of May, 1758. This eminent warrior, though of low
extraction, had a most brilliant career. He worked as a sailor
for four years. At the age of seventeen he quitted the marine
and joined the Royal Italian Regiment, in which he served for
a period of fourteen years, attaining the rank of adjutant under
officer. That was the highest post he could obtain; there was
no further advancement to satisfy his ambition open to him in
the Sardinian army.

In the early days of the French Revolution, on the 1st of February, 1792, he joined the second battalion of the National Guards of the Var as adjutant, and speedily rose to high rank.

In his long conversations at Saint Helena, Napoleon said with regard to Massena that he was a " general endowed with a rare courage and remarkable tenacity, whose talent augmented with the greatness of the danger; who, when overcome, was always ready to begin afresh as if he had not been vanquished."

Massena was one of the most artful of Italians, and the foremost amongst Napoleon's marshals. He was a general of real genuine ability, and before his unsuccessful campaign in Portugal was in France deemed equal to Napoleon as a general, and by not a few held to be even Napoleon's superior. He was a real leader of men—that is, he had the gift of rousing his soldiers to great exertions when everything conspired against him, when the circumstances were so disastrous as to cast the whole of the army into gloom and despair. He had the power of infusing in his men his determination not to be beaten; he could make them believe thoroughly in their superiority over the enemy.

After Jourdan's defeat at Stokach on the 25th of March, 1799, Massena had been appointed to the chief command of the French forces in Switzerland. There he had to contend with serious difficulties, nevertheless he held his ground stoutly against the Archduke Charles. At Zurich, on the 25th of September, he gained a brilliant victory over the Russians, and averted from France all danger of invasion.

Bonaparte, who had a genius for understanding men, and was well acquainted with Massena's ability and spirit, recalled him from Switzerland and confided to him the supreme command of the Army of Italy. Having been born in the Riviera, and having taken part in the campaigns of 1795 and 1796, Massena was well acquainted with the Ligurian coast and with the issues from the Apennines. He was, moreover, the fittest officer for command in mountain warfare, in which he had quite recently shown signal ability.

It must be confessed that the command of the Army of Italy was poor recognition for Massena. He was compelled to quit victorious troops, to assume the command of a few thousand men scattered over the hills around Genova, to command an army in which misery and disorganization held supreme sway; an army without supplies, magazines, or money.[*]

On the 3rd of November, Joubert, in assuming the command of this army, wrote to the Directory: "I have the honour to inform you, citizens Directors, that General Brune has left me the Army of Italy in as good a state as circumstances permitted." But the citizens Directors were famous for bringing any army to ruin; so when Massena arrived to take command of the Army of Italy he found but a shadow of an army. The troops were unpaid, their uniforms worn to shreds, themselves barefooted and dying of starvation or from epidemic brought about by continuous privations. His predecessor, General Championnet, was so overcome by grief in having to behold the privations which his soldiers had to endure that he sickened and died [†] of an epidemic which broke out amongst the troops; a last scourge of an army once so flourishing and splendid. With his death had disappeared what little remained of self-respect in the army. When Massena took over the command of the French troops, nothing could equal their state of destitution. Everything at that moment forebode inevitable disasters. On every side it was impossible to avoid seeing the germs of disorganization and death. There were no chiefs and no discipline. The officers quitted their posts, the soldiers broke and sold their arms. Marbot, who served with this army, writes: "The troops were unpaid, almost unclad and unshod, receiving only quarter rations, and dying of starvation or epidemic sickness, the result of privations. The hospitals were full, and medicines were lacking. Bands of soldiers, even whole regiments, were every day quitting their posts, and making for the bridge over the Var. They forced their way into France, and scattered about Provence, declaring themselves ready to return to their duty at once if they were only fed. The generals had no power against such a mass of misery; every day their discouragement grew deeper, and they were all asking for leave, or resigning on the ground of illness." [‡]

---

[*] Massena's ill success in Portugal arose from the same causes. He experienced immense difficulties in getting provisions. He had to advance through a deserted country, where everything which the inhabitants could not carry away was delivered to the flames. This was the principal cause which compelled him to abandon his enterprise and to withdraw into Spain.

[†] Championnet died on the 22nd of December, 1799.

[‡] "Mémoires de Baron de Marbot," vol. i. p. 66.

The venality, avarice, and fraudulent embezzlements of the Directory were conspicuous. They always managed to neglect their troops. The utter carelessness they showed in the maintenance of their armies in the field was the subject of Bonaparte's first proclamation to the Army of Italy in 1796. In 1799, for want of food, many brave soldiers, the heroes of Lodi and Arcole, the conquerors of Castiglione and Rivoli, were driven by starvation to beg on the roads of the Apennines. Some even went to a greater length, and affiliated themselves to bands of brigands, to procure for themselves the simple necessaries of life, which their Government made no efforts to give them.

The troops were for the most part in a miserable condition. The disasters of the previous campaign had depressed their spirits. The artillery was in a bad state, the cavalry was much in need of remounts.

An officer who was with the army describes in the following words the appearance of the troops at that time : " The soldiers, pale, languid, disfigured, starving, naked, discouraged, and dejected, presented the appearance of so many miserable spectres. The streets were covered with the dying and with corpses ; and such of the former as succeeded in crawling as far as a hospital found themselves in worse conditions, without straw, without the least morsel of food, without attendance of any kind—a berth on the stony cold floor, and in the midst of filthy corpses (for latterly in many hospitals the dead were buried very late). There they met with a death more ready, more cruel, and more certain than if they had remained in the unhealthy fields, or on the roads they had quitted."

Massena made a great sacrifice in accepting the command of this unhappy Army of Italy. He well knew the sad condition that army was in, and how the Government could do next to nothing for it. Nevertheless, he went to Paris, and did not quit the capital until he had made sure of being given such articles of primary need as he knew for a certainty would be required by the army now placed under his command. Always keeping in view the requirements of that army, when passing through Lyons and Marseilles, on his way to join it, he took measures to obtain provisions, clothing, horses, etc. All the way down, as he passed by Toulon, Fréjus, Antibes, and Nice, he worked hard to see how he could put a term to the disgraceful desertion which he believed to be the outcome of the privations and

H

sufferings to which the soldiers had for a long time been subject.

When discipline is lost, it is with difficulty that it can be restored. The primary source of all the trouble was the neglect paid to the proper maintenance of the troops. Still, a very unsoldierlike spirit had more or less seized hold of all ranks. This had to be repressed with a strong hand. Massena punished the deserters severely, shot a few of their principal leaders, degraded and expelled such officers as had secretly connived at this disgraceful abandonment of their posts. His firm rule soon had the desired effect. It inspired confidence throughout the ranks, for the soldiers, always ready to obey an officer with a high reputation and a name, soon regained all their habits of obedience and self-respect.

Massena reached Genova on the 20th Pluviôse (10th of February). There he was soon to make himself a glorious name. His obstinate courage and the superhuman efforts he made to hold that place had very important consequences, for the entrance of the Army of Reserve into Italy might have become a serious task indeed had the Austrians been free to meet the French as they issued from the valley of Aosta.

From the Col di Tenda, where the mountains make their great bend to the northwards, near the sources of the Tanaro, a vast range branches off from the Alps. This, known as the Apennines, forms after a time the watershed between the Mediterranean and the Adriatic. This great range, as it runs inland for a considerable extent to the extremity of Calabria, bears different names, which have been given to its different sections by modern geographers. The section known under the name of Ligurian Apennines overhangs the gulf of Genova in the immediate vicinity of the sea.

"The majority of the chief towns of Italy," George states, "owe their importance very largely to their geographical position, while one or two are conspicuous exceptions to the general rule that geographical considerations mainly determine which seats of human habitation shall grow in importance. It was inevitable that a large maritime town should grow up somewhere on the strip of coast between the Apennines and the Western sea which alone gives access to Italy without the necessity of crossing a mountain-chain. That Genova should be the place was decided by two facts, that it possesses a pretty good harbour, and that the easiest route across the Apennines into the basin of the Po starts from thence." *

The city of Genova is the chief commercial seaport of Italy. Vessels of the largest class can enter inside the harbour, and, notwithstanding the heavy swells occasioned by the south-west wind (the Libeccio), the harbour is remarkably safe. But the series of moles and piers which protect the harbour were constructed long after the Austrians besieged the city in 1800. As one of the first commercial ports in the Mediterranean, Genova is a formidable rival to Marseilles.

The people possess all the qualities of a commercial and maritime community, and had been long remarkable for a spirit of enterprise and freedom, which strongly characterized the period of the ancient Republic.

Some hold that the name of the city was formerly Genua, being probably a corruption of *Janua* (a gate), to indicate that it was the gate of Northern Italy. Others declare that its name was derived from the fact that the shape of the coast here resembles that of a knee (*genu*).

The city presents a very imposing appearance when beheld from the sea.

> " Ecco ! vediam la maestosa immensa
> Città, che al mar le sponde, il dorso ai monti
> Occupa tutta, e tutta a cherchio adorna."
>   Bettinelli.

Genova had participated in the Crusades, and secured to herself a busy trade in the Levant. She once possessed colonies at Constantinople, in the Crimea, in Syria and Cyprus ; and the rivalry of the Genovese and Venetians was a fruitful source of war.

The Genovese are proud of claiming Columbus, the discoverer of America, as a native of their city, though it is contended that he saw light first, not in the city of Genova, but somewhere in the neighbourhood. Tradition points to the village of Cogoletto as being Columbus's birthplace, but Savona also lays claim to that honour. In any case, proud as the Italians are of Columbus, they took no part whatever in his voyages.

The Genovese have a greater right of being proud of the famous Andrea Doria, who in 1528 freed his country from foreign invaders and restored to Genova republican institutions.

* H. B. George, " The Relations of Geography and History," p. 196.

Doria was offered the ducal authority for life, and there is
no doubt that he might have acquired the absolute authority,
all of which he refused. However, in 1797, the people put an
end to Doria's constitution, and, not satisfied with this, an
excited mob burnt the Golden Book and destroyed the statue
of the greatest hero of Genovese liberty—a barbarous act,
which caused great displeasure to Bonaparte.

It will not be considered irrelevant here to narrate how
the general's first acquaintance with the Republic of Genova
was fraught with important consequences.

In July, 1794, Bonaparte was sent by the representatives
of the Convention upon a secret mission to Genova. At that
time the younger Robespierre was in supreme command at
Toulon. He had conceived a very high admiration for Bonaparte, and urged him to throw over his mission to Genova
and to accompany him to Paris, where he was returning to
support his brother. He offered him the command of the
National Guard, to supersede Heriot, of whose capacity the
Committee of Public Safety had become somewhat doubtful.

To his brothers, who strongly recommended him to close
with the offer, Bonaparte replied: "I will not accept it: this
is not a time to play the enthusiast; it is no easy matter to
save your head in Paris. Robespierre the younger is an
honourable man, but his brother is no trifler; if I went to
Paris, I should be obliged to serve under him. Me serve such
a man! Never. I am not ignorant of the service I might be
in replacing the imbecile commander of the National Guard of
Paris, but I do not choose to do so; this is not the time for
engaging in such an undertaking. What could I do in that
huge galley? At present there is no honourable place for me
but the army; but have patience: the time is coming when I
shall rule Paris." *

His defence of Genova will always be reckoned as the most
brilliant part of Massena's illustrious career. And not without
good reason; for when we take into account the wretched state
of the garrison, the epidemics and sickness, the serious discontent of the population, caused by the stoppage of their
business and occupation, as well as by starvation and death,
it seems miraculous that he managed to hold out as long as he
did. His supreme contempt for his adversaries, the result of

* Alison, " History of Europe," vol. iv. chap. xx.

the several victories he had gained over the Austrians, was
shown in the words he spoke to Lord Keith : " Give me some
provisions, and none of these gentlemen, I declare, will ever set
foot in Genova." * He disdained the idea of a capitulation ;
but he had to bow before necessity, for he had to keep his
troops alive. The enemy never succeeded in subduing him.

In place of an army of 60,000 men which he was told he
would have under his orders, there were not more than 30,000
men between Mont Cenis and Genova on whom he could count.
On the 28th Nivôse (7th of January) we find Massena writing to
the minister of war on this point : " You have no real knowledge
of the actual strength of this corps, for it is very far from what
it is shown in the returns which you gave me in Paris."

Having received some slight reinforcements, reorganized his
army, and re-established some measure of order and system of
provisioning, Massena was ready to confront the Austrians. He
was to present a stubborn front to the enemy for two months, and,
though he fought fiercely, a starving army and a starving city
proved the most redoubtable enemies he had to contend against.

At the end of the eighteenth century, Genova was the only
important place which remained to the French in Italy. After
the disasters of the past campaign, the residue of the Army of
Italy was left to defend that noble city. The Aulic Council
attached great importance to its capture, more so as all the
odds were dead against the French. Had fortune befriended
her, Austria would have become mistress of the whole of Italy.
She would then have regained her former positions on the
Maritime Alps, would have been in a position to attack Switzerland, or reinforce her army on the Rhine.

Austria undertook the conquest of Genova by enlisting everything in her favour, and in this was much aided by fortune.
The French, on the other hand, had to contend against an enemy
three times as numerous, and were doomed to play a passive *rôle*
so as to insure a full success in other points. To make up for
inferior numbers and scanty resources, they had only genius and
valour. Not only were they in inferior numbers and in straitened
circumstances, but a large and influential part of the inhabitants
were strongly attached to the cause of the Imperialists, and did

* Crossard, who inspected the city, felt convinced of the difficulties which an
attack by main force or by escalade would have experienced. To hold the city, it
only needed supplies and troops for manning the extent of its defences.

not cease to be a source of serious embarrassment to the general. The working classes who had lost their occupation, owing to the blockade established by the English fleet, were also seriously disaffected.

Writing to Bonaparte on the 28th of February, 1800, and expressing his opinion that the Emperor of Austria was seriously bent on capturing Genova, Moreau says : " If General Massena has organized his army, with a little skill and plenty of vigour he can save the place." Well did the rugged warrior play his part in the great war of 1800, fighting desperately amid famine and death all through two wearisome months, striving by all he knew to subdue the despondency of his officers and men. History has few examples of a more stubbornly contested struggle than Massena's defence of Genova. He was enjoined to offer a stubborn defence, and to occupy and detain the enemy as long as possible, so as to facilitate the offensive enterprises of the other two armies. He did what had been prescribed to him, and with most consummate ability.

The principal passes which lead from Piedmont to the shores of the Mediterranean are three in number—the Col di Tenda, Cadibona, and Bocchetta. All are practicable for artillery. Operating by the first, the Austrians would have left nearly the whole of the Army of Italy on their flank, they would have missed their special object, which was to divide it, and were, besides, liable to encounter more obstacles and to run greater risks. Advancing by the Bocchetta, the entire French army would be found concentrated on their front, and they would have secured no advantage whatever from their position. That of Cadibona alone offered, without incurring any risk, every possible advantage. If in the end the most was not made of these advantages, the reason can be found in the slowness of the Austrian movements.

Massena had given the most minute instructions to his subordinates, who were enjoined to concentrate their divisions at the first aggressive attempt the enemy should make. Genova, the too-evident objective point of the allies, was indicated as the rendezvous of the three divisions of the right wing.

From the 5th to the 12th of March, Bonaparte had written to Massena several letters full of forethought. He had, in a special way, recommended him not to occupy too extended a line, to keep four-fifths of his troops in Genova, and to occupy the Alps, Nice, with its surrounding forts, and the Col di Tenda with detachments. The Austrians, he believed, would issue from the passes on the French right in the neighbourhood of Genova, or on the centre in the direction of Savona, if not from both points at the same time. Massena was recommended to avoid one of these attacks, and to throw himself with all his forces on the enemy on the other. The ground would not permit Melas to draw any advantage from his superiority in artillery and cavalry. Bonaparte considered that a clever manœuvrer in a country like Liguria could beat 60,000 men with one-half that number. He ends one of the letters by reminding Massena that his opponent, Melas, being inferior to him in activity and talents, there is no cause for being afraid of him. He will not dare to go far, with Massena in Liguria, ready to fall on his rear or on the Austrian troops left in Piedmont.

In the beginning of March, Admiral Lord Keith established a blockade of the harbour of Genova. On the 5th of April following the entire British fleet cast anchor before that city, and cut off every means of communication by sea.

Massena had been deceived by the apparent immobility of the Austrians, and had come to believe that their troops, like his own, had been seriously weakened by the effect of contagious diseases. But at the commencement of April, the concentration and movements of troops which had been taking place for the last ten days, and the frequent reconnaissances made all along their front, left no longer any doubt in the mind of the French that an attack was imminent. This surmise was strengthened by the intelligence brought in that the Austrians had established magazines in different localities. Massena, however, did not expect to be attacked yet for another fortnight, and was very busy collecting supplies and ammunition.

Melas was very keen to secure the assistance of the population. He accordingly, on the 5th of April, issued from Acqui a proclamation to the Ligurians. In this he announced that he was about to reconquer their country, and called on all patriots to rise *en masse* against the French.

All of a sudden an order was issued for all the Austrian corps to concentrate at their headquarters. All were put in motion together, and by well-combined marches directed on the localities they were to occupy in the plan of operations sketched out. Melas himself transferred his headquarters first from Turin to Alessandria, and later on to Acqui. The greater portion of his forces had assembled in the valley of the Bormida. On the 5th of April he went from Acqui to Cairo, and thence to Carcare, Malale, and Cadibona. His intention was to cut the French line of defence in twain as near as possible to Genova, with the object of isolating Massena, and then, with the co-operation of the British fleet, to starve him out. If he succeeded in doing this, nothing would be left to Massena but to surrender the city. By this manœuvre the French left wing would be entirely separated from the rest of the army; and, as Suchet would find it impossible to feed his troops in the Riviera di Ponente, he would find himself compelled to retire behind the Var, in order to avoid the risk of being cut off from France. Melas's scheme was calculated to see the speedy evacuation of the Genovese territory by the French.

Massena occupied a very extended line of operations; with the left at Finale, under Suchet, 12,000 strong; the centre (12,000 more) at Cadibona and Bocchetta, under Soult; the reserve (2200 men) under his own command at Genova; and Miollis, with his division, on the right at Recco and Torriglia.

He had a difficult question before him: Was it best to make the Army of Italy depend entirely on France, or to abandon his communications with France, and make Genova his pivot of operations? It was open to him, in the first case, to provide Genova with a garrison of 7000 or 8000 men, keeping the rest of his troops concentrated between Savona and Finale; in the second alternative he could hold in hand some 30,000 men, with the left at Savona, and the right at Genova ready to confront the Austrians. The latter arrangement recommended itself only if he could make sure of collecting in Genova sufficient provisions for the subsistence of his army.

Massena did not follow either of these alternatives. With 30,000 troops he occupied a line 50 leagues in extent from the Col di Tenda on the left to the gulf of Levante on the right. This was a long and narrow strip of land, extending parallel to the sea and three leagues in breadth, having one single line of communication with the base which ran parallel to its front. It was a dangerous position, being easy to be overcome at any one point. Indeed, it was one of the many fortuitous circumstances of this campaign that all the danger of this position turned in favour of the French. It was not from option that Massena occupied it. He was in a certain way compelled to do so, for either of the two alternatives mentioned above hardly satisfied the requirements of the peculiar circumstances in which he was placed.

The operations sketched out by General Zach, and fixed to commence on the 27th of February, were adjourned. The Austrians were deterred by a heavy fall of snow which occurred on the 13th of February, and began to be alarmed lest the ships which were to come from Leghorn with provisions for the Austrian army might not be able to reach Savona in time. For these reasons the execution of the plan was put back for six weeks—a fatal delay, which in the end brought about the loss of their possessions in Italy.

Jomini, with very good reason, observes that circumspection was the favourite virtue of the Austrians. There is no doubt that all through this campaign lack of enterprise was equally conspicuous.

The Austrian staff were fully acquainted with the feebleness of the French troops. Reports of their misery and of their state of disorganization had reached the headquarters of the Austrian army. Melas, who after the fall of Coni had spread out his troops over Piedmont, Lombardy, Tuscany, and the Romagna, to get them to recover from the hardships of the past campaign and to repair their *matériel*, had fully restored the efficiency of his men. The disparity in the condition of the two armies was such that when the Austrian forces were ready for the contest it was a great blunder to give time to the adversary. And what made the adjournment more strange was that there were already rumours about of large forces being assembled by the French in the Valais to come in aid of the Army of Italy.

Had the Austrians commenced operations only a fortnight earlier, which was not at all impossible, they might have overcome Massena, and had plenty of troops at their disposal for confronting Bonaparte as he issued from the valley of Aosta.

Melas commenced the campaign by making his appearance simultaneously before Genova and Savona. His plan was very ably conceived, and the attacks were well combined.

His preparations were so ably concealed that Massena had not the least notion of what was about to happen. To distract his attention from the principal point, Ott had been directed to make a threatening demonstration against the extreme French right on the 5th.

On the 6th, the entire French line was attacked by a number of columns, and the contest was carried out from Nervi to San Giacomo.

In the operations of the 6th of April, Ott, who commanded the Austrian left wing, had 15,000 men. He issued from the valley of the Trebbia, and was directed to move on Monte Cornua, attack the forts on Monte Faccio, and operate against the French right. Hohenzollern, at the head of other 10,000 men, was to endeavour to force the Bocchetta pass. Melas, with the centre, consisting of three divisions, 25,000 men, was to advance by the valley of the Bormida, and make for Savona by way of Altare and Cadibona; his object, as we have said, being to separate the French left wing from the rest of the army. Elsnitz, who commanded the Austrian right, and Morzin, with two more divisions computed at 18,000 men, were to attack the French left at Monte San Giacomo's intrenchments, and to assist in making the telling movement of the centre a success.

Palfy, with a division, commenced by attacking the fortified position of Cadibona. He moved to the attack, passing by Altare and Torre, whilst General Saint Julien, at the head of his brigade, moved on Sassello and Montenotte with the object of supporting the attack. Gardanne, with 4000 men, was in position at Stella, Santo Bernardone, Madonna di Savona, and Vado; further away on the heights he occupied the redoubts of Montenotte, and behind it the intrenchments of Cadibona. He resisted the dashing onsets of Palfy's division all the day, and then fell back on the positions of Cadibona.

Saint Julien, having carried the heights of Montenotte and Monte Negrino, pursued the French in the direction of Madonna di Savona.

The Austrians, having cleared away the first impediments, rushed on the enemy and drove him back in disorder. Soult occupied Monte Moro, which covered Savona. This position was carried by a frontal attack, aided by a turning movement. The French retired precipitately, and were so closely followed by the Austrians that both entered pell-mell into the suburbs of Savona. Night alone put a period to the fighting.

By sheer force of numbers Melas had succeeded in beating Massena back towards Genova and separating Suchet from the French main body. Both sides fought with great determination,

HEADQUARTERS STAFF (HEADQUARTERS, GENOVA).

MASSENA, Commander-in-Chief of the Army.

Oudinot, General of Division, Chief of the Staff.

Andrieux, Adjutant-General, Under Chief of the Staff in the absence of Brigadier-General Franceschi.

Thiébault, Reille, Gautier, and Campana, Adjutant-Generals employed under the Commander-in-Chief.

Degiovanni, Ottavi, Adjutant-Generals, and Hervo, Acting Adjutant-General, employed on the general staff.

Aubernon, Chief Executive Commissary.

Artillery.	Navy.	Engineers.
Lamartillière, General of Division, Commanding Royal Artillery. Sugni, General of Division, Chief of the Staff of the Artillery.	Sibilla, Chief of Division, commanding the naval forces of the army.	Mares, Chief of Brigade, Commanding Engineer. Couche, Captain, Chief of the Staff.

DISTRIBUTION AND STR

Division Miollis.	Men.
Headquarters—Albaro.	
Held San Alberto and Recco with the 8th half-brigade of light infantry.	
Strength	600
Tortiglia and Scofera with the 24th of the Line.	
Strength	800
Monte Cornua with the 74th.	
Strength	1100
Albaro and Nervi with the 106th.	
Strength	1700
Total	4200

Division Gazan.	Men.
Headquarters—San Quirico.	
Held Cazella, Buzalla, and Savignone with the 3rd of the Line.	
Strength	1300
Teggia with Piedmontese Grenadiers	90
Voltaggio and Carasio with the 5th Light Infantry.	
Strength	500
Campo Marone Rivarolo and Ronco with the 2nd of the Line.	
Strength	1600
La Bochetta with a company of artillery	40
Campo Freddo Marcarolo and Masone with the 78th.	
Strength	1300
San Quirico with three companies of Pioneers.	
Strength	90
Total	4920

Division Marbot.	Men.
Headquarters—Savona.	
Commanded by Gardanne, Marbot being sick.	
Held Stella and la Madonna with the 3rd Light Infantry.	
Strength	900
La Vagnola and Monte-Notte with the 62nd.	
Strength	1500
St. Bernardone and the Madonna of Savona with the 63rd.	
Strength	500
Savona with the 93rd.	
Strength	500
Vado and Cadibona with the 97th.	
Strength	1300
Total	4700

STAFF OF THE RIGHT WING (Headquarters at Cornigliano).

Soult, Lieutenant-General, Commanding.

Gauthrin, Adjutant-General, Chief of the Staff.

Unattached Officers.

Fressinet, Brigadier-General.

Trivulzi, Adjutant-General.

Cerisa, Adjutant-General.

First Division.	Second Division.	Third Division.
lis, General of Division, mmanding.	Gazan, General of Division, Commanding.	Marbot, General of Division, Commanding.
rnaud, Petitot, Generals of igade.	Poinsot, Spital, Generals of Brigade.	Bujet, Gardanne, Generals of Brigade.
tor, Adjutant - General, ief of the Staff.	Noel Huart, Adjutant-General, Chief of the Staff.	Saqueleu, Adjutant - General, Chief of the Staff.
	D'Aoust, Squadron Commander on special duty.	

OF THE DIVISIONS.

Reserve.	Men.	Garrison of Genova and Gavi.	Men.	Total.	Men.
Reserve held Samerdarena with the nd.		Adjutant-General Degiovanni commanded in Genova, and had for garrison—		Division Miollis	4200
Strength	500	The 41st, strength	350	Division Gazan	4920
ri di Ponente and rnigliano with the th Light Infantry.		The 55th, strength	250	Division Marbot	4700
		The 73rd, strength	500	Reserve	2200
Strength	1700	The 45th, 500 strong, was at Gavi	500	Garrison of Genova and Gavi	1600
Total	2200	Total	1600	Total	17,620
				Deducting the garrisons of Genova, Gavi, and Novi	2,300
				There remained for the active army	15,320

All deductions made, the three divisions and the reserve could only put 12,000 men in the field. With this slender force, this wing of the Army of Italy had to guard a front of sixty miles. It could not do otherwise if the most practicable passes were to be occupied and communication maintained with the rest of the army.

[To face p. 106.

and the Austrians experienced an obdurate opposition, but their great superiority in numbers was bound to tell.

At two in the morning of the following day, having placed in the citadel of Savona a reinforcement of 600 men and furnished the place with a supply of provisions, Soult evacuated Savona and retired towards the heights of Albissola. The enemy was already there, but not being in any great strength was quickly brushed aside. Savona, Cadibona, and Vado were occupied by the Austrians.

Suchet was attacked on the 7th of April; the movements of the previous day had already turned his position on Monte San Giacomo. He made the Austrians pay dear for their success and the possession of that post, but, attacked by superior forces, he had to retire to safeguard his communications. The fight was spirited, and several redoubts were taken and retaken more than once. At Melogo the Hungarian grenadiers were not successful. Suchet was now completely detached from the rest of the army, and retired fighting step by step, disputing every inch of ground, but always compelled to give way.

Whilst Melas was pursuing his success in the direction of Savona, Ott expelled the French from Monte Faccio. General Darnaud in vain offered a serious resistance to Gottesheim, but this important post was eventually captured. Monte Faccio, so closely situated to the city, was in a military point of view, and owing to the moral effect caused by its loss, the most decisive gain the Austrians had scored on that day. Petitot was not more successful at Torriglia and Scofero, and had to give way before Leczeni's brigade. Gazan's division occupied many posts between the valley of the Orba and of the Scrivia. Fighting went on gallantly at all these points, until Gazan at the approach of superior forces, fearing he might be overlapped and turned, retired, and occupied a position at Buzetta, between the Monte Giovi and the Scrivia. Hohenzollern, whose task was to carry the Bocchetta, displayed little energy. He tried to outflank the French on both wings, but his movements lacked the unity necessary for success. He took Ronciglione and the hamlet of Marcarolo, but he was soon after chased from these positions.

Ott also carried Monte Ratti, and invested the forts of Quezzi, Richelieu, and Santa Tecla, within cannon-shot of the walls of the city.

Massena found himself in a serious predicament, but he was

not a man to be easily daunted. He knew how expedient it was to keep the field outside the works as long as possible, and how desirable it was to beat the enemy within sight of the Genovese, who had been witnesses of the Austrian successes, and were greatly inclined to favour the Imperialists.

The same night the Austrians, to convey a great idea of their strength, displayed a large number of fires on the Monte Faccio. This was done with the intent of inciting the population of the city and surrounding country to rise against the French. Emissaries had been also sent to visit the villages and to induce the people either by promises or by threats to take up arms.

Massena made his preparations during the night of the 6th, and at daybreak on the 7th sallied out of Genova, attacked the Austrians on the Monte Faccio with great vigour, and recaptured that important position. Miollis, coming with his right from Quinto, his left from Parisone, and supported by a reserve column in the valley of the Bisagno, drove the Austrians brilliantly out of the Monte Cornua and Monte Faccio. The second division moved as far as Borgo di Fornari and Savignone, and the third deployed from Varaggio to Ciampani. Torriglia and all the passes of the Apennines were lost to the Austrians that day, with 1500 men taken prisoners.

Besides the prisoners captured by the French, the brilliant results of the day's battle reanimated the patriots, and had a great effect in deterring the discontented and the agitators. The population from the walls of Carignano and from the fields of the Bisagno had been entranced spectators of the combat, and Massena's return to Genova was a real triumph.

The success gained on the 7th of April was not enough to satisfy Massena. When he heard of Soult's retreat on Genova, and how Suchet had evacuated the posts of Melogno, Sette Pani, and Finale to concentrate his forces at Borghetto, he determined to re-establish the connection with his left as being the measure which pressed the most. He decided to assume a vigorous offensive with the object of raising the blockade of Savona and effecting a junction with General Suchet.

This gave rise to so many engagements, delivered in many and divergent directions, that it is rather difficult to relate them in proper sequence, and this may somewhat confuse the student.

The operations between the 9th and the 18th of April were carried out on the rugged ground of the Ligurian hills. Besides the ordinary impediments, mountain warfare is surrounded by embarrassments of a character more serious than the mere difficulty of movement. There is the difficulty of concealing the march of the troops and the difficulty of insuring complete harmony of action. Operations of this nature abound in perplexities. Of all the French armies in the field in the campaign of 1800, the Army of Italy was the one which saw most constant and stubborn fighting, and that on most difficult ground. Nor should we overlook the low physical condition to which the troops had been reduced by want of sufficient nourishment, epidemics, and general discouragement. It was a difficult task to get them to keep the field and to call on them to undergo fresh privations and great fatigues. How well it was accomplished this chapter will show.

Massena carried his plan into execution on the 9th of April. Miollis, with the brigades of Darnaud and Spital (7000 men), was left to guard Genova and keep Ott in countenance. The rest of the troops were divided into two columns—one of 5000 men under Gazan, directed to move by Voltri on Sassello; the other, of 4500 under Gardanne, was to follow the coast route. Soult went with the first, Massena with the second. These two columns, with the object of dividing the enemy's attention, were to march by different roads, in the hope that the enemy would split up his forces; then, after having passed Varaggio, Gardanne by a rapid march was to effect a junction with Soult on the heights of Montenotte, with the prospect of crushing any Austrian troops that might happen to be there, or to meet at Savona or Vado, pounce on Melas's magazines, and join hands with Suchet, who had been ordered to suspend his retreat and to come from Borghetto and manœuvre in the direction of Cugliano between Vado and Savona.

Melas, however, had resolved to march on Genova, and having established Elsnitz on the heights of Vado, so as to hold Suchet in countenance, he set out to encounter Massena and connect with Hohenzollern. He rightly judged that his adversary would direct his principal efforts to re-opening communications with France and the left wing of his army.

Melas, who led his right column, directed Bussy on Varaggio, Lattermann on Prasi, and Sticker on La Stella. Bellegarde's, Saint Julien's, and Brentaro's brigades marched on his left on the mountain position of Sassello and La Verreria. A column coming from La Bocchetta had pushed advanced posts as far as Ponte-Decimo. Another body coming from the huts of Marcarolo was marching to occupy the post of Madonna dell' Acqua Santa, three miles only from Voltri.

On the night of the 8th of April, all the troops which were to form Soult's column were directed on Voltri. The population of Genova and the neighbourhood was badly disposed towards the French, and all round the city that night the alarm-bell sounded. Signal rockets were also fired from Carignano and San Pier d'Arena, in response to signals made on the mountains and at sea. Both commanders had decided on an offensive movement. Neither one nor the other was able to carry his conception into effect. The two generals manœuvred on wrong suppositions, relying on results which could no longer be attained. The difficulty of penetrating the adversary's intentions, and of carrying out the directions received, made the various columns fall on each other according to the more or less favourable nature of the ground.

The movements of the columns coming from La Bocchetta and Marcarolo had the effect of diverting Soult from his objective. As he was about to leave Voltri for Sassello, he deemed it necessary, first of all, to drive the Austrians from their positions at Ponte-Decimo and Madonna dell' Acqua Santa, so as to gain complete security for his rear. This move affected the plan laid down by Massena.

In accordance with this decision, Soult marched by Acqua Bona, Martino, and San Pietro del Orba on Sassello on the 10th; whereas he should have been there the previous day. Saint Julien was at that moment marching on La Verreria, with the object of making for Ciampani on Massena's rear, and cutting off his retreat on Voltri. Soult took post at Pallo, on the road which leads from the Verreria to Pouzonne, whilst a portion of his division attacked briskly and cut off at Sassello General Saint Julien's rear-guard. In Sassello he captured 600 men of the Deutschmeister regiment, with three guns and a convoy of ammunition. Saint Julien arrived at La Verreria with the bulk of his troops, but he found his forces paralyzed, being almost separated from his centre.

Massena had marched in two columns. The one on the right, commanded by Sacquelen, was to ascend by Santa Giustina; the one on the left, with which he himself moved, marching under Gardanne's orders, issued from Varaggio, and proceeded past Castagnebo towards La Stella.

Whilst Bellegarde developed his attack, closing with the French columns, Lattermann, following the coast, attacked and carried Varaggio. Massena had stopped his movement, and taken post at Santa Croce. There he stayed to await the result of Soult's attack; and there, with 1400 men, he had to contend for several hours against an immensely superior force.

Receiving no news from his right, the reinforcements he expected from Genova failing to put in an appearance, and being overlapped on all sides, after directing General Fressinet to cover the retreat, Massena quitted the left column, and, with his adjutant-general Thiébault and two other staff officers, went across country, at a great risk of being captured by the Austrians or killed by the peasants, to the right column. This column had been delayed by the length and arduousness of the march, and by the slowness experienced in distributing provisions. It had consequently not yet engaged the enemy, and was directed to reoccupy the position it held in the morning in rear of Varaggio. In the evening of this day Massena ordered his troops to fall back, and take up a position in front of Cogoletto.

Massena remained steadfast in his design. But the excessive fatigue and the disorder prevailing in the ranks prevented his carrying out a desperate resolve. He had intended nothing more nor less than to march to his right during the night, and effect a junction with Soult; then to attack and crush Melas's left, and to push forward on Loano, so as to join Suchet. Lastly, to march with all his forces united in the direction of Genova, and free Miollis. This junction of forces, being unexpected, would, he deemed, cause the destruction of the corps which was opposing Soult, and might lead to happy results. The darkness would hide his movements, and four hours would have sufficed for the success of this bold enterprise.

The troops of Gardanne's column, however, were demoralized; and when the time came for setting them in motion it was found that they had scattered about, that they were tired and famished, and that not a few had gone across the mountains back to Genova. When day broke, the report of the generals confirmed this sad state of things. At about ten o'clock Adjutant-General Gautier arrived from the right column, and persuaded the general-in-chief that Soult was in imminent need of reinforcements.

Seeing the steady progress of his adversary's column, Massena found himself compelled to hold the position of Cogoletto, so as to detain as many of the enemy's troops as possible before him. He detailed four battalions for this purpose. The remaining six battalions, under General Fressinet, he detached to his right to reinforce Soult. By a singular chance Melas was at that identical moment employed in sending his centre and part of his right to reinforce Saint Julien at La Verreria, so that for four miles the Austrians and French marched on parallel crests within cannon-shot of each other.

Soult would not let Saint Julien effect his retreat in peace. Having left a detachment beyond Sassello to watch the roads leading from Ponzone and Acqui, he marched with the rest of his troops on La Verreria, and attacked the regiments of Lattermann, Deutschmeister, and Vukassevich, that held that place. The Austrian general could only effect his retreat on Ponte Ivrea after having lost 2000 prisoners and seven flags. The defence was really stiff, but the extraordinary bravery of the French, combined with the excellence of their dispositions, made them overcome all the obstacles of locality and numbers. Soult did not follow far in pursuit, and rallied his troops on the hillock of Grosso Pasto, an eminent position parallel to the mountain of L'Ermetta, which he believed the enemy would be sure to occupy before long.

Soult, informed during the night that Saint Julien had left for L'Ermetta, whilst La Verreria was only guarded by a detachment, got Gazan's division to carry that post at two o'clock in the morning. Saint Julien, reinforced by Bellegarde, occupied a position on the mountain of L'Ermetta, and endeavoured to turn Gazan's right, as that general led his division to the attack. The combat was stubborn, and the result doubtful; but the victory seemed if anything to be inclining towards the side of the Austrians, when, after a five miles' march, Fressinet's column appeared on the scene of action. These troops appeared on the Austrian right, overthrew everything which stood in their way, and joined Gazan's division on L'Ermetta. Saint Julien, protected by Bellegarde and Brentano, fell back with them to Santa Giustina.

On the afternoon of the same day, Melas, with all his right, attacked the four French battalions at Cogoletto, drove them out of the place, and pursued them vigorously as far as Voltri. The Austrians neglected to make the most of their advantage. They failed to occupy Voltri, and withdrew to their previous positions. The French on the hills were within an ace of being cut off from Genova; but in the early hours of the 12th Massena brought up a brigade of 2000 men, drawn from Miollis's column, and strongly occupied the post. By this skilful measure Massena saved one of his divisions from a dire disaster.

Soult, ignorant of Massena's retreat, was confronting the enemy. To do so needed daring, for the troops he commanded were without provisions and ammunition. Bellegarde and Brentano, in possession of Monte Faiale, kept Soult from extending to his right. He determined, therefore, to carry that position. This he did on the 12th, and whilst Poinsot was threatening Saint Julien at L'Ermetta, two columns, one led by himself, the other by Fressinet, attacked Monte Faiale, and after immense efforts wrenched it from the enemy. Soult carried his attack further on, but the two Austrian brigades, reinforced by fresh troops, turned and drove him back to the position he had so gallantly captured. He remained there all the 13th, but on the following day, learning that the Austrians were employed in effecting a concentration, he endeavoured to take advantage of this, and to capture their camp at Giustina. But in this he failed.

Melas resolved to reinforce his left and to withdraw his right. On the 14th, Bussy's brigade was added to the others on the mountain, whilst Lattermann was directed to withdraw to the strong position of Albissola, and there to keep on the defensive. The Austrians concentrated five brigades on Montenotte and Monteleggino, with the object of lending a hand to Hohenzollern's corps and of driving the French before them into Genova. The operation was ordered to take place on the 15th.

Soult, the purpose of whose operations had been all along to enter into communication with Suchet by way of Sassello, anticipated the Austrian attack, but found himself confronted by superior numbers; and his operations for capturing the position of Ponte Ivrea ended in complete failure. The combat was renewed on the 16th. The French fought with conspicuous gallantry, though borne down by fatigue and want, not being in any way as well provided with food and ammunition as their

opponents. Melas employed most of his forces; two brigades
were directed on Sassello; Bellegarde took the direction of La
Verreria; two other brigades went to L'Ermetta. Soult soon
perceived that he could not contend against such overpowering
forces, so he tried to place himself in communication with
Massena, whom he expected to find somewhere about Savona.
With this intent he moved in the direction of Monte Pasto, but
only to fall in with Bellegarde's column, whose chief summoned
him to surrender. Soult was in a critical position, attacked in
front and in rear; eventually he was compelled to order a
retreat. There was yet time for this. In a dense mist he
gained the heights of La Verreria, and from that point made
for Voltri, only disturbed by small parties of the enemy, which
he easily brushed aside.

Whilst Soult was fighting for the position of Ponte Ivrea on
the 15th, Massena set out from Voltri to attack Lattermann at
Albissola. After a combat which lasted three hours, he was
repulsed, and retired on Varaggio, closely followed by the Austrian
Grenadiers. Hearing then that Hohenzollern was marching
with four battalions against his right flank, he ordered the
retreat to be continued as far as Arenzano.*

Both French columns were in retreat, and came together
at Voltri on the 17th. Being unable to effect anything in the
direction of Savona, Massena decided to place his troops under
the protection of the guns of Genova. The retreat thither
was ordered; but it was delayed to clear what there still remained in Voltri of stores and provisions. This delay cost the
French a certain loss of men.

From the summit of Monte Faiale Melas had been able to
survey the position occupied by the French, then encamped
between Acqua Santa and Arenzano. He decided to profit by
this knowledge, to crush them by a combined attack, and to cut
them off from Genova by anticipating them at Sestri, whilst
Bellegarde and Lattermann would occupy the enemy's attention
along the coast. Melas descended from Monte Faiale, and
marched on Voltri with Bussy's brigade; whilst Ott, coming
from Masone, made for the same place. Sestri di Ponente was
a most important point for the Austrians, but it was not

---

* Oudinot declares that though Massena's and Soult's troops had been fighting
for some days, they had suffered more from hunger than from the engagements
which they had sustained or delivered.

strongly occupied by Ott. It was owing to their inability to appreciate all the value of this point and their tardiness of movement that the Austrians failed to score a signal success. Ott was the first to attack Voltri. His troops drove the French before them, and seized one of the bridges, but the French reserve attacked his column to favour the return of the troops engaged on the mountain and of those coming from Arenzano, which were much harassed by Bellegarde. The fight was carried out at close quarters, both sides losing heavily.

On being apprised of the enemy's march on Sestri, Soult hastened the retreat, judging it far more important to outstrip the enemy at Sestri than to hold out at Voltri. This made his rear-guard and reserve in succession maintain themselves in Voltri, to gain time for the arrival of the column coming from the mountain and the troops arriving from the coast. The battle continued until late in the night, and was conducted by the light of torches.

The French had anticipated the enemy, and by deploying on the heights of Sant Andrea, covered the passage of the Polcevera at the bridge of Cornigliano, by which their army fell back on Genova.

In the fortnight during which this heavy fighting had been going on, Miollis had had daily combats with the Austrians in the neighbourhood of Genova.

However ably the French occupied the ground in all these operations, the numerical superiority of the enemy always told heavily against them. After a fortnight of constant and determined fighting, Massena was at last shut up in Genova. All hope of co-operation on the part of Suchet or of receiving reinforcements from France could be absolutely dismissed.

General Thiébault sums up the operations of these two weeks in the following words: "But soon he (Massena) resumes the offensive, and, not satisfied with beating the enemy under the walls of Genova with eight or nine thousand debilitated men, he goes as far as the walls of Savona, to contend the victory with thirty thousand men picked out of the finest army in the world, and keeps the field for fourteen days. The brave men he commands kill or wound more than eight thousand men of the enemy; fall back around Genova without Melas being able to cut them off; lead back more than six thousand prisoners, and amongst other spoils bring away with them six standards and five guns as tokens of their victory." * For want of sufficient escorts, many of the Austrians captured on the Ligurian hills and during the blockade managed to effect their escape and get back to their corps.

The Austrians now occupied all the heights around Genova. All the defiles of the Apennines had been forced, and nothing remained for Massena to do but to concentrate his small army. On the 21st of April, the blockade of Genova was established.

Melas was soon on the Var, and all the Genovese territory, save the citadel of Savona and the city of Genova, *Genova la Superba*, was lost. Great was the alarm in Provence; Toulon and Marseilles did not consider themselves safe.

General Ott was placed at the head of 25,000 men, and to him were confided the operations for the reduction of the city. As to the remainder of the troops, they marched in the direction of Vado, for Melas's intention was to combine with General Elsnitz and drive Suchet back across the frontier of France.

The ancient city of Genova, which has occupied a distinguished place in the history of modern Europe, with a population of more than 100,000 souls, lies on the shores of the Mediterranean, at the foot of the southern slope of the Apennines, seventy-nine miles south-east of Turin. Built in the shape of a horse-shoe, the city rises like a superb amphitheatre on the lowermost spurs of the Apennines, and the bleak summits of the loftier ranges are capped with forts, batteries, and other works which constitute a line of fortification of great strength and extension.

Owing to the configuration of the ground, which rises on all sides, it became necessary in fortifying the city to include in the zone of defence the various heights which, rising in succession from the seashore, end in Monte Diamante at 1500 feet above the level of the sea.

Two torrents placidly meander round the city, La Polcevera and the Bisagno. They have their sources in the highest peaks of the surrounding mountains, and their names frequently recur in the narratives of the siege.

The city has two inclosures, one exterior, and one interior. The latter, which protects Genova more thoroughly, is formed of an irregular line of bastions.

* General Paul Thiébault, "Journal des opérations militaires du siége et du blocus de Gênes," p. 220.

The exterior line of ramparts is divided into nine principal sections. To the west are the Lanterna fort, which borders on the water battery of the same name, the section of the Tenaglia, and that of Degato. On the north there is but one section, that of the Sperone. On the east there are five, that of Castellozzo, of the salient above San Bartolomeo, of the important height of Zerbino, of the curtain by the Porta Romana, and lastly of Carignano, which descends to the sea. On the south a parapet extends from the lighthouse gate to San Tommaso.

The Sperone, lying at the top of the great triangle, was reputed to be the key of the position, because from that point the whole line of the ramparts could be enfiladed and taken in reverse. In front of the Sperone are two hills called Spino and Pellato, otherwise called the Monte dei Due Fratelli, on which a work had been constructed called Forte del Diamante.

On the east, the spur of the Apennine, which forms the left strand of Bisagno from Monte Cornua up to Nervi, is studded with three forts, Santa Tecla, Quezzi, and Richelieu. These were constructed on a projection named Monte Ratti.

On the south-east, on the heights of Albaro, is the only locality where regular approaches can be made. From that direction also it is possible to bombard the populous quarters of the city, which on that side approach more closely to the ramparts than on any other.

With respect only to the state of its defences, Genova was badly prepared to withstand a siege. Still the zeal, talent, and activity of General la Martillière, Sugni, and Marès fully made up for this drawback. All the most necessary repairs of the fortifications were speedily executed, and a general system of defence laid out.

Massena could barely hope to compete against an enemy whose forces were three times as numerous as his own. But he devoted his energies to strengthening his position and to discovering what means of subsistence the city could command.

The troops were divided into two divisions—one under Miollis, 4500 strong; the other under Gazan, numbering 3500 men. Besides these two divisions there was a reserve. But this comprised only 1600 men. In the terrible combats of the last fifteen days the army had lost fully one-third of its numbers.

Massena called out the National Guard to assist in maintaining order. Besides this, he organized a legion composed of Italian refugees and of some hundreds of Poles found amongst the prisoners captured from the enemy. This arrangement enabled him to keep in hand all the forces capable of engaging the Austrians beyond the walls.

The country round about Genova had been for three years subject to a terrible scourge—the presence of numerous armies. The local resources had become exhausted, and there was no way of drawing means of subsistence from so miserable a region.

Massena did his best to purchase all the grain which could be got on the spot. He also wrote for it to Corsica, to Marseilles, and to Suchet. He established a very rigorous supervision over the manufacture of the bread and over its distribution, and had a census made of all the horses.

The three divisions of the French entered the city of Genova, which was blockaded on the land side by the Austrians, and by the English on the sea. For two months both the garrison and the inhabitants suffered unheard-of privations and hardships. During that period the ravages of famine, typhus, and war were on a very large scale. The garrison lost heavily. Every day 700 to 800 corpses of the citizens—individuals of every age, sex, and class—were picked up in the streets, and buried in an immense trench filled with quicklime, and which stood behind the church of Carignano. The number of victims during the blockade surpassed 30,000, the great majority starved to death.

"It would not be possible to describe in detail," writes Gaston Stiegler, "the famous siege, with its sorties, its incessant combats, the sufferings of its inhabitants, the riots of the women, the endurance of the soldiers, the famine, the necessity of eating loathsome articles, herbs, unclean beasts, and, under the illusive name of bread, a mysterious compound of starch, linseed, and cocoa."

At that period there was not in the city of Genova a single private bakery, all the bread being baked in state ovens. The dread which the old Genovese Government had entertained of the population was the origin of this singular arrangement. To maintain the population in submission, the Government had from time immemorial claimed a monopoly of grain, flour, and bread. The bread was baked in an immense building guarded by soldiers and cannons. Under this system, whenever the Doge or the Senate wished to prevent a revolt or to punish the people, they had only to close the state bakeries, and the people were soon starved into submission.

These bakeries habitually provided bread for a population of more than 120,000 souls, but, for want of grain, they remained closed for forty-five days out of the sixty during which the siege lasted.*

When hostilities commenced, all the wheat, all the grain and pulse that could be discovered was collected. It was then estimated that the city could withstand a fortnight's blockade. More thorough searches were made during those fifteen days, and by vigorous measures grain and other substances were found with which the people and the troops could be fed for fifteen days more.

On the 30th Germinal (20th of April) it became necessary to eat bread made of rye and oats. The cavalry horses were also sacrificed. The staff gave up their reserves for the help of the sick, who were overcrowding the hospitals. This was of very slight assistance, for through want of medicines the mortality soon became appalling.

On the 15th Floreal (5th of May), a small ship ran the blockade and brought grain to last five days ; but on the 20th, as the supplies were beginning to run short, the grain was all reserved for the troops. The rations were reduced, and no more bread was issued to the inhabitants.

The troops received a miserable ration of ¼ lb. of horse-flesh and ¼ lb. of what passed by the name of bread. This was a compound of damaged flour, sawdust, starch, hair-powder, oatmeal, linseed, rancid nuts, and other substances, to which a certain consistency was given by the admixture of a small portion of cocoa.

Neither bread nor meat was publicly sold for forty-five days. The more wealthy of the inhabitants were able, during the first part of the siege, to obtain a little codfish, sugar, figs, and other provisions. Oil, wine, and salt never failed.

Men were compelled to shoulder a musket and enrol themselves amongst the combatants, in order to claim the wretched ration which was distributed to the soldiers. At the commander-in-chief's table, bread, roasted horseflesh, and dried pease, were served once a day. The portions were extremely minute.

* Genova had a population of about 120,000 souls. Of this number some 40,000 belonged to Albaro, San Martino, Bisagno, and San Pier d'Arena.

Massena allowed his officers to retain only one horse; the rest had to be sent to the butcher. As the horses were lean from want of forage, the flesh was not of much account. Even diseased horses were killed, and the flesh issued as rations.

All the dogs and cats in the town were soon eaten; rats fetched a high price. Whenever the French made a sortie, crowds followed them outside the gates, and set to work to cut grass and nettles, and to collect leaves, which were subsequently boiled with salt. Rich and poor, women, children, and old men, took their share in this work. The local Government had the grass which grew on the ramparts mown, and afterwards cooked in the public squares and distributed to the sick people who were not strong enough to procure this coarse food and cook it themselves.

Some few vessels from Toulon, Marseilles, or Corsica, succeeded in deceiving the vigilance of the English fleet, and got into port. But these were very rare cases indeed.

Men, women, and children were paid by the discontented to saunter along the streets in a state of almost entire nudity (representing a pretended state of destitution), uttering heart-rending cries and heavy moans, with the object of shaking by this counterfeit of distress the resolution of the authorities.

Leather and skins of every kind were consumed, and, horrible to relate, numbers of the starving wretches sought support from the dead bodies of their fellow-citizens.

From the nature of the ground, Genova offers almost insurmountable obstacles to a regular siege. At this period the Austrian operations were retarded by a deficiency of transport. Transport, without which no military operations can be carried out with vigour, was scarce. If there was little of it for the conveyance of provisions, there was less for a siege-train and artillery park coming from Turin or Alessandria. Without guns no impression could be made on the city.

Before starting on the 27th for his expedition against Finale, Melas decided to occupy San Pier d'Arena. The column of attack, led by the Nadasti regiment, advanced with that object on the 23rd. But the French, reinforced by the reserve, drove it back in disorder beyond the Polcevera, with the loss of 400 prisoners. Ott the same day occupied Rivarolo, and Hohenzollern failed at Forte Diamante. Miollis drove Gottesheim out of Monte Parisone, but failed in an attempt to turn the camp at Castagna.

On the 30th of April, Ott made a general attack with the object of chasing the French from the exterior line of defence. He planned a general assault on Massena's defences on the Bisagno, the Polcevera, and the fortified summits of the Madonna del Monte, and the Monte Ratti. The attack was successful only at first, for whilst on one side Ott had not a sufficient force, Massena on the other turned skilfully to account the immense advantage which his central position in an intrenched camp gave him. Both sides fought with great resolution, and for a time success was doubtful. In the end the Republicans remained victorious on the Monte Ratti, which, with its forts and 400 prisoners, fell into their hands. By taking advantage of the ravines, Soult had penetrated in rear of the Due Fratelli; and Hohenzollern, attacked in rear by the garrison of Forte Diamante, and in front by a body of fresh troops, was broken. The Austrians had to abandon all the ground they had gained from their opponents, excepting the Monte Faccio, losing 1800 prisoners.

On the following day, Massena attacked the fortified heights of Coronata, but was repulsed with great slaughter, and driven back to Genova.

For the next ten days nothing occurred of any special importance. Such, however, was the dire condition of the beleaguered city that Massena could not remain inactive. He determined to make a sally on the 11th of May. The Austrians had been celebrating Melas's success on the Var by a *feu de joie*, and Massena determined by a vigorous effort to show them that the spirits of his troops were not sinking. Miollis was to attack Monte Faccio on the front of the Sturla, and Soult, ascending by the bed of the Bisagno torrent, was to take it in flank. Soult was successful, and the Austrians were only able to force their way through their pursuers by leaving 1300 prisoners in the hands of the French.

Massena was very keen to undertake an expedition to Portofino, with the intent of laying a hand on the corn which was known to have been collected there. However, at a special meeting held to consider the question, he was, much against his will, persuaded to give it up, and in its stead endeavour to carry the camp of Monte Creto, the most prominent and commanding point of the Austrian lines. The loss of this place would possibly have obliged the besiegers to fall back from Genova and retire behind Voltri and Sestri di Levante, to evacuate Portofino, and to abandon all the guns they had at Cornigliano and Sestri di Ponente.

Nothing was neglected that might secure the success of such an important enterprise, Massena being thoroughly alive to the fact that this was the last offensive movement he could attempt. The troops were picked for it, and the best leaders were chosen.

As the enemy fully realized the vital importance of Monte Creto, he had posted there and in the vicinity the greatest portion of his forces. The intrenched camp on Monte Creto had been fortified with care, and Hohenzollern, backed by a powerful reserve, was intrusted with its defence. The attackers were divided into two columns. Soult led the right column direct on Monte Creto, and this column, having quitted Genova by the Porta Romana, moved along the valley of the Bisagno. Gazan, who led the left column, issued from the Sperone, and passed by the Due Fratelli.

The French advanced to the attack with intrepidity. At first both Soult and Gazan were successful, but a violent storm which lasted three-quarters of an hour interrupted the operations. The rain fell in torrents, the French got drenched, their uniforms got soaked, and the roads became bad and slippery. Meanwhile, the Austrians received reinforcements from the valleys, which had escaped the fury of the storm.

The assailants had lost the resolution necessary for carrying strong works by force, for the dire effects of rain and want of food combined had taken all the energy out of them. Fresh efforts were called for, and the officers set a noble example, but all to no purpose. The troops were exhausted. Enthusiasm, the great motor of all combatants, and of such consequence for the French, had subsided.

A fresh reserve came forward under Hohenzollern, charged, and dispersed the French. Soult and his brother strove to rally them, but in vain. In this attempt Soult was seriously wounded in his right leg. He then ordered the retreat. The ground was in such a slippery state that his soldiers could not bear him away. Seeing this, he sent his sword to Massena, and remained on the battlefield, where the enemy captured him.

The French, thoroughly broken and in the utmost confusion, fled to Genova. The ill success of this attack, the decline of the soldiers, and, above all, the greatly felt loss of Soult, left no hope to Massena of tiring out the assailants. With this fight all defensive action beyond the walls of the city ended. Massena had to look after the safety of Genova, had to evacuate Monte Faccio, and to draw his posts closer in. He could labour under no illusion of being able to cut his way through his foes. The port, hermetically closed by the British fleet, dispelled all hope of obtaining supplies. Death was the only prospect. Massena might have waited for it calmly, but the citizens were not inclined to die of starvation; and if they were to die, the soldiers preferred to die fighting.

The Genovese are a shrewd, active, and laborious race. They make skilful and hardy seamen, energetic traders, and thrifty husbandmen. When the main part of their occupation was maritime, one may picture to one's self what a blow a rigid blockade of their port must have been for them. To the enemy outside was soon added an enemy within, for the dearth of food and the threats of a terrible bombardment had exasperated the people. The citizens murmured, and were much inclined to revolt against the authority of the commander-in-chief. Massena, however, was too determined a man to be trifled with. To prevent any attempt at a rising, he proclaimed that the soldiers had received orders to fire on any assemblage of the inhabitants which numbered more than four individuals. In addition to this he took other precautions. He made some arrests, caused whole regiments to bivouac on the squares and principal streets, and defended the approaches by guns loaded with canister.

It required a very determined mind to uphold authority under such dire circumstances. But Massena was firm, and at the same time that he stifled any attempt at a revolt he overawed the murmurs of the soldiers. He ate the same scanty fare as the troops,* and was foremost in braving the enemy's fire.

Notwithstanding all the horrors and the hopelessness of the situation, Massena remained impassible and calm. He clung

---

* The repast set before the commander-in-chief and his staff on the 15th Prairial (4th of June) consisted of a soup of herbs, some boiled horseflesh, and a dish of boiled French beans.

obstinately to the defence of Genova, having heard from Bonaparte that he was busy collecting an Army of Reserve, at the
head of which he intended to descend from the Alps; how he
purposed to surprise the Austrians by falling on their rear
whilst they were busily occupied with their operations in
Liguria. This stubbornness was partly in keeping with
Massena's character, and partly in compliance with the First
Consul's orders, which were to hold the city as long as possible,
since to do so was at that moment of immense importance to
France.

Massena had opposed to the largely superior forces of the
enemy the most brilliant tactics. He had turned to account all
the defensive positions of the mountains in his front. He was
always ready to resume the offensive as far as he could, whilst
defending the ground inch by inch; following, in short, the
proper principles of the art which enjoin that when a general
is in command of inferior forces his ability lies in imposing on
the enemy and in gaining time.

Firmly resolved to give Bonaparte time to arrive, he made
the most ingenious dispositions. He determined that the
resistance should be maintained as long as possible, and
resolved in any case to save the honour of the Army of Italy,
by sacrificing the very last soldier, and by dying himself, if that
proved necessary.

The credit due to Massena for his gallant defence of Genova
is enhanced when we reflect how his gallant bearing was
seconded by half-starved and sickly troops.

Not only was there a great scarcity of provisions in the
beleaguered city, but the ammunition also was running alarm-
ingly short. Massena took great pains to have some manu-
factured. But during the blockade no more than 12,000 lbs.
of gunpowder in all were obtained in that manner. When the
troops evacuated the city there were only 4000 lbs. of good
and bad powder in the arsenals. For the field guns and the
guns of position there remained not more than ten rounds
per gun.

Massena's greatest talent lay in finding in a city, where
before the blockade there never was more food than was sufficient for three days' consumption, enough to last for sixty days,
and that notwithstanding a most rigorous blockade. He gave
further evidence of his ability by discovering warriors, and even

heroes, amongst soldiers who seemed to be incapable of with-standing the hardships of a single march. By his talent, example, and pluck, he had secured general admiration, which gave him a moral force of immense value. During the sixty days' blockade he gave unremitting attention to every matter, and his personality made up for everything else. The respect which he inspired was shared by all alike. He was a model commander. He asked for no more than the scanty fare of his men. He shared their fatigues and their dangers, and had at all moments to be on his guard against discontent and treachery. He alone, in short, was the individual who retained the Austrians such a long time before the walls of Genova.

Outside the walls scarcely a day passed without a fight. The French, highly disciplined and judiciously posted, did much harm to the assailants. Some well-directed red-hot shot com-pelled the English fleet to draw further back from the shore.

There were battles without number, sorties, assaults, and repulses; desperate fighting, in which brave men lost their lives. To these were added other horrors, hunger and pestilence. The food grew less and less, till at length there was left next to nothing. It came very nearly to what the soldiers had predicted, that, before giving in, their general would make them eat their boots.

All the horrors of famine and pestilence were not enough, for the French could not secure an instant of repose. They were harassed on the land side by the Austrians throughout the day, and battered by the guns of the English, Turkish, and Neapolitan fleets all through the night.*

Massena had sent Major (Chef d'escadron) Franceschi, Soult's aide-de-camp, to Paris to report on the state of affairs at Genova. This daring officer succeeded both on going and returning in passing through the enemy's fleet. Suchet in his report states that Franceschi quitted Genova in the evening of the 8th Floreal (28th of April) in a rowing-boat. Befriended by darkness, the boat succeeded in passing through the British fleet, but at break of day was descried and chased by a corvette. When on the point

---

* For, as Holy Writ declares, "The sins of the fathers are visited on the children, unto the third and fourth generation of them that hate Him." Who can say that all the gallant blood shed and misery endured in this and in the rest of the Napoleonic wars may not have been a punishment for all the barbarities com-mitted by the French in the frenzy of the Revolution? What made it even more poignant was that these heartrending sacrifices were in the long run all in vain.

of being captured, Franceschi tore up most of his despatches, placed his sword between his teeth, threw himself into the sea, and was fortunate in being able to land safely near Finale, which point was then occupied by some of Suchet's troops.*

De Cugnac relates that, having quitted Genova on the 27th of April, he arrived the same day at La Pietra, still occupied by Suchet's troops, and informed that general how the commander-in-chief had resolved to shut himself up in Genova, where provisions sufficient for a month existed, and that the inhabitants were animated by the best dispositions.

Franceschi pursued his route, and reported himself to Berthier, then at Chalons, on the 3rd of May. Berthier sent him to Paris. He arrived on the 5th, and delivered to the First Consul a letter from Massena.†

Bonaparte writes to Massena on the 5th of May: "Your aide-de-camp has arrived, and I have received your letter."

The following day a courier sent by Suchet arrived in Paris with a despatch, written from La Pietra some hours after Franceschi's departure.

From Franceschi Bonaparte learnt all about Massena, and how he had provisions only enough to last him till the 25th or 26th of May.

On his side the First Consul, on the 1st of May, had directed the war minister to send a very intelligent staff officer of engineers on a mission to General Suchet, and who was afterwards to pass on to General Massena.

This officer was to inform them that the Army of Reserve was in full march, and about to issue from the Alps, that it would be in Piedmont by the 11th of May.

No letter was to be given to him lest by chance it might come in possession of the enemy. But the officer was to be made familiar with all the details of the march of the Army of Reserve. He was, moreover, to instruct both generals that when the enemy was weakened by having to make head against the Army of Reserve, it was expected of them to regain the lost ground.

The officer intrusted with this task was Brigadier Vallongue, of the corps of engineers. He joined General Suchet, and remained with him during the operations on the Var.

---

* Gachot, "La Deuxième Campagne d'Italie," p. 31.

† De Cugnac, "Campagne de l'Armée de Reserve en 1800," vol. i. p. 280.

Franceschi left Bonaparte at Lausanne on the 14th of May, and returned to Genova with a letter from the First Consul. He had seen something of the Army of Reserve, and was instructed to tell Massena that he would be relieved in the first decade of the month Prairial (21st to 30th of May), according to what the First Consul had written to the other consuls on the 13th of May.

On the 1st of May, Bonaparte wrote to the minister of war. He directed him to order Saint-Hilaire, who was commanding the 8th Military Division at Marseilles, to push all the available cavalry towards Nice,[*] in order that, when the arrival of the Army of Reserve in Piedmont released Massena, he might at once undertake the pursuit of the enemy.

Embarking at Antibes, Franceschi succeeded in steering through the British fleet at night in an open boat worked by three oarsmen. At dawn he was sighted, when he was about a mile from the shore. The cruiser's guns opened fire, and wounded some of the boatmen. The daring aide-de-camp saw no other way of saving his despatches than by taking to the water. He promptly removed his clothes, took his sabre in his teeth, and swam towards the harbour, reaching land in a state of exhaustion. The soldiers received with joy the news brought by Franceschi of Moreau's successes in Germany, and of the passage of the Army of Reserve over the Alps.[†]

Massena made the following communication to the Army of Italy and to the Ligurian Government:—

" One of the officers that I have despatched to the First Consul in Paris returned this night.

" He quitted General Bonaparte as he was descending the Grand Saint Bernard, having with him General Carnot, minister of war.

" General Bonaparte intimates that from the 28th to the 30th Floréal he will have arrived with all his army at Ivrea, and from there he will proceed by lengthy marches to Genova.

" At the same time, General Lecourbe accomplishes his movement on Milan by the Valtellina.

" The Army of the Rhine has scored fresh successes on the enemy. It has gained a decisive victory at Biberach; it has captured many prisoners, and has directed its march on Ulm.

---

[*] De Cugnac, vol. i. p. 240.   [†] " Mémoires de Masséna," tom. iv. p. 204.

"General Bonaparte, whom I have made acquainted with
the behaviour of the inhabitants of Genova, assures me of all the
confidence he reposes in them, and writes thus : 'You are in a
difficult position, but what puts me at my ease is that you are
in Genova. That city, led by an excellent spirit, fully cognizant
of its own interests, will soon find in its deliverance the reward
for all the sacrifices which it has made.'

"MASSENA."

The friendly part of the population was cheered by such
news, and followed on maps, which were exposed in the shop
windows, the movements of an army on which it reposed full
confidence, led, moreover, as it was, by a beloved general. From
the experience of the preceding campaigns it was well known
all that might be expected from this army.

Massena endeavoured to take advantage of the momentary
enthusiasm of the troops. A rumour having gained ground to
the effect that the enemy was falling back, anxious not to lose a
single moment, he ordered for the 28th of May a reconnaissance
to be made in the direction of Nervi, Monte Faccio, Monte
Ratti, and Bisagno. This reconnaissance led to serious fighting. The effort, however, was far beyond the strength of
the men. The French, as is their wont, advanced gallantly
enough, but were received at the foot of the redoubts by a
tremendous fire of grape and musketry. They became broken
and dispirited, and were easily driven within the walls of the
city. The French lost heavily, but the Austrians more heavily
still. It was ascertained by this sortie that the Austrians round
Genova were as strong as ever.

Notwithstanding the vigorous searches already made for
eatables, provisions were still hidden in the city. About this
time the report that Bonaparte had gained a great victory ran
through the place. This rumour brought out again some
articles of food, for which covetous dealers asked an excessive
price, but even these signs of abundance did not prevent several
individuals from falling down in the streets to die of starvation.

A couple of days later (the 30th of May) a small sail laden
with sixty sacks of grain contrived to enter the port. The
owner declared that he was followed by fourteen more, but none
of these ever arrived.

"We were reduced," writes Oudinot, in describing the horrible situation of the city, "to such a state of distress that our soldiers were too glad to eat the straw of the hospitals. Soon this last resource gave out, and we were only able to keep up our strength by drinking the generous wines which we discovered in quantities in the cellars of the town. One saw sentinels, unable to hold themselves erect, mounting guard seated in gilt armchairs, and drinking claret in their misery."

General Gazan's aide-de-camp reported to the commander-in-chief on this same 30th of May, that the sound of guns had been heard in the direction of the Bocchetta and of small arms on the side of Monte Freddo. The excitement caused by this news soon became intense. All Genova was in a delirium of exultation. The troops were all under arms, keen to see if the enemy made any movement. The report, however, was not true, the thunder of a distant storm was evidently the sound which had been heard. The hopes revived were soon abandoned, and discouragement again seized hold of the population.

Can there be a more pitiable sight than that of brave soldiers, eager to sally and meet the foe, day after day miserably succumbing to famine and disease? The conditions had grown rapidly worse. The garrison had made its last effort; but this very day the end of their misery commenced, inasmuch as Massena received an invitation to a parley with Lord Keith, Generals Ott and Saint Julien. Andrieux, one of the adjutant-generals, was sent to ascertain the object for such a demand, and he returned to Genova bearing a letter from Melas to the Commander-in-Chief of the Army of Italy, in which he renewed his offers of a most honourable capitulation.

At first Massena thought of refusing such a proposal. But he reasoned that all hope of being relieved had already gone, that the moment had arrived when Bonaparte knew that the place must inevitably fall. He judged that possibly all that he expected from the defence of Genova was to facilitate for the Army of Reserve an easy issue from the Alps and an undisputed advance into Piedmont. Besides these considerations, there remained not one complete ration per head of the substitute for bread, bad as it was. All the horses had been eaten, and it was high time to attempt something for the relief of troops which had done their duty so well. All their efforts, all the unheard-of sufferings, were sufficient to show that it was not weakness which made him give in.

K

Massena was in such dire straits that he could not remain deaf to any proposals. Though he made a semblance of reject-ing it with disdain, this offer of Melas was in the actual circum-stances very opportune. Nevertheless, there was also a chance that this humane desire of the enemy might be intended to veil his ambiguous position. No spies, no emissaries, had been able to come to him, to cross the enemy's lines, and of Bonaparte's actual position, beyond the capture of Ivrea, nothing was known.* But what aggravated the state of affairs, and possibly decided Massena more than anything else, was the suffering of the troops, and that the helplessness of the situation was causing many good soldiers to desert. A report had become current that several regiments had determined to put an end to their suffer-ings, and had arranged to quit the city and to give themselves up to the Austrians.

The English, wishing to add pressure to the Austrian proposals, bombarded the city on the night of the 30–31st of May. Their fire was more appalling than injurious; for all that, it caused considerable commotion amongst the people.

Massena had formed a project of leaving Miollis in Genova with the sick, and of opening himself a passage into Tuscany at the head of 7000 or 8000 men. To this forlorn hope he gave the name of *colonne d'affamés* (column of the famished). He had prepared all the details of the march, but when he proposed to his officers to cut their way through the enemy he was dissuaded by their unanimous voice. All declared that though they were only too ready to follow him, the soldiers were not in a physical condition to undertake either a combat or an ordinary march. This last resort, which the gallant general had cherished so fondly, being denied to him, he addressed a proclamation to his troops. He advised patience, and a few days more of endurance, and urged that they should not lose in one moment of despair the fruit of all their efforts, of all their glorious sacrifices.

But the soldier does not exist who can continue a hero for ever, animated always by the same spirit of daring, revelling in the dangers of personal encounter, and despising death. Such

---

* " *On croyait généralement à Gênes que le premier Consul, profitant de l'entêtement du Général Melas à couvrir le blocus, tâcherait de surprendre Mantoue, se jeterait de là dans le Tirol ferait en continuant son mouvement sa jonction avec le Général Moreau, et à la tête des deux armées irait à Vienne dicter les conditions de la paix. Mais il portait des coups plus sûrs et plus rapides.*"—Thiébault, " Journal des Operations Militaires," footnote, p. 199.

enthusiasm cannot last for an indefinite period. When the soldier has to fight almost every day, when he is unceasingly exposed to danger and privations, when he has to pass the nights watching or reposing in miserable bivouacs, he begins to get sore tired of war; he begins to long for some rest, for some comfort.

There is nothing finer in the history of sieges than this defence of Genova, in which most of the sorties had been victories. But by this time many of Massena's boldest soldiers had fallen, many were in hospital incapacitated by wounds, many had succumbed victims to epidemics and want. As he gave battle after battle, the worth of his army gradually lessened, for as it is always the most enterprising and bold who lead in an attack, the Army of Italy had left many of its bravest officers and soldiers in front of the Austrian redoubts and strong positions which surrounded the city of Genova.

Whilst matters were in this unsettled state, on the evening of the 31st of May, Melas despatched two letters to Ott, who was ignorant of what was occurring in Piedmont, directing him to raise the blockade. Of these letters one was a positive order to march during the night, whilst the other simply desired him to make ready to march, but to await more positive instructions before setting out. Singularly enough, there was nothing in the tenor of these letters to indicate which of the two was the one to be acted upon.

The messenger who brought these letters had crossed in his way a messenger sent by Ott bearing despatches for the commander-in-chief, in which Ott announced the impending surrender of the city, asking at the same time if he should be severe or lenient in the negotiations, and not unnaturally, for he was not well posted on the exact situation of the Austrian army.

Melas, in a letter to Count de Tige at Vienna, states that Ott had written to him to the effect that at the moment he received, at Sestri on the 2nd of June, his despatch with the order to raise the blockade, Massena appeared inclined to capitulate; that the conferences had began that very day, and that Ott thought that he should delay his departure for a few days to see the end of the negotiations.[*]

Prince Sulkowsky, who arrived before Genova on the 3rd of

* De Cugnac, " Campagne de l'Armée de Reserve en 1800," vol. ii. p. 229.

June, was the bearer of Melas's reply to Ott's letter. In his letter Melas depicted the positions occupied by the Army of Reserve, and frankly confessed that only a battle could re-establish the affairs of the Austrian army, but that there was no time to lose. Sulkowsky on his way thither had gathered the first news of the disasters which had overtaken the Austrian forces in the Riviera di Ponente. These he communicated to Ott, who became alarmed lest the negotiations should be broken. This appeared likely, for on the morning of the 3rd Massena had not decided on anything, and had even sent word that pressing business would prevent him from attending the conference at the hour agreed upon. Ott began to fear that on arriving at Savona Suchet might, by a brisk cannonade, intimate to the right wing that he was within reach and could render assistance—an event that might induce Massena to break off all negotiations.

Ott had been greatly upset by the receipt of the order to raise the blockade. It was distracting, coming just at a moment when he was about to reap the fruit of so much bloodshed, of fatigues, dangers, and privations undergone with such unheard-of fortitude. He reflected that when Melas had indited the order he had not contemplated the possibility of an early surrender, such as he now saw every prospect of realizing. This disparity in the conditions of the two letters he received from Melas he took to mean that there was no real urgency. As the report he had sent to the commander-in-chief might lead to a counter-order, it was, he considered, proper to wait for more positive injunctions.

The noble and unfortunate Army of Italy was to pay dearly for the success of the Army of Reserve. All its privations, all its sufferings, all its losses, were not enough; to all these was to be added a painful evacuation. Massena thoroughly under-stood the *rôle* which had been assigned to his army, but there is a limit to all resistance, more so in a case like this, when the army believed that it had done all that could be expected of it.

Notwithstanding all Massena's efforts to support the drooping spirits of his soldiers, the fact that there remained nothing beyond the last morsel of food stared him in the face; and that all hope of being relieved was gone. The rapid progress of the epidemic, the number of the dead, the dreadful misery of the living,* the general discouragement and discontent at last prevailed. Alive to these dire facts, he commissioned Andrieux, under pretext of treating about an exchange of prisoners, to ascertain what the terms the enemy was minded to propose would be. He was authorized to lend a willing ear to all such as would be made to him as long as they did not contemplate a capitulation. As the negotiations went on, fearing that Andrieux was not sufficiently able to safeguard the interests of the army, Massena gave him as an aide Morin, his secretary, an astute and clever man, on whom he conferred full powers of debating. His concise instructions were, " Demand that the army may be free to return to France with arms and baggage ; if not, tell them it will make its way through with the bayonet."

Massena agreed to an evacuation at the very moment that Ott had received the order to raise the blockade. No doubt, if he could have held out two or three days longer things would have taken a different turn. Massena would have seen the enemy in his front diminishing in numbers, he could have made some sort of a sortie, effected a junction with Suchet, and have caused the Austrians serious trouble. An army, however, cannot undertake anything without provisions. The French were *absolutely starving* when Massena agreed to an evacuation, and it would have puzzled the critics who suggest such brisk operations to indicate where the French were to obtain the provisions required for a march to Savona and onward.

The soldier has a tender point—he has a jealous regard for his reputation ; and who will reproach Massena for having resented his being entirely abandoned by the First Consul, and having been consequently forced to evacuate the city ?

Ott could hardly conceal his joy when Andrieux proposed such a thing, for he was in dire straits. The news he had received from Melas was sufficiently alarming. There was not a moment to lose. He already knew that the Army of Reserve had crossed the Ticino and was on its way to Milan, that it was time for him to march in the direction of the Po. To prevent a junction between Massena's forces and those of Suchet, which would have been sure to operate against him, he proposed that the former should convey his troops to Antibes by sea. This

---

* The mortality amongst the Austrian prisoners amounted to from 45 to 50 per cent. per day. Massena had begged Ott to supply them with bread; he refused, alleging that these provisions might be consumed by their captors.

proposition was disdainfully rejected. Massena held firm, and declared he much preferred cutting his way out. At last it was arranged that all who were strong enough to carry their arms should go by land. These amounted to between 8000 and 8500 men. The rest, being convalescents, were sent by sea.

Massena delayed ratifying the convention as long as he could. Up to the very last moment he hoped he would be relieved, but when any further delay would have made him break his word he agreed to the terms proposed.

The principal clauses of the evacuation signed on the 4th of June were the following :—

" The French garrison marches out of Genova with arms and baggage to rejoin the Army of Italy.

" 8110 men proceed by the land route, and march in the direction of Nice.* The rest of the troops, effective or con-valescents, will be transported by the English fleet to Antibes, and fed on the way.

" The artillery and munitions belonging to the French will be conveyed in the same manner to Antibes or to Golfe Jouan.

" All the Austrian prisoners captured by the French are released.

" The population of Genova will be provisioned with the least possible delay.

" The artillery and the munitions belonging to the city of Genova will be surrendered to the allies."

Massena has been reproached for not having detected by the extremely favourable terms they offered him, and by their fulsome adulation, what straits the allies were in, and how anxious they were to bring the blockade to an end. The acquiescence of General Ott and Admiral Keith—under pretence of rendering the greatest possible honour to the brave defenders of Genova—to allow the garrison to march out with arms and baggage without being prisoners of war, was unusual. Napoleon argues in his " Mémoires " that this fact alone should have put Massena on his guard. It was an indication of the critical position the allies were in. Massena thereupon should have instantly broken ;off all negotiations, sure enough that he would have been relieved in four or five days. When he wrote this the

---

* On the 6th the troops marched out with arms and baggage, but with no cannon. Massena embarked for Antibes with 1500 men and 20 guns. The sick and wounded remained in the city, cared for by the French medical officers.

emperor entirely overlooked the fact that there was barely food —and such food too—for one day more when Massena agreed to march out.

Napoleon's strictures on the evacuation of Genova were written in after-years. Immediately after the event he uttered no reproaches, no complaint; on the contrary, he was lavish in his praise, full of gratitude.

Massena took ship for Antibes, but for a good reason; for, being ignorant of the details of Suchet's pursuit of Elsnitz, what could be more natural for him than to believe that Suchet was still on the Var? With that idea in his mind he conceived that by repairing quickly to Antibes he would soonest be able to resume operations.

The memoirs accuse him of having sent 8500 men by land, but without guns, and of having embarked with twenty field-guns and 1500 men, and landed at Antibes. *Son devoir était de partager le sort de ses troupes, et il devait bien comprendre l'intérêt que mettait l'ennemi à l'en séparer.* After the treatment Massena received from Bonaparte, this stricture seems more than uncalled for. It is well known how reluctant he was to descend into the plains of Monferrato without artillery and cavalry. And where was he to find horses for drawing his twenty field-guns when all his horses had been slaughtered for food? And where was he most likely to find teams for his guns but at Antibes or at Nice? Massena, with his stubborn defence of Genova, did much towards helping the progress of the Army of Reserve. When his troops evacuated Genova, they were not in a condition to undertake anything. The sufferings of hunger, the influence of disease, the depression caused by numerous losses, by the terrible sights which had been constantly under their eyes, cannot but have seriously lowered the *morale* of the troops. Bonaparte expected from them further efforts without allowing them any time to recuperate. He demanded what was impossible.

The occupation of Genova, after all, was far from being an advantage for the Austrians, for it compelled them to leave a strong garrison to hold the city, whilst it freed several thousand tried soldiers who, under the terms of the treaty, were at liberty to take the field once outside the city walls. Jomini states that the Austrians left 16 battalions in Genova and 6 in Savona, or 22 in all. In his report to Massena, June 24, 1800,

Suchet states that when he took over the city from Hohenzollern three brigades, infantry and cavalry, forming a total of about 8500 men, marched past him.

Jomini also states that Lord Keith had been solicited by Hohenzollern to call up the British corps from Minorca to relieve his troops, but that Keith replied that he had no authority to control its movements, and could do nothing till Abercromby arrived and assumed command. This, as we have seen in Chapter IV., only took place on the 22nd of June.

It has often been said of the Great Emperor's marshals that when left to themselves at the head of an army they found their task too great for them. This cannot be said of Massena, after his spirited defence of Genova. With regard to most of Napoleon's generals, can we wonder that they were not always up to the mark, when we reflect how, in most cases, their professional education had been purely practical, how they lacked that knowledge which a long study of history imparts, and without which their master declared it to be impossible for any one to become a great commander? How assiduous was Bonaparte can be gathered from the following anecdote. Being at Marseilles, and in company with a party of young people, he had retired into a corner of the room with a book, while the rest were dancing and amusing themselves. In vain they solicited him to join in their youthful sports; his reply to their entreaties was: "*Jouer et danser, ce n'est pas là la manière de former un homme*" ("Playing and dancing is not the way to form a man").

How thoroughly it is known that Bonaparte spent the best years of his youth in storing knowledge by studious and attentive reading! It was his genius, backed by deep study and reflection, that made him the incomparable general he was.

CHAPTER VI.

SUCHET'S DEFENCE OF THE VAR.

Suchet separated from Massena and opposed to Elsnitz—Attacks the Austrians at Melongo—Unsuccessful attack of Monte San Giacomo—Oudinot sails through the blockading fleet—According to Massena's orders, Suchet attacks Monte San Giacomo, but is beaten back—Melas reinforces Elsnitz—Reaches Savona on the 29th of April—Attacks Suchet on the 2nd of May—Suchet retires during the night—Melas attacks the French again on the 7th, outnumbers them at all points, and compels them to retire—Being outflanked, Suchet retires to the Var—Melas enters Nice—The Austrians make a feeble attack on the 13th—Melas receives alarming news, and quits Nice on the 18th— Austrians attack the bridge of Saint Laurent on the 22nd of May—Make a second attack on the 27th—After this last failure they retire—Suchet cuts them off at Col di Tenda—Pursues them up to Ormea—Elsnitz makes a hasty retreat, suffers heavy losses, and finally reaches Ceva on the 7th of June—Suchet and Gazan join forces.

In 1800, another brilliant commander was wielding the sword in defence of the Republic on the Western Riviera. This officer was Suchet, one of the three Napoleon classed as the best of the French generals.* His military talent was of the highest order; he had served as chief of the staff to Joubert and Championnet, and when Moreau was about to quit Italy to assume the command of the Army of the Rhine, he said of him that Suchet was one of the best chiefs of the staff the French army possessed.

When Massena arrived from Switzerland to take up the command of the Army of Italy, he brought with him Oudinot as his chief of the staff. On his way to Genova, Massena fell in with Suchet at Fréjus, and as he had known him for a long time

---

* " I then asked Napoleon," writes O'Meara, in his " Memoirs," " which of the French generals was in his opinion the most skilful? ' I should find it difficult,' he replied, ' to decide ; but I am inclined to name Suchet. Massena was formerly the most skilful, but we may now consider him as no longer in existence. Suchet, Clausel, and Gérard are, I think, the best French generals.' " What great soldiers fought with the Army of Italy in 1800 ! There were Massena, Suchet, Soult, Clausel, Oudinot, Mouton, and others.

and appreciated his abilities, he was anxious to retain him, and
so conferred on him the command of his left wing. In this
manner Suchet found himself at the head of two or three
divisions; but so weak in numbers that the whole did not
approach in strength a really complete division.

In Melas's successful operations of the 6th of April, Suchet
had some encounters with Elsnitz's command. Threatened as
he was by very considerable forces, and hearing of the capture
of Savona, he determined to retire from the Apennines, to concentrate at Borghetto. Gorupp had harassed his left in the
valley of the Tanaro; Ulm had occupied Sette Pani; Fort San
Stefano had fallen into the hands of the Austrians, and Elsnitz,
with Morzin's division, occupied Monte San Giacomo. Separated from Massena, Suchet was now left to contend against
greatly superior numbers. For a month he had to fight against
Elsnitz's corps, and later also against Melas, when, advancing
from Vado, the latter combined his forces with those of Elsnitz.

The Court of Vienna, alarmed at the great superiority of
the French army on the Rhine, and by the immense preparations the First Consul was making to carry the war to the
Danube, was urging Melas to make a powerful diversion in
Provence. Melas judged that the so-much-wished-for moment
had arrived for entering France, and moved his forces towards
the Var. He advanced at the head of 30,000 men against
Suchet.

Massena fully recognized the great importance of re-estab-
lishing his connection with Suchet, and determined to effect
this by assuming a vigorous offensive. His orders to Suchet
were to co-operate as much as it lay in his power with the
efforts he was about to make on the 10th at Montenotte, with
the object of reuniting the two wings which had been driven
asunder by Melas's attack on the 6th.

Suchet thereupon took the following steps. Leaving Pouget
to protect Borghetto, he moved on Bardinetto and Calissano
on the evening of the 9th, and with little trouble dislodged the
Austrian posts. Séras's brigade was left to guard the issues of
the Bormida, and Clausel was directed to march on Melongo.

Elsnitz occupied a favourable position; his left rested on
Finale, the Austrians occupying the small fort there. With
the centre he held Monte San Giacomo. On his right at Sette
Pani lay the camp of Ulm's brigade.

Under cover of a dense fog, Clausel sent General Compans to carry Melongo, separated Ulm from the rest of the Austrian forces, and attacked him with vigour. Elsnitz, made aware of Clausel's attack, reinforced the garrison of Fort Finale, and gathered the bulk of his forces round San Giacomo with the object of supporting Ulm in case the latter should be seriously attacked. Suchet, who had come up during the night with rein-forcements,¦reanimated the spirits of the troops. On the following day General Compans led the 7th Light up the mountain before daybreak, and, favoured by a fog, totally surprised Ulm's troops. Ably seconded by Clausel's forces, he hurled the enemy on Biestre with a loss of between 1300 and 1400 prisoners.

The whole of that day, Suchet heard a heavy cannonade in the direction of Sassello, and having by demonstrations before San Giacomo riveted the attention of the Austrians to that point, might during the night have moved thither, and thus have effected a junction with the right wing. Such a masterly movement, notwithstanding the important results which might have accrued from it, might, looking at the lassitude of his troops and at the great dearth of provisions, have placed him in a highly dangerous situation. Suchet considered it preferable to attack Monte San Giacomo, and after carrying it to descend on Savona.

Suchet ordered Monte San Giacomo to be attacked on the 12th. The attack was carried out by three columns, com-manded by Generals Compans, Solignac, and Séras. Elsnitz, however, was in a state to meet the attack; his defence was brisk, and the French were soon compelled to retire with heavy loss. During the night Suchet withdrew his forces to Melongo and Sette Pani. On the following day he extended his right by coming down to Finale. The left he pushed towards Garessio, so that the enemy might not be tempted to turn his position by advancing along the valley of the Tanaro.

The uncertainty as to how Massena's attacks had fared kept Suchet inactive for two or three days. Massena, on his side, after his check at Albissola on the 15th of April, was dis-turbed at not hearing from Suchet. Seeing how impatient his chief was to learn the result of Suchet's operations, Oudinot volunteered to go and confer with him and to be the bearer of any fresh instructions.

Oudinot, conducted by a certain Bavastro, captain of a

privateer, and accompanied by his aide-de-camp, left Varaggio on the 16th, passed through the blockading fleet, and, after having a hundred times risked capture or destruction from the enemy's fire, succeeded in landing at Loano in safety. Writing to Bonaparte on the 17th of April, Oudinot confesses how Massena was fully alive to the danger which encompassed the enterprise, and how it was simply owing to the darkness of the night that he was able to carry it into effect. He reached Suchet's head-quarters at Melongo. Having given him his orders to attack the enemy and to make a brave attempt to reach Savona, Oudinot faced the same risks, and returned to Genova, bringing to Massena a detailed account of the position occupied by Suchet, and of the total of his effective forces.*

Acting on the orders Oudinot had brought with him, Suchet called in all his posts from Murialto, Ronchi, and the heights in the neighbourhood of Monte San Giacomo, and on the evening of the 19th took post about the village of Bormida.

The mountain was to be carried during the night. He formed three columns; one under the orders of Brigadier-General Mazas was to take the right, General Jablonowsky was to lead the centre one, and Compans and Clausel had charge of the main attack on the left. Séras and Blondeau commanded two small reserve columns marching in the interval of the other columns.

After the combat at Voltri, Melas had, on the 18th, sent the brigades of Bellegarde, Brentano, and Lattermann to reinforce Elsnitz. These brigades had not yet arrived, but knowing that he was about to be reinforced, and warned by what had occurred the previous day, Elsnitz got before daybreak sufficient troops under arms to overcome the French. Suchet's columns quitted Bormida at one o'clock in the morning, and took the directions assigned to them. Jablonowsky, however, in place of waiting until the lateral columns had reached the foot of the mountain, pushed beyond Mallere and showed himself to the Austrians. Elsnitz then sent down a mass of men which overthrew the

---

* Oudinot, the commander of Napoleon's grenadiers, was always to be found in the front rank in a fight, and wherever danger was thickest, risking his life in the *mêlée*. His body was covered with scars and wounds received in hand-to-hand conflicts. Of all Napoleon's marshals few could boast of so marvellous a military career, of such frequent and narrow escapes from death, of so much blood spilt for the honour of his country. Justly proud of being commanded by such a brave man, the Grenadiers called him their father.

brigade and drove it back on Mallere, where Séras's forces were just arriving; then, profiting by the time the French took to rally, Elsnitz charged in succession Mazas's and Clausel's columns, and routed them completely. Had Elsnitz shown more enterprise he might have captured one-half of the French forces. The thing was not difficult. He had only to direct a column between Mallere and Bormida.

When all hope of forming a junction with Soult came to an end, Suchet realized that to relieve the strain on Genova it behoved him to find work for as large a number of Austrian troops as possible. As he had become a thorn in the side of the Austrian general, Melas decided to get rid of him definitely. Having left Ott with a body of 25,000 men to undertake the blockade of Genova, he marched, on the 27th of April, with Lattermann's brigade to join Saint Julien somewhere about Savona, and to assume supreme command of Elsnitz's column.

At that period Kaim was holding Piedmont with 25,000 men. Melas considered that at a season when the snows had not melted such a large force was wasted in Piedmont, and could be more advantageously employed elsewhere than keeping watch on Turreau's division. What the French had at that period were some 6000 men of General Turreau's division on the Mont Cenis, and a small detachment under Lesuire encamped on the Col di Tenda. There was no reason to be anxious on their account. So Kaim was ordered to send some of his troops to reinforce Melas. He sent some troops and Piedmontese militia to reinforce Gorupp's force, then operating on the Tanaro before Ceva. Knesevich's brigade, moving by Vernante, had to threaten the Col di Tenda, while detachments were to show themselves towards the passes of Finestre and Vinadio.

Suchet was holding a dangerous position about Borghetto, and had decided to defend it, and, if beaten, to retire behind the Roya. He had a very small force, quite insufficient to occupy a line six leagues in extent. Clausel's division had its right on the sea in front of Borghetto, and the left at Castel-Bianco. His outposts held Loano and the heights of Bardinetto and Rocca-Barbena. Pouget occupied Castel-Bianco, Caprauna, and Ponte di Nave in the Tanaro valley. Blondeau, with two half-brigades, was in reserve at Lecco. Suchet's headquarters were moved to Albenga on the 27th.

In commenting on Suchet's activity, Mathieu Dumas remarks

how that general remained faithful to the following precept: that when one is engaged in mountain warfare he should not consider himself bound to observe a strictly passive defensive; but, on the contrary, should increase his movements and attacks, because, even given that their issue is not always favourable, their effect at least is certain, inasmuch as the adversary is everywhere harassed, everywhere discovered, and is often disconcerted at the very moment when he believes he is about to deliver the most telling strokes.

Melas had arrived at Savona * on the 29th of April, with the troops intended to reinforce Elsnitz, and his presence imparted fresh vigour to the operations. The Austrians quitted Monte San Giacomo, and occupied Melongo and Sette Pani. On the 1st of May, General Lattermann drove the French advanced posts out of Loano, whilst Morzin, at the head of three brigades, moved on Monte Calvo. Elsnitz, with two more brigades, marched by Bardinetto so as to assail Monte Lingo, as soon as Gorupp was seen to be advancing on Monte Galera; then he was to menace the French left.

The general attack was fixed for the 2nd. Séras, threatened by Elsnitz on the side of Monte Lingo, and overpowered by Morzin, who had issued smartly from Monte Calvo, could not hold out long against such superior forces, and deemed himself fortunate in being able to reach Sambucco in fair order. As Gorupp arrived at Galera, Elsnitz hastened to join him. On the side of the sea Lattermann, assisted by the fire of some British frigates, carried Borghetto, but could not quite overthrow the French right beyond it. The day had gone against the French, and Suchet, fearing lest he might be turned, ordered the retreat, which was carried out during the night.

After this the French took post: Pouget at Rezzo and Mezza-Luna, with his right resting on Monte di Toria; Clausel, with four half-brigades, occupied the ground between Mezza-Luna and Diano in front of Oneglia. A thousand men, under Séras, were posted at Triola, to cover the Col Ardente and to connect Pouget's troops with those under Lesuire.

By this time Suchet had heard of the advance of the Army of Reserve on Geneva, and how Turreau had captured Mont Cenis. He hoped that the news would compel Melas to lead a

* On the 17th of April, the citadel of Savona held a French garrison of 750 men and supplies for ten days.

portion of his troops back into Piedmont, allowing the French some rest in the valley of Oneglia, as long, at least, as the Col di Tenda remained in their hands.

The Austrians remained inactive for four days. Very early on the morning of the 7th of May, all their columns moved simultaneously. Gorupp led for Col Ardente. A portion of Morzin's division and Lattermann's brigade under Zach attacked the French right. Elsnitz was told off to carry Monte di Toria and the heights of Cessio, while Knesevich had to carry the Col di Tenda.

Melas had gathered together from 15,000 to 18,000 men, and the French were outnumbered at all points. Zach drove Clausel's division back as far as San Lorenzo. Elsnitz was even more fortunate, for he defeated Pouget, enveloped his right on the Monte di Toria and Cessio, and captured 1400 prisoners. Pouget was fortunate in being able to effect his retreat from Monte Calvo by Borgo Mario and Carpasio. Gorupp occupied Col Ardente and Mezza-Luna, and Knesevich's column drove Lesuire from the Col di Tenda and joined Gorupp's force at Saint Dalmazio.

The Austrian dispositions were faulty. Situated as the enemy was, with a flank resting on the sea, and that flank exposed to attack by the British men-of-war, the most sound process would have been to have brought all weight to bear on the French left. In the combats of the 2nd and 7th no attempt whatever was made to seize the French line of communications. It was an error simply to drive them back on their natural line of retreat, when the longer they remained on the coast the more certain became their capture; whereas the further Suchet was driven back and the nearer he approached the French frontier, the more likely he was to obtain reinforcements. Nothing demonstrates better how wrong Melas had been throughout not to operate strongly on the French communications than Suchet's speedy retreat the moment he learnt that Knesevich had got possession of the Col di Tenda.

Suchet in his retreat was not only molested by the Austrians, but also by the inhabitants of the valleys, who had risen and made common cause with their would-be deliverers.

The combat of the 7th of May did great honour to the French troops. The Austrians displayed great vigour and combination in their attacks, and the French would have been

surrounded and destroyed, had not all the troops during this
bloody contest fought with the courage of despair. But what
redounds still more to their credit was that they had been
seriously enfeebled by want and privations. Such was the
dearth of provisions that a ration loaf was divided amongst
fifteen men.

Nothing does so much honour to the soldier as when he
fights hard and strives to do his duty gallantly with scanty
nourishment, with barely enough bread to keep body and soul
together.

When Suchet became aware of the capture of the Col di
Tenda, and how Knesevich had advanced beyond Saorgio, he
owned that the line of the Roya was no longer capable of being
disputed, and that no time was to be lost in regaining the
frontier. He had fought stubbornly, but with the principal
positions in the hands of the enemy, and outflanked on his
left, he determined, and with ample reason, to fall back behind
the line of the Var. Time was precious, consequently the
retreat had to be carried out as speedily as possible. The
troops, which after the combat on the previous day had retired
behind the Taggia, continued to fall back on Ventimiglia on the
night of the 8th. Having destroyed the bridge on the Roya,
placed a garrison in the fort, and sent Coussaud with 800 men
to reinforce Lesuire, Suchet continued to retire by Mentone,
Villafranca, and Nice.

Lesuire, after abandoning Sospello, had taken post at St.
Pons on the 10th of May, so that the French forces were now
all on the left bank of the Var. On the 11th, they abandoned
Nice, and crossed the Var.

Suchet set at once to reorganize his forces, to which were now
being added some reinforcements. He divided the troops into
four divisions. One, commanded by Clausel, was posted on the
left bank of the river, to protect the completion of the bridge-
head; the second, under the orders of Rochambeau, lined the
Var from its mouth as far as Pujet; General Ménard, with the
third, took post by Le Broc; Garnier commanded the fourth,
located between Le Broc and Malaursène beyond the Esteron,
connecting by small detachments with Entrevaux, then held by
part of Turreau's division. General Quesnel commanded the
reserve, composed of some squadrons of cavalry and stationed
at Saint Laurent, in rear of the bridge on the Var.

Having made a resolution to defend the bridge over that river to the very last, Suchet despatched his aide-de-camp Ricard to Paris with despatches for the First Consul, asking for adequate reinforcements. Ricard had to follow Bonaparte to Dijon, Geneva, and Lausanne. In the last of these towns he overtook the First Consul, and strove to picture to him the dismal situation of the small corps which was left to protect the department of Provence. But Bonaparte relied on Suchet's energy and mettle, and was pleased to hear that Melas was dipping more and more into the territory of the Maritime Alps, leaving to him the plains of Lombardy uncovered. He folded the despatch, and listened to what the aide-de-camp had to say with the greatest complacence. At that moment he was interrupted by the entrance of one of his ministers. Bonaparte advanced to meet him with a mirthful look, exclaiming, " I hold Melas in my pocket " (" *Je tiens Melas dans ma poche* ").

Suchet did the best he could with the forces he had. His corps barely amounted to 8000 combatants, nevertheless these troops were inured to war, and were led by zealous and able commanders.

General Saint Hilaire, who commanded the 8th Military Division, hastened to the Var, collecting on his way at Marseilles and Toulon all the available troops. Several companies of National Guards placed themselves under his orders. Soon the troops concentrated on the Var were raised by conscripts and National Guards to 14,000 men.

The Austrians closely followed the French. On the 11th of May, the same day that Suchet crossed the Var, Melas made his entry into the city of Nice. We can well picture to ourselves the feeling of pride which filled the troops, both officers and men. At last they had set foot on the territory of the Republic, after having suffered humiliating defeats by her armies, and seen them victorious at the gates of Vienna. An English man-of-war had brought the welcome intelligence that the English troops had embarked at Mahon, and were on their way to invest Toulon. This report, however, turned out untrue.

The Austrians took post parallel to the river, their line extending from the sea as far as Aspromonte. They took the precaution of covering their camps with intrenchments and abatis.

On retiring before Melas, Suchet had left garrisons in the

fort at Ventimiglia, in the castle of Villafranca, and in Fort Montalban. The last of these was situated on a height which separated the bay of Villafranca from the roadstead of Nice, and dominated both towns and the course of the Paglione. On the fort was mounted a semaphore, and in this way Suchet managed to have in rear of the Austrians an instrument which reported all their movements, either on the side of Genova by way of the Turbia, or on the road to Turin by the valley of the Paglione.

The position on the Var first of all demanded attention. The Var is a mountain stream generally fordable, but which by heavy rains becomes swollen into an impetuous torrent in a few hours. The fords consequently are not safe. Suchet's line of defence was short: the left rested on some rugged hills ; the right, some 1300 yards beyond them, on the sea. The position which it was Suchet's purpose to defend had been always considered a weak one, for it could only be made safe by extending the defences as far as the French Alps, which at that point are ten or twelve leagues from the sea. The French generals, however, had for four years after their entry into the country of Nice spent considerable attention in protecting the approaches to the bridge by the construction of a number of batteries on the right bank of the river. A bridge-head was now hastily constructed on the left bank, and armed with some heavy ordnance, which had been brought up from Antibes; these pieces were manned by some gunners belonging to the coast artillery. The bridge-head was by this and other measures made the centre of the defence. Batteries were run up and armed on the right bank of the stream, and mortars placed near the river mouth, to keep British ships from approaching the shore and bearing upon the French position. Having by these and other measures rendered the position tenable, Suchet confidently awaited Melas's attack.

He had not long to wait. On the 13th of May, Elsnitz, Lattermann, and Bellegarde attacked the bridge-head, but, though the new defensive works had been not more than traced, the Austrians were driven back. This first success inspired confidence in the defenders, who pushed on their works with great energy.

The post continually brought from Paris news of the progress of the Army of Reserve, from which the *morale* of the troops and the spirits of the population were raised; both had become very hopeful.

On the 18th of May, on the receipt of alarming information from Kaim, Melas decided on quitting Nice and repairing to Turin. He left Nice on the 20th of May, and by the 26th was at Turin. Elsnitz, with 18,000 men, was left to confront Suchet. His men were divided into five brigades. Lattermann and Weidenfeld were on the left towards the Bridge of Saint Laurent; Ulm and Bellegarde in the centre towards Aspromonte; Gorupp on the right, on the Tinca. A sixth brigade, commanded by Saint Julien, joined Elsnitz's force after the capitulation of Savona.

Elsnitz did not dare undertake anything against the bridgehead on the Var, as his artillery had not been able to come by the Corniche road. He had consequently to rest satisfied with some paltry demonstrations. The time was not wasted by Suchet. Aided by General Campredon, an officer of great ability and energy, he completed the defensive works, and made them strong enough to resist a determined attack.

The apparent necessity of soon having to call Elsnitz's troops back to Piedmont to confront the French columns which were descending from the Alps, decided Melas to attempt an attack of the bridge on the Var, in the hope that the capture of that important post would thoroughly paralyze Suchet's forces.

The Austrian heavy artillery had at last been landed at Nice. It was drawn hence, and placed in batteries, which had already been prepared. At the break of day on the 22nd of May the guns suddenly opened fire. The brigades of Lattermann and of Bellegarde, six battalions of infantry and eleven of grenadiers, advanced in three columns against the French works defended by Rochambeau. These columns were protected on their right by a powerful battery of twelve guns, and on the left by the fire of several frigates and smaller British ships, armed with heavy guns. Thus, with both flanks well protected, the Austrians delivered two vigorous attacks, but unsuccessfully; for the French, informed of the assailants' proceedings by the semaphore of Fort Montalban, made suitable dispositions, and met each attack with great courage.

The attack was stubborn, the defence brilliant. The assailants were mown down by grape and canister, and were received by a heavy and well-directed musketry fire. The bravest of them fell, the rest were severely shaken and disheartened. After a time the impossibility of carrying the position was recognized; the troops were withdrawn, and fell back on their camp, having suffered very sensible losses.

The Austrian commander after this check decided to try to cross the Var further up, and had he succeeded in turning the French position, there would have remained nothing for Suchet to do but to fall back on Cannes and the defiles of the Esterelles. However, from this he was saved by the news which reached Melas at Coni. On the 22nd, he heard there of Turreau's attack on Susa, how Bonaparte had crossed the Great Saint Bernard at the head of an imposing army, and how his advanced guard under Lannes had captured Ivrea.

A strong French column had made its way down the valley of Aosta, and at this date Melas simply conjectured that it was a powerful diversion intended to let him relinquish his hold on Genova and relieve the pressure on Suchet. In support of this, we find him on the 23rd of May writing to Lord Keith from Sevigliano : " The enemy has encompassed the fort of Bard, and has advanced up to the castle of Ivrea. It is very clear that his aim is to release Massena." Even Turreau's advance by Mont Cenis was explicable enough, for were the French Government bent on relieving Genova, what would be more natural than for them to send a force from Lyons by that route? In fact, this column so thoroughly showed its object that Kaim went to Avigliano to reconnoitre Turreau's real strength. Zach, led into error, had Kaim's corps, which was already stronger than Turreau's, reinforced by Knesevich's brigade.

When Melas started from Nice with his reserve, he ordered Elsnitz, in case he was threatened by superior forces, to withdraw the remaining troops and to take up a position in rear of the line of the Roya with the right resting on the Col di Tenda, the centre on the heights of Breglio, and the left on Ventimiglia. A number of Engineer officers and a detachment of sappers had been already sent there to prepare intrenchments for covering the retirement from the Var.

The instructions given to Elsnitz had reference to two distinct contingencies. If threatened by a superior force, he was to withdraw his troops beyond the Roya. Should he be forced from that line of defence, and Genova still held out, he was enjoined to dispute the ground stubbornly up to Savona, and there he was to defend himself up to the very last. In case, however, Genova should have fallen, he was ordered to leave 2000 men in Liguria, and with the remaining 16,000 men to follow the road of the Col di Tenda.

Elsnitz, like Ott at Genova, could not resist the desire of scoring a victory. This may have been thought quite a natural ambition after so much brave blood spilt, still it showed that neither of them had a proper military insight nor the ability to appreciate the situation to a nicety. The Austrian generals did not recognize how imperative it had become, when an able and daring general had descended into Italy with a fresh army, to concentrate their forces, which were mostly scattered at that time along the Riviera di Ponente.

Elsnitz did not comply with the instructions he had received from Melas. He had arranged with the English a plan of attack against the position held by Suchet, and did not at all relish having to abandon the undertaking without making an effort. He longed to burn the bridge, and to destroy the intrenchments lining the right bank of the Var. Suchet, nevertheless, made him pay dear for his attempt, which was not crowned with success. Elsnitz decided, before breaking up his camp and complying with the orders he had received, to deliver a fresh attack, as the best way for carrying out the intentions of the commander-in-chief. Considerable forces took part in this attack on the French position on the 27th of May, but the Austrians were no more successful on this than they had been on the former occasion.

They opened fire at about three in the afternoon with twenty guns, mostly of heavy calibre. The cannonade was kept up till ten in the evening, when the assault was delivered. The French, informed betimes by the semaphore of Montalban, were ready to receive the enemy. The Austrian grenadiers moved to the attack with great resolution, but were stopped by a heavy fire of musketry and artillery. The assault, suspended for an hour, was resumed with greater fury. The Austrian columns advanced, preceded by 200 pioneers furnished with fire-balls, fascines, and hatchets to cut down and demolish the abatis, but all in vain : these brave men never got beyond the foot of the intrenchments, their supports were swept away by the artillery ; all their gallant endeavours failed, and they had to be recalled from their dangerous position.

The next day Elsnitz, afraid lest the French should forestall him at the Col di Braus and at Sospello, ordered a general retreat. First, however, he caused two brigades of grenadiers to attack Clausel's troops, which had advanced beyond the bridgehead of Saint Laurent. That same day, the 28th, Ménard attacked the brigades of Ulm and Saint Julien close by Aspromonte. At 11 p.m. that same day, the whole of Elsnitz's forces set out for the Col di Braus, covered by Lattermann's brigade, which had been directed to occupy Monte Grosso to the north of Nice, and afterwards to fall back on the heights of La Turbia overlooking Monaco. Elsnitz had shipped his heavy ordnance, and sent it direct to Leghorn. The heavier of the field-guns had marched for the Col di Tenda, and he did not keep with the troops more than ten or twelve very light pieces.

Suchet followed to the letter the instructions he had received from Bonaparte ; these were "to keep in check a body equal to your own," and it was this and more that Suchet did.

The reinforcements brought by General Saint Hilaire had raised his force to 13,465 men of all arms. This was divided as follows :—

		Men.	
Brigade Quesnel	...	640 ;	cavalry advanced guard.
,, Séras ...	...	942	Clausel's division, right.
,, Brunet	...	1451	
,, Jablonowsky	...	1305	Rochambeau's division, centre.
,, Solignac	...	1525	
,, Lesuire	...	1441	Mengaud's division — Left wing
,, Delaunay	...	1600	under
,, Calvin...	...	1420	Garnier's division — Ménard.
,, Jonais-Laviolais		780	
,, Beaumont	...	1611	
Artillery and Engineers		750	
Total ...	...	13,465	

The bridge on the Var and the communications with France had necessarily to be guarded, and in resuming the offensive Suchet was not able to mobilize much more than 9000 men. Elsnitz had still with him 15,000 men, all fine infantry. To the superiority in numbers on the Austrian side should be added superior quality, for many of Suchet's men were young soldiers

and National Guards inexperienced in war. Rose * quotes a
report from Lord W. Bentinck to the Admiralty dated Alessandria, June 15th : " I am sorry to say that General Elsnitz's
corps, which was composed of the grenadiers of the finest
regiments in the (Austrian) army, arrived here in a most
deplorable condition. His men had already suffered much from
want of provisions and hardships. He was pursued in his
retreat by General Suchet, who had with him about 7000 men.
There was an action at Ponte di Nave, in which the French
failed; and it will appear scarcely credible, when I tell your
lordship, that the Austrians lost in this retreat, from fatigue
only, nearly 5000 men ; and I have no doubt that General
Suchet will notify this to the world as a great victory." †

The moment the semaphore at Fort Montalban announced
that the Austrians were retiring, Suchet issued from his intrenchments and took up the pursuit. He may possibly not have
known the exact reason for their withdrawal, but he justly
surmised that if they were retiring it was a clear sign that
grave events had taken place in Piedmont or in Lombardy.
Every consideration demanded that he should follow on their
track, drive them back, and inflict on them considerable
losses.

Suchet did not repeat Melas's error when driving back the
French a few weeks before. He quickly detected how the best
plan consisted in manœuvring by his left, so as to deprive the
enemy of the important communications with the rest of their
army by way of the Col di Tenda. By doing so, he would menace
Elsnitz's retreat, would compel him to withdraw from the Riviera
di Ponente, and rid Massena of him. By acting in this manner
he would also more readily join the First Consul, should his
army be operating in Piedmont.

When Suchet issued his orders to his divisions, those on
his left, 4000 men under Ménard, were directed to advance on
Duranus and Lucerame ; those of Rochambeau, with Brunet's
brigade, marched in the direction of Sospello. Clausel led Séras's
weak brigade on Monaco, following the coast route ; at a distance
of half a day's march came Beaumont's reserve. To Clausel

---

* Rose, " Napoleon Bonaparte," vol. i. p. 253.

† The date of this report appears somewhat strange, for the events of the
previous day—the total defeat of the Austrian army—hardly made the above facts
worthy of being reported.

had been assigned the task of moving along the seashore with the object of molesting the Austrian left.

When Elsnitz quitted the Var he took position on the line of the Roya, which from the Col di Tenda stretches to Ventimiglia and the sea, a total distance of twenty-five leagues.

To turn the right of the Austrians and to gain possession of the main road leading through the Col di Tenda, Suchet engaged in a series of combats which the nature of the country more than the relative situation of the two sides necessitated.

Suchet's left, under Ménard, was divided into two columns. One of these moved up the valley of the Vesubia, the other went by Col de la Pietra in the direction of the camp of Mille-forche to Monte Lauthione. The object of the manœuvre was to turn the Colle di Brouis, which the Austrians seemed intent on defending obstinately. General Rochambeau in the mean while was reconnoitring the valley of the Bevera, keeping touch with the scouts of the right wing.

The intention was to seize Tenda, and with this object in view Suchet ordered Ménard to carry the position of Col di Braus, whilst Rochambeau advanced on Baolet and La Penna, so as to surround the Austrian rear-guard, which held the Colle di Brouis, and so cut off its retreat.

The manœuvre was quite successful. Ménard carried the Col di Braus and captured 400 prisoners; the enemy's rear-guard was cut off and captured almost to a man. Bellegarde and Gorupp, who were at Breglio, just escaped, but with the loss of their baggage.

The position of Saorgio had lost much of its importance since the fort had been razed. Nevertheless, the difficulties of the ground rendered that locality, with those of Milleforche, of Monte Lauthione, and of Col di Braus, formidable positions only, however, when sufficiently manned. The Austrians had overlooked this last condition, and had disseminated their force injudiciously.

The capture of the Col di Braus led to that of the redoubts on Monte Lauthione, and on the camp at Milleforche, where the Austrians lost 600 prisoners. The posts of Saorgio and Fontana had been evacuated. Ménard occupied the road to Tenda, closing the way to such of the Austrians as were moving in that direction.

On the 3rd, the French occupied the Col di Tenda, which

had been turned by way of the Col Sabione ; it was feebly contested. Rochambeau's two columns advanced rapidly, one by
the Colle Ardente, the other in rear of Ventimiglia by the left
bank of the Roya. Elsnitz was compelled to beat a hasty
retreat, abandoning some prisoners, his baggage, and artillery,
which could not quit the Roya valley in time.

Suchet, who was keen to draw Elsnitz away from the coast
road, pushed forward three brigades to Pieve, a point of great
importance for the Austrians in the communications between
the valleys of Oneglia and the Tanaro. Their retreat to the
north or south of the Apennines depended at that moment on
news arriving from Genova.

About that time Melas had despatched a courier to Elsnitz,
bearing orders to fall back at once on Alessandria. The courier
found himself at Tenda at the moment of Gorupp's defeat ; his
progress was stopped, and he was only able to reach Elsnitz's
headquarters by making a considerable *détour*.

Suchet marched by the Colle Ardente to the valley of the
Taggia. On the 4th, he occupied Badelucco, Andagna, and
Mendalica on the parting of the waters of the Arosia and
Tanaro. Ménard came down the Col di Tenda by the sources
of the Tanaro, and occupied Ormea, thus menacing Elsnitz's
new line of operations had he chosen to march north of the
Apennines.

Having left 200 men in the fort at Ventimiglia, Elsnitz
marched rapidly on Pieve. There he concentrated his forces,
and awaited the entire evacuation of the posts on the Riviera di
Genova, and of an immense convoy of baggage and ammunition,
which employed about 5000 mules, and which was already wending
its way slowly to Ceva. The appearance of Ménard's advance-
guard making for Ormea, and the rapidity of Rochambeau's
and Clausel's movements, which were directed on Pieve, made
the Austrians accelerate their retreat. On the 5th they still
had a rear-guard at Pieve ; this was attacked and overcome by
the columns of Ménard, Mengaud, and Clausel. The French
captured 1500 prisoners and six standards, pursuing the rest
up to the valley of the Tanaro.

Suchet had no enemy now before him, and only very few
marches more remained to be made, and then Massena could
hear the sound of his guns. Elsnitz had been pretty well cut
up in his retreat from Nice ; he reached Ceva on the 7th of

June with 8000 men. Reckoning that he had quitted the Var with 15,000 men, this disastrous retreat had cost him nearly one-half of his force, or 7000 men.

In his report to the Archduke Charles, dated Piacenza, 19th June, 1800, Melas admitted that the 19,000 men Elsnitz had at Nice and on the Var had been reduced to 6000. He thus admits a loss of 13,000 men.* Jomini sets down the loss of the Austrians at 10,000 men.

Whatever may have been the exact figure of Elsnitz's losses, the result cannot be measured from that alone. His hasty retreat and the inability of the Austrian officers to stay Suchet's vigorous pursuit must have told on the entire column. The self-respect of the troops and the confidence in their officers received a rude shock from which Elsnitz's troops certainly did not recover by the 14th of June.

Suchet surmised that the reasons which had made Elsnitz beat a hasty retreat would also put an end to the blockade of Genova, and that the two parts of the Army of Italy would soon be able to effect their junction. Convinced that henceforth there would be no obstacle to bar the road to Genova, Suchet, who had advanced between Albenga and Garessio, marched for Monte San Giacomo, but was soon apprised of the fall of Genova and of Gazan's march to Voltri. The two forces came together on the 6th of June between Finale and Savona, and the French at once established their outposts on Montenotte.

When he recovered the ground lost in May, Suchet astonished the inhabitants by his forbearance. They were already surprised by the very rapid change of fortune of the French, and expected to be punished for having risen in arms against them, but Suchet conciliated them by mild treatment, got them to lay down their arms and keep the communications unmolested.

If Suchet's retreat to the Var in the face of very superior numbers was considered a very creditable achievement, how much more praise does he not deserve for his operations after he resumed the offensive? In less than a week he reconquered every inch of ground he had been compelled to abandon to the Austrians since the 1st of May, and he did this acting in a very difficult country, defeating time after time an enemy whose strength was nearly double that of his own, and driving them with very considerable loss from positions naturally strong.

* De Cugnac, vol. ii. p. 437.

After being joined by Gazan's division, Suchet proposed to
Massena to cross the Apennines, to throw themselves on the
rear of the Austrians, and to strive to co-operate with the First
Consul in the battles which he foresaw to be imminent. Massena,
however, had injured himself when landing at Finale ; besides,
at that time he was very wroth with Bonaparte for not having
at once, after entering Italy, proceeded to his help when so
sorely pressed at Genova.

Massena had some good grounds for discontent. Bonaparte
had deceived him, for he had promised by the despatches sent
by Franceschi to proceed after his arrival at Ivrea, from the
28th to the 30th Floréal, by lengthy marches to Genova. More
than sufficient time had elapsed, still he did not put in an
appearance ; and when he did move from Ivrea, he marched in
the opposite direction, leaving the beleaguered city to its fate.

Massena's part in the campaign was to detain the Austrians
in the Riviera of Genova till Bonaparte had time to cross the
Alps and strike them in rear. Owing, however, to his march
on Milan, that much-to-be-hoped-for event, their defeat in battle,
had been put off for twenty days.

His troops, as well as those of Suchet, had experienced
hardships untold, had suffered heavy losses both during the
siege and blockade, and in the retreat to the Var and pursuit
of the Austrians. They needed rest, and possibly were not
equal to any very great exertion.

Of all the French generals, Suchet was the most upright
and honest. He was keen to take part in the decisive operations which Bonaparte was about to carry out, and it was with
some difficulty that he prevailed on Massena to allow him to
take the road to Acqui. His first orders had been to march
to the Col di Tenda, and to bring up the artillery which could
not come by the Corniche road. The presence of some of his
troops at Acqui had an important effect on the battle of the
14th of June, as we shall see in Chapter XIII.

CHAPTER VII.

THE ARMY OF RESERVE.

Bonaparte desires to blot out all the misfortunes which had lately befallen the French arms in Italy—Weak state of the Army of Italy—An Army of Reserve decreed on the 7th of January, 1800—Raised with great rapidity—Berthier appointed to its command—Berthier's ability—Bonaparte deceives the spies at Dijon—All preparations studiously concealed—Strength and distribution of the Army of Reserve—Marmont dislikes to command the artillery—The transport service—Berthier's instructions for the supply of biscuit—The First Consul quits Paris for the army.

By the end of 1799 France had two armies in the field, one of about 120,000 men on the Rhine, the other of something between 25,000 and 30,000 men in Liguria. In the interior of the Republic most of the available troops were occupied in the Vendée.

Bonaparte was devoured by an eager desire to see the Austrians out of the fair provinces which had been the cradle of his first renown. Shortly after his elevation to the Consulate, when his overtures for peace had been rejected by England and Austria, he began to put his plans into execution. In the winter of 1799–1800 he had avowed that he would wrest Italy from the Austrians. He did what he had promised, and in less time than it seemed possible for any one else to do it. What he said was not an empty boast, for he knew the extent of his genius and the wideness of his power.

His great design was to obliterate all the misfortunes which had befallen the French army in Italy, and to restore to it all the prestige of past glories. To do this, to carry his plan into effect, a third army was needed, and this he set about raising. His design, which for any one else would have been rightly considered absolute folly and temerity, was for Bonaparte a real stroke of genius. And these soldiers, which he seemed to have raised from nothing, were the conquerors of Marengo.

In the early days of the year 1800, France had an army in Italy not only numerically inferior to that of the Austrians, but dispirited from the defeats sustained during the past year. A very narrow strip of country on the Riviera di Genova was all that remained to her of her former conquests. How to render prompt and effective assistance to the Army of Italy was a problem bristling with difficulties. That army needed very large reinforcements, but the troops could only arrive after long and painful marches. Once in Liguria there was nothing for their subsistence. There was not even enough to feed and pay the troops that were already there.

The difficulty was even greater for the cavalry, of which a large number was needed. Such was the dearth of forage, that the little of it procurable was not more than was required for feeding the horses of the generals and their staffs.

How could the army be reinforced in artillery when there were no roads fit for its passage ? Besides, here again cropped up the question of forage.

The sea, the only way of getting large cargoes into port, was in every direction patrolled by the enemy's ships of war; and it was out of the question to think of establishing large magazines in a country devastated by sickness.

The actual state of the Army of Italy was so deplorable, that with great difficulty could the *morale* of a reinforcing army be kept from being undermined. The troops marching along would hear nothing but bad news and horrible details, which could not but have an extremely lowering effect.

We may well imagine that all these points did not escape the perspicuous mind of the First Consul, who was familiar with the territory occupied by the Army of Italy. In contrast to all this there were the special advantages presented by an advance on the central positions occupied by the enemy's army, by an irruption from the side of Switzerland into Upper Piedmont, which the configuration of the frontier permitted.

With all the semblance of wishing to maintain a purely defensive attitude, Bonaparte prepared in secret to assume a vigorous offensive. He succeeded in this, and deceived every one. For whilst pretending that he was neglecting the interest of the army, he was in reality studiously working and paving the way to attain its well-being and glory. His forces were, however, to be studiously kept hidden from sight, and to come in view only at the moment when they would for the second time be descending from the slopes of the Alps into the plains of Italy.

With consummate foresight the documents which referred to his preparations were carefully removed from the War Office. Plans shared, the saying goes, are easily spread; and plans spread are easily baulked. Bonaparte desired nothing so much as to conceal his plans. The secret was in the keeping of a very few trusty officers, on whose discretion the First Consul could fully count. In 1796, he had failed in surprising the Austrians in their winter quarters; now he trusted he would be more fortunate, and be able to appear in their midst when least expected. Bonaparte thus writes on the 25th of January to the minister of war : " You will keep thoroughly secret the formation of the said army, even amongst your office staff, from whom you will ask nothing beyond the absolutely necessary information."

At that moment there were in Holland, in the Vendée, and in other parts of France, enough men to form a third army, and this is what Bonaparte set all his energy and talents to create. A reserve army was silently and unostentatiously formed from selected veterans, skilfully blended with young and promising conscripts. The divisions could attract no special observation, mobilized as they were in different places, and to all intents forming part of no special unit.

Bonaparte's unrivalled power of administration was straining every nerve to raise the French forces from the state of disorganization into which they had been allowed to fall by the incompetence and neglect of the past Government.

As long as Genova held out and Massena was there, he did not despair of being able to meet the Austrians in Italy.

To operate against them with any prospect of success it was necessary to have a respectable army, an army capable of doing great things. It was, moreover, prudent to raise this army in such a manner that no one would ever credit its existence.

Brune had succeeded in pacifying the Vendée. The French in that province had been brought to terms, so that the Army of the West could be reduced in numbers. In the Vendée and elsewhere Bonaparte found the men he so much needed to weld into an army, which, when suddenly transferred by a master hand to the theatre of war, would thoroughly make amends for the disasters of the past campaign, and bring back laurels for France.

The patriotic enthusiasm of 1792, alas! was no more. It had disappeared with the circumstances which had brought it into existence. It was no longer possible to create an army out of nothing, to work on the feelings of the masses until thousands and thousands of brave volunteers rushed suddenly to arms and proceeded to the threatened frontier.

Besides the troops to be drawn from the Vendée, much also could be demanded from the Army of Holland, since the disposition of the Batavian Republic had become extraordinarily conciliating.

Whilst bent on carrying out military operations in Italy, the First Consul was bound also to protect the coast of France from invasion. To that end he left Augereau in Holland with a force half French and half Dutch. Once it was placed beyond doubt that no hostile movements were to be dreaded in that country, Augereau's force was to ascend the Rhine and cover the rear of Moreau's army in Germany.

The Army of Reserve had been decreed by the Consuls on the 7th of January, 1800, on the 16th Ventose, an VIII. It was to be formed at Dijon, and an order went out for 30,000 conscripts to concentrate about that city. This army was destined to support either the Army of Italy or the Army of the Rhine, just as circumstances might require.

The first class of the conscription of the year VIII. was called out, without exception of rank or fortune. By this measure 120,000 men came to be put at the disposal of the Government. All the men who had been paid off or discharged during the last eight years were called to submit their papers to a rigid scrutiny ; * 30,000 men were thus secured, the majority being broken to the hardships of war. By the offer of advancement and other rewards, men on the retired list and veterans were induced to resume active service.

The First Consul then detailed the most wasted half-brigades †

* In the preceding months the army had been largely reduced by desertions. Twelve thousand discharges had been granted to the soldiers, but discipline had become very slack, and more than ten times that number had left their colours and lived without concealment at their homes. The number had become so considerable as to render it neither prudent nor practicable to attempt enforcing their return to duty. They had to be won back gently.

† The term " demi-brigade " replaced in 1793 that of " regiment." At that time

160 Marengo and Hohenlinden.

to perform garrison duty in the unsettled provinces. Even from these half-brigades he withdrew the most efficient soldiers, which he replaced by conscripts who were to learn their duties whilst performing garrison work. These troops, cavalry, artillery, and infantry, commanded by able officers, he gathered into five camps, with instructions that they should be prepared to march at the shortest notice. Of these camps two were left in Belgium, one at Liège, the other at Maestricht; the other three were at Lille, Saint Lo, and Rennes. The camp at Rennes was the largest, and numbered from 7000 to 8000 men. The remaining did not muster more than 4000 or 5000 men. The whole force, which originally constituted a body of troops 30,000 strong, was to be doubled on the arrival of conscripts.

From the troops left in the Vendée Bonaparte drew 30,000 excellent soldiers. From these he formed three splendid divisions, two in Brittany, one at Rennes, the other at Nantes. The third was formed in Paris. The vigilance of the British cruisers had kept the depôts of the army in Egypt from fulfilling their intended purpose, viz. repairing the waste of their respective corps in that country. Out of these a fourth division was ordered to be formed at Lyons. The troops were drawn from Toulon, Marseilles, and Avignon, and formed fourteen excellent battalions.

To gain the good will of the Italians, Bonaparte decided to avail himself of an Italian contingent. To escape from the fury and persecution of the Austrians which followed Scherer's defeat, Lechi had fled to France. There he had soon collected a brave and soldier-like body of his countrymen, and this was to be employed with the Army of Reserve.

The rapidity with which this Army of Reserve was raised and put on a war-footing appears almost miraculous. It is easy, nevertheless, to conceive that this army would never have been organized in such a short time without the intervention of two very rare circumstances. First, that the army was raised by an individual of extraordinary talent—the greatest organizer the world has ever seen—and secondly, that this man of transcendent genius found himself at the time at the head of the Government.

a demi-brigade was formed of an old regiment and two battalions of volunteers. It was not till the 24th of September, 1803, that, by an order of the Consuls, the name of regiment was restored in the French army.

The very title "the Army of Reserve" was calculated to deceive the enemy. It appeared to indicate that it was an army which had been raised with the sole object of reinforcing the Army of Italy, then in the field on the Riviera of Genova. There was nothing to suggest that it would enter Italy as a complete army, and engage independently of the Army of Italy.

Whilst driving Suchet back and narrowing the grip round Massena at Genova, Melas was mystified and deceived, for no movement was made in the valley of the Maurienne nor in that of the Tarantaise. The frontiers of the Dauphiné gave no indications whatever of any military preparations.

Nevertheless, Bonaparte had set about destroying the Austrian army in Upper Italy. By an article of the Constitution of the year VIII., none of the Consuls could command an army in the field beyond the frontiers of France. Bonaparte overcame this difficulty, for there was nothing in the enactment against one of the Consuls being present with one. He collected from all parts numerous soldiers and distinguished generals, and formed them into an Army of Reserve, at the head of which he placed Berthier, who was styled *General-in-Chief of the Army of Reserve*. In this manner he solved the difficulty; Berthier by all appearance commanded, whilst he himself directed the operations. As Marmont observes, by this arrangement Bonaparte retained Berthier as his chief of the staff, though under another denomination.

Berthier, the faithful depositary of the secrets and projects of his chief, was not well pleased with his appointment. Whether he disliked to part from Bonaparte, who was detained in Paris, or to give up the influential post of minister of war, or that he did not consider himself fit to direct the undertaking, he did not conceal his vexation. However, Bonaparte soon appeased his bad humour, and he quickly came to understand the exact *rôle* he was to play. For whilst Bonaparte made a show of considering him and representing him as the *de facto* commander-in-chief, Berthier studiously abstained from assuming powers to which he knew he could claim no real right. The letters from one were letters from a superior to a subordinate, and the style of the other that of a subordinate when corresponding with his chief.

Carnot, the conqueror of Wattignies, the organizer of victory, a man of extraordinary talent and resolute character, replaced

M

Berthier in the ministry of war. As a suspected Loyalist, he had been sentenced by the *coup d'état* of the 18th Fructidor, an V. (4th of September, 1797), with Barthélemy and others, to deportation. But he escaped to Germany, and the 18th Brumaire brought him back to Paris. He was greatly feared by the enemies of France, and his return to the direction of military affairs produced a great effect in Europe. His energy, skill, and fertility of administrative resource, helped to achieve the brilliant results in the Italian and Rhenish campaigns.

In his "Précis de l'Art de la Guerre," Jomini, referring to the orders issued for the campaigns of 1806 and 1815, writes : "It was for a long time believed that Berthier * was the crafts-man of these instructions conceived with so much precision, and ordinarily transmitted with so great lucidity. I have had a hundred opportunities to assure myself of the incorrectness of this assertion. The emperor was himself the real chief of his staff; armed with a compass open to a scale of seven or eight leagues in a direct line (which on account of the windings of the roads always means nine or ten), leaning, sometimes lying, on his maps, on which the positions of his army corps and those presumed of the enemy were marked by pins of different colours, turning his compass quickly, he ordered his movements with a certainty of which it would be difficult to form a correct idea. Moving his compass briskly over this map, he judged in the twinkle of the eye the number of marches necessary to be made by each of his corps to arrive at the point where he wished it to be on a given day; after which, placing his pins in these new localities, and combining the speed of the march which was necessary to assign to each of these columns, with the date of their possible departure, he dictated his instructions, which of themselves alone would form a claim to glory."

Baron Lejeune, who for many years served on Berthier's staff, wrote in a different strain. This is what he says on the subject of the Marengo campaign: "It was the First Consul who inaugurated every plan, improvised the means for carrying it out, and by imbuing all with his own zeal made everything possible. It was General Berthier who identified himself thoroughly with the plans of his chief; divided and subdivided the work to be done, assigning to each one his particular task by fulfilling which he was to co-operate with every other member

* For Berthier's character, see "Houssaye, 1815," p. 56, 19th edition.

of the army; he strove to remove obstructions and provide for every contingency. His anxious solicitude, which kept him ever on the alert, his undaunted co-operation, were never relaxed until success was achieved."

It is commonly understood that Berthier was incapable of comprehending the great designs and views of his brilliant master, and that he was absolutely nothing without Napoleon. Nevertheless, he was capable of undertaking endless work. He was as indefatigable in the field as at his desk, expert in all the details of the mechanism of an army. Bonaparte generally issued his orders by brief directions, which Berthier took down there and then. He often had to trust to his memory for what had fallen in conversation; from this he detailed, developed, and transmitted to the general officers the whole of the necessary directions.

The Army of Reserve, about which there was so much talk and clamour, was supposed to be assembling at Dijon. Bonaparte knew that that city was full of emissaries from other Governments, and all these he was determined to deceive. He consequently gave out his intention of reviewing the Army of Reserve. He proceeded to Dijon for this purpose, and there he was followed by a number of foreign spies. At this review some 3000 or 4000 men, and not in the best condition for campaigning, were present. The very want of caution in making the enemy free with his designs threw Austria and England off their guard. So very insignificant was the show, that it cast ridicule on the First Consul, and the absurdity of the whole thing soon found its way abroad. It was but natural that information so positive, coming from many sources, as to the non-existence of the much-vaunted Army of Reserve and of the limited preparations, should have deceived the Court of Vienna and General Melas. Carrion de Nisas declares, " There was not a single diplomatic correspondent who did not indulge in ciphering daily to his court, that the First Consul made a great fuss about his Army of Reserve, but that there was nothing else at Dijon but a handful of men badly armed, badly equipped, and undrilled; and that in whatever direction a similar reinforcement might proceed, it would to a certainty be of very feeble help to the army which received it." *

These reports were exact, but the real object of the Army of

* De Nisas, " Mémorial du Dépôt de la Guerre, Campagne de 1800," p. 42.

Reserve was so studiously concealed, that Moreau himself
believed for some time that the corps which were said to be
assembling at Dijon were in a great part destined for the
immediate reinforcement of his own army.

In January, 1800, Bonaparte issued an order prohibiting
journalists to print anything in their newspapers which had
the slightest reference to movements of the army and of the
navy. The existence of the Army of Reserve was steadily
denied even at the war department, and for good reasons.
First, because the war department had been diligently kept out
of the secret; secondly, because all orders were sent to the
commanders of corps direct from the office of the First Consul.

In our days, with telegraphs, railways, and the increased
habit of travelling, the secret could not have been kept. To
keep such a large number of men and such stupendous preparations from prying eyes would be next to impossible. We
have only to bring to mind the performances of some of our
special correspondents, how, for instance, in 1877, Archibald
Forbes rode sixty miles for three consecutive days to get at the
wires and to send his news home ; we have only to recollect how
the better and more educated classes are now commissioned to
gather items of intelligence for the public press, and how no
money is spared in getting news, to realize the present impossibility of imitating Bonaparte's concealment of his design.

Bonaparte's plan was a daring one, and it was this very
daring that kept it from being divulged; for who but a genius
would have ever dreamt of carrying an army, with its artillery,
cavalry, and materials, across the Alps in the middle of May?
What spy or emissary could have fathomed the conception of
the First Consul?

With the rude way of travelling which obtained at that
period, no spy or emissary would have dreamt of crossing the
passes at that very early season of the year.

" *L'homme médiocre regarde comme chimérique ce que l'homme
supérieur regarde comme un moyen assuré de triompher.*" * Melas
could well imagine that all the news which reached him was
merely loud talk intended to make him abandon the siege of
Genova. Even when some few weeks later the French troops
were signalled on the snow-clad crests of the Saint Bernard,
the Austrian general was confirmed in his error, and believed

---

* Bulow, " Histoire de la Campagne de 1800."

them to be the 3000 or 4000 men who had been passed in review by the First Consul at Dijon.

The ridicule thrown on the Army of Reserve by the Austrian authorities was unparalleled. They broke out in jests and caricatures. The cavalry were represented as mounted on asses, the infantry composed of old men, invalids and infants, armed with sticks bearing a bayonet at one end. The artillery were furnished with pop-guns. In fact, the success the Austrians had quite lately obtained over the French had made them haughty. There was no extravagance in which they did not indulge. The French troops, they said, were imbeciles, their generals totally void of military talent.

From the moment that Bonaparte quitted Paris, every one, and all the newspapers, declared that by the end of the month he would appear on the plains of Lombardy, and possibly be in Milan. On hearing such predictions, the Austrians smiled; they persisted in remaining blind to all warnings.

This general report did not much please Bonaparte, as can be gathered from his letter to the Consuls of the 19th of May. In that letter he complains that the journals have made him write a letter to his mother declaring that he would be in Milan short of a month. Bonaparte desires them to publish a denial in the *Moniteur*. He reminds them that such avowals were not in keeping with his character. "Very frequently," he remarks, "I do not say what I know; but it never happens that I say what will be."

Though beset by numerous occupations, Bonaparte worked unremittingly at the organization of the Army of Reserve. The preparations were growing apace. Hardly a day passed that he did not write one or more letters to Berthier, entering into the most minute details. His letters show what a thorough master of organization he was. His purpose was very clearly laid down, nothing was omitted. He thought of everything, he provided everything. He never ceased to urge on and to stimulate every one. As an incentive to gallant deeds in the field, he decreed the distinction of swords of honour, which were to be conferred on conspicuously brave soldiers.

The strength of the Army of Reserve was summed up by the First Consul in a despatch he wrote to Berthier on the 26th of April—

"Loison's division, composed of the 13th Light, the 58th and 60th of the line: 6000 to 7000 men.

" Chambarlhac's division, composed of the 24th Light, 43rd and 96th of the line : 9000 men.

" Boudet's division, composed of the 9th Light, 30th and 59th of the line : 7000 to 8000 men.

" Watrin's division, composed of the 6th Light, 22nd and 40th of the line : 6000 to 7000 men.

" These four divisions were available and ready to march by the 30th of April.

" The 5th division, that of General Chabran, to be formed of nine of the battalions belonging to the Army of the East, which you will form into brigades as I had already projected. That will give you a division of 6000 men, which should be able to march soon after the first four divisions.

" The 6th division, which may set out from Dijon between the 15th to the 20th of May, will be composed of the 19th Light, 70th and 72nd of the line : 6000 to 7000 men.

" The 7th division will be composed of the 17th Light, and of the six remaining battalions out of the fifteen of the Army of the East.

" Finally your 4000 Italians, leaving a depôt, as a point of formation for the 3000 or 4000 Italians which are still in different parts of France, and will congregate at Dijon the moment the movement is unmasked.

" It thus appears to me that on or about the 5th of May you may reckon on having at Geneva ready to go wherever it may be necessary—

1. The first four divisions ... 28,000 to 30,000 ⎫
2. The 5th division, Chabran's   5,000 to 6,000 ⎬ 40,000
3. A few days later, the Italians ...   4,000 ⎭ men.

" On the 20th of May you might have at Geneva—

" The 6th division : 6000 to 7000 men.

" And towards the 4th of June the 7th division : 6000 men.

" General Turreau might aid you with 3000 men.

" The troops of the Army of the Rhine, who are now in the Valais (Béthencourt) : 3000 men.

" In this way you might arrive at Aosta and at Susa from the 10th to the 20th of May with 44,000 infantry, being followed within ten days by a complete division of 8000 men ; and within twenty days 6000 more men ; independently of the *detachment from the Army of the Rhine* proportionate to the circumstances in which the said army will find itself, which may vary from 30,000 to 10,000 men according to events.

" In this way I see you firmly established, having at your disposal from 50,000 to 60,000 infantry.

" In so far as the cavalry is concerned, you have—

The 11th and 12th Hussars
The 2nd, 7th, 15th, and 21st Chasseurs
The 8th and 9th Dragoons
The 2nd, 3rd, and 20th Heavy Cavalry
} 4000 men.

" This is sufficient cavalry for your first ten or fifteen days' operations.

" The 11th Hussars, the 15th Chasseurs, 9th Dragoons, and 3rd Heavy Cavalry are ready to start at the commencement of the decade ; these four will form 1000 men, who will join you in good time.

" The 1st Hussars, 1st and 5th Heavy Cavalry, and the 5th Dragoons will set out during the month ; they will have with them six guns, and the four will make up 1800 men well mounted and equipped.

" Thus you will have at once 4000 men, and 3000 more which will join you in good time.

" Do not attach to your divisions aught but chasseurs and hussars, and keep all your dragoons together.

" I have issued orders for the 19th Light, the 70th and 72nd half-brigades, and the 20th Heavy Cavalry to expedite their march.

" SUMMARY.

Infantry at immediate disposal   44,000
Cavalry   ,,   ,,   ,,   4,000
Artillery   ,,   ,,   ,,   2,000
} 50,000 men.

" In your rear—
Infantry   8,000
Cavalry   3,000
} 11,000   ,,

Total   61,000   ,,

" 7th division, to be kept in account.

" *Behold 60,000 men who, after the follies which the Austrians are committing in shutting themselves up in the Riviera of Genova, place you in condition to act without having to recur to anybody.*

" As for the artillery, you have forty-eight pieces ; this makes eight guns for each of your first five divisions, and a small park.

" Reduce the number of your howitzers and increase the number of your 4-prs. as you have them at Auxonne. That will render you good service, and will make the transport more easy.

" General Turreau's column may bring five or six pieces from Briançon.

" There will be time to prepare at Auxonne the guns necessary for your sixth division.

" Yesterday, to-day, and to-morrow, 600 horses have been started, or will start, from Versailles.

" The six pieces belonging to the Guard are very well horsed. You can attach them to the cavalry, and utilize the spare teams for the other divisions.

" With regard to cartridges, Briançon can well supply you ; let all those now at Grenoble and at Briançon be conveyed to Geneva. Have a manufactory established at Geneva. By being a little enterprising, and with a little money, one should be able to find in a city like Geneva enough lead for a million cartridges.

" Leave all the depôts at Dijon and on the Saône, so that as the conscripts arrive they may receive a first training, and thence feed the army.

" Leave the cadres of six battalions of the Army of Reserve ; they will be completed by conscripts as they arrive, so that in the course of June (Prairial), the 17th Light and the two half-brigades formed by these six battalions may form for you a seventh division.

" I shall be at Geneva, where I will make all the substitutions in the troops which the events that may occur in the Army of the Rhine may render necessary, leaving Chabran's division on the defensive in Switzerland, and directing some of the better-organized half-brigades to march.

" The divisions are sufficiently strong with three half-brigades. You should have on hand at least five or six divisions. Two 4-prs., three 8-prs., and a howitzer seem to me, in all fairness, sufficient to make up the artillery for a division ; and, if you have not sufficient draught animals in a division, reduce the number to three 4-prs. and two 8-prs.

" Let General Marmont (commander of the artillery) send

a superior officer to Besançon, and another to Grenoble, to put in movement all that is possible. General Marmont should be furnished with a return showing the cartridges and artillery munitions which are to be found at Besançon and in the strongholds of the Dauphiné.

" To-morrow I will order 200 of my Guard to start.

" Send General Marescot (commander of the engineers) to the Saint Bernard, so that he may be back in Geneva by the 5th of May, with some exact surveys of the road. Should he have any pioneers, let him take them with him.

" If nothing prevents it, I expect to be at Dijon on the 30th of April or 1st of May."

The Consular Guard, under the orders of General Bessières, was composed of two battalions, two squadrons, and six guns.

The cavalry was organized by brigades under the supreme command of Murat. To Rivaud was given the light cavalry brigade, which was to cross the Alps with the advanced guard. Champeaux commanded the dragoon, Kellermann the heavy cavalry brigade. These two brigades were to bring up the rear when crossing the Alps, and to take the lead under Murat as soon as they came out on the plain.

In the infantry, the first arrangement by division was subsequently changed, and the divisions were grouped by two, each two being placed under the command of a lieutenant-general. After Montebello, Desaix was given the command of Boudet's and Monnier's divisions, Victor those of Gardanne's and Chambarlhac's.

The artillery was organized at Auxonne, Besançon, and Briançon.

General Saint Remy was to have had command of it, but he fell ill. Marmont relates in his "Mémoires" how Bonaparte offered him the direction of the artillery, how he had conceived certain prejudices against that arm, and would have preferred to command a body of troops, as being the only means for acquiring renown. What he might have looked to, according to his rank, was the command of a brigade; but, as Marmont goes on to explain, the command of a brigade leads, later on, to the command of a division, and the command of a division is the school of high tactics. One is then in a good position to judge of the total of the operations; by directing 8000 or 10,000 men one learns to handle troops with skill.

Bonaparte overcame Marmont's repugnance, and assured him that the work about to be undertaken, the transport of the artillery across the Alps,* was a difficult task ; that he had confidence in his activity, in his resources, that he appreciated his imagination and force of will, and that he desired he would accept. For Marmont there was nothing left but to comply.

Being himself young and active, Marmont was already convinced that in most cases the word "impossible" is only an excuse for want of enterprise ; all working with a will, he had no reason to anticipate a failure.

In the beginning of the year 1800, Bonaparte introduced a very important change in the field artillery. The pieces and the ammunition-waggons had hitherto been drawn by animals and drivers taken from the transport companies. The drivers, not having the least interest in the fate of the batteries, could, at the first signal of danger, cut the traces and decamp with the horses. Bonaparte arrived at the conclusion that it was very desirable to turn the drivers into a constituent part of each battery, to dress the men in the uniform worn by the gunners, and to imbue them with the same *esprit de corps.* He thus made it clear to the men that the drivers not only ran the same risk as the gunners, but rendered just the same services, that it was incumbent on them to display the same zeal in running the guns up within range of the enemy and in withdrawing them as the gunners had in loading and aiming them.

The Army of Reserve crossed France in fine order, with drums beating and colours flying. Their martial appearance inspired confidence ; and after the disasters of the preceding year's campaign, the people were in need of this reanimating sight to rouse them from their state of despondency.

An army can seldom dispense with the resources of the country through which it marches, be it in provisions, manual labour, or transport. Active operations are impossible without a sufficiency of the latter; and, as a large mass of troops cannot move nor operate creditably without transport, the transport service has been justly called the soul of an army. Lasting success cannot be obtained without transport ; never-

---

* On the 28th of April, the park comprised 24 four-prs., horsed, 12 eight-prs., sledges and munition-boxes holding 7000 muskets, 2 howitzers, 10 bullet-moulds, 6000 shot, 400,000 cartridges for infantry, and a complete transport train.— *Gachot*, p. 23.

theless, the raising of an efficient transport is a matter which presents much difficulty. Generally speaking, most of it is obtained from the country which constitutes the theatre of operations, and by requisition. In any case, the transport should be organized before the actual commencement of the operations, for the transport service is undoubtedly a question of time. In the crossing of the Alps there was little prospect of finding overmuch transport to requisition, whilst collecting it had necessarily to be left to the last moment for fear of putting the enemy on the *qui vive.*

Bonaparte, being well aware how ready money was the surest way to allure the assistance of the hardy mountaineers of the Alps, had sent forward considerable remittances in the shape of cash. Baron Lejeune, in his "Memoirs," relates how he was instructed to take several bags of gold to the *curés* of the Valais, with which to pay the peasants who were to help in dragging the artillery over the Alps, and in other cognate work.

In this way, but only on the last days, all the transport of the country, all the mules, and all the peasants were made to converge to Martigny. Bread, biscuit, forage, wine, and spirits, had been transported from Villeneuve to Martigny, and had now to be forwarded from Martigny as far as Saint Pierre, at the foot of the final ascent.* A sufficient number of live cattle had also been conveyed there. This accumulation of stores was indispensable, for the crossing of the Alps involved a march of several days, without any possibility of finding resources on the way. With a good deal of foresight, Bonaparte had also won to himself the monks of Mount Saint Bernard, and had got them to collect a certain quantity of provisions for his troops.

On the 6th of May, 1800, Berthier issued the following instructions to the chief controller :—

"Procure all possible means of transport, be they by water or by land, so that by the evening of the 18th there may be at Villeneuve 400,000 or 500,000 rations of biscuit, and double that amount on the 20th.

"You should hire mules at once in the Valais, taking them by requisition if they cannot be had in any other way, for conveying 30,000 rations to the village of Saint Pierre ; you can also take local chars-à-bancs. It is urgent that these 30,000

---

* Several villages of the Valais put in large claims for damage done, and principally for mules requisitioned to carry firewood, provisions, etc.

rations be at Saint Pierre by the 20th or 22nd; the transport to return to Villeneuve to take up a fresh load, which should arrive at Saint Pierre on the 25th. If you can command transport to this extent, our provisioning will be well assured.

"Afterwards it will be desirable to establish a depôt of biscuit in some village between Saint Pierre and the foot of Mount Saint Bernard. In this same village you will set up a hospital, from which the patients will be transferred to others established at Saint Maurice or Villeneuve. There is not a moment to lose in organizing these three hospitals. My plan is to concentrate four divisions at Villeneuve. About the 19th the troops will take over from that place biscuit to last them for four days; at Saint Pierre for three, which should suffice up to Aosta. In the meanwhile we shall continue to fill the depôt at Saint Pierre, to provide for transmission or against a retrograde movement, should such a step be forced on us. The cavalry, the drivers, the staff—in short, all who are mounted—will be made to pick up biscuit for eight days' consumption. Oats must be conveyed to the foot of the Saint Bernard, as well as to the convent.

"You will easily perceive that you have not an instant to lose in having the extraordinary supplies carried to the depôts of Villeneuve and Saint Pierre.

"I recommend to your attention especially the boots, for which we have a most pressing need. Independently of the dispositions you are about to make, and of the orders you are going to issue, take such steps as will make the execution of your measures perfectly sure."

It was a strange oversight not to have used as a line of supply the road leading from Savoy over the Little Saint Bernard into the valley of Aosta, which was fit for wheel traffic. As an alternative and a supplementary line to the one passing over the Great Saint Bernard, it would have been of great assistance; more so had a retrograde movement forced the French to retire behind their frontier.

In spite of all the trouble taken, the transport fell short. When the first real piece of engineering had to be done, at Fort Bard, we find the chief engineer of the army, General Marescot, complaining that he had no tools, as all those drawn from Besançon, or bought at Geneva and at Martigny, had been ordered to be left at Villeneuve and Sembrancher for want of transport. What transport there was available had been entirely given up for the use of the artillery and supplies.

In the wars of the Revolution the French had considerably reduced the number of waggons and carriages in rear of their armies, which always constitute one of the greatest impediments in war. This made their forces much more free in their movements, above all in retreats. On the other hand, it necessitated a greater appropriation of the resources of the theatre of war, and, very frequently, led to pillaging. The soldier must be fed, and, when he is starving, will lay his hands on such articles of food as he finds within reach.

Bonaparte remained in Paris till everything was in readiness for the advance of the army. Berthier wrote to him from Geneva: "I wish to see you here. There are orders to be given by which the three armies may act in concert, and you alone can give them on the spot. Measures decided on in Paris are too late." On the evening of the 5th of May, a council was summoned at the Tuileries, at which the consuls and ministers were present. It was at this council that Bonaparte notified his intention of joining the army. "A grand stroke," he said, "is contemplated, but the campaign will be short." He had it given out that he might go as far as Geneva, declaring at the same time as his resolve to be back within fifteen days.

When, later on, his intention of assuming the military command became patent to all, there was no audible discontent. Some of the leading men, however, discussed the consequences should the First Consul happen to be killed.

At two o'clock in the morning of the 6th, Bonaparte quitted Paris. The magnificent hopes which he cherished made the dangers he was about to encounter seem insignificant. As he journeyed towards Dijon, he talked all the way of the great warriors of antiquity with all the ardent enthusiasm of boyhood.

CHAPTER VIII.

THE CROSSING OF THE ALPS.

France to be dazzled by a stupendous deed—Moreau's distaste for acting under Bonaparte's guidance—The road over the Great Saint Bernard selected for crossing into Italy—Routes for the other armies—Survey of the Great Saint Bernard route—Bonaparte receives Marescot's report, and decides to advance—Lannes marches with the advanced guard on the 15th of May—Arrangements for the conveyance of the artillery—The soldiers entertained by the monks at the Hospice—The crossing favoured by fine weather—Austrians abandon Aosta, and are driven away from Châtillon—The French are stopped by Fort Bard—Description of the fort—Difficulties of the French—They find a way over the Albaredo—Bonaparte crosses the Great Saint Bernard—Capture of the village of Bard—Passage of the artillery through Bard—Assault of the fort—Ill success of the French—The Austrian commander finally surrenders.

Bonaparte had come into power, but had not yet obtained absolute power; and no one knew better than he did that to be able to impose his will on the French people, after the feelings and aspirations which the events of the Republic had evoked, it was absolutely necessary to dazzle France by some superb and entrancing deed. As it was only to an extraordinarily great man that the multitudes would be disposed to submit, a warlike feat was needed which would at the same time amaze the French by its lustre, and show to the whole of Europe the surpassing brilliancy of his genius.

To a man like Bonaparte, who had so recently been dreaming of an empire in the East, of revolutionizing all Asia, and seating himself on the throne of Constantine, it was not a difficult matter to conceive a superb achievement, some exploit that bordered on the marvellous.

His thoughts very naturally reverted to Italy, the theatre of his first exploits, to the fertile provinces which his talent had wrested from Austria, but which the incapable rulers of his country had not been able to retain for the Republic. To conquer them for a second time in a short campaign, to lead the French colours again to victory, was a worthy conception, and pregnant with results of the weightiest moment.

The Austrians and Russians in 1799 had expelled the French from Italy. All that remained in their hands was Genova and a narrow strip of territory along the Ligurian shore. All Northern Italy up to the summit of the Alps was occupied by the Austrians.

In the condition in which affairs were in Italy, it was necessary to re-enter the country, otherwise to cross over into Germany, and deliver such a decisive blow on the Danube as would make it possible to recover the Italian provinces by dictating peace to Austria. It was possible for France to recover Alessandria and Milan at Vienna, and such had been Bonaparte's original intention. Moreau, however, had plainly shown a distaste for commanding under the guidance of the First Consul, and it was generally believed that had Bonaparte gone to the Army of the Rhine, the troops would have positively refused to countenance his plans. It was this difficulty which decided him to leave Moreau to act against Austria with the best army France could dispose of, whilst he led a mass of conscripts over the Alps into Lombardy.

Bourrienne, who was privileged to be the first to hear the exposition of Bonaparte's plan, as he fixed black and red tipped pins in Chauchard's large map of Italy, failed to grasp the full import of his design. Melas and his staff did not realize to what measures a man of genius could resort.

Bonaparte's plan for the reconquest of Italy was stupendous. The march over the Alps astonished even Desaix, who on reading an account of it exclaimed, "He will leave us nothing to do." It embraced the whole section of the Alpine region which extends from Mount Genevre to the Saint Gothard, and threatened the plains of Piedmont and Lombardy with invasion. He trusted that Massena and Suchet would hold out in Genova and on the Var, and by doing so would keep Melas occupied till he could come himself to attack him both in flank and in rear. Bold and wonderful was this conception, but had Melas been more prudent, more active, and, above all, better informed, it might have miscarried.

In a long mountain chain there are scores of passes over which a small party of travellers on foot and laden animals can make their way. Folard remarks that a man can pass where

a goat does, and that a corps can pass where a man can.   But
armies which include infantry, cavalry, artillery, and trains
cannot use most of these passes, owing principally to the
narrowness and abruptness of the track.

As far back as the time of Hannibal it was shown that there
was no really insuperable difficulty in conveying an army with
its impedimenta across a great mountain range.   The arduousness of the operation in this instance was great, but it was
nothing compared with the difficulty of keeping the preparations
concealed; for the least suspicion aroused was likely to lead to
a failure.

Bonaparte could select for the march of his army any of
the passes which lead from France, Savoy, and Switzerland
into Italy.   His troops could cross by the Cottian Alps, Mont
Genevre, and Mont Cenis; by the Graian Alps, Little Saint
Bernard; by the Pennine Alps, Great Saint Bernard; and by
the Lepontine Alps, Simplon, and Saint Gothard.

There was, therefore, the choice of several ways for crossing
the Alps and descending into Italy.   Mainoni, writing to Berthier,
indicated eleven points of passage between the Saint Gothard
and Courmayeur, and states that there were still others leading
to Piedmont and to Italy.   As a preliminary, all the advantages
of the different routes across the Alps had to be carefully thought
out.   It was on the strength of Marescot's report that the First
Consul decided to adopt that of the Saint Bernard.

Bonaparte recognized the necessity of appearing in Italy
from the side where he would be the least expected.   The
execution of his plan demanded most profound secrecy, the
utmost possible celerity, and unusual boldness.

It was obviously his interest to take the shortest way to
Genova, and it was the impending fall of that city, and the
limited time at his disposal for giving effective succour to
Massena, that made him accord the preference to the Saint
Bernard route.   At one time he had thought of the Simplon,
so as to turn the whole of Piedmont, but an operation from that
point would necessarily have been too long, and the first effect
would have been felt by the Austrian army too late to be of any
use in relieving Genova.   It was then that he determined to cross
the Saint Bernard, that route having the advantage of giving
him an entry into the very centre of Piedmont.   Besides which,
it had an important advantage over the Simplon route, inasmuch

as it had only five leagues of road impracticable for artillery, whereas in the other there were nearly double that number.

The most direct route from the lake of Geneva to Milan runs over the Great Saint Bernard. At the Hospice the road is 8120 feet above the level of the sea.

Not far from where the Hospice buildings now stand once rose a temple to Jupiter Poeninus, from which the mountain derived the name of Monte Joux or Monte Giove, and the range is called the Pennine Alps. The Roman consul Varo erected a statue of Jupiter at the top of the pass. At this point, which marks the boundary between the Valais and the valley of Aosta, in the year 962, Saint Bernard de Menthon founded a hospice, with the very charitable object of affording assistance to travellers overtaken by storms and foul weather. This is the most elevated point in Europe which is inhabited all the year through.

Most travellers consider the Great Saint Bernard less attractive than most of the other Alpine passes. The track over the mountain was used in 1800 by the people of the Lower Valais going to Piedmont and Italy by the valley of Aosta, and *vice versâ;* all merchandise and goods being carried by pack horses and mules. Armies have likewise crossed the Alps at this point. A Roman army did so in the midst of winter during the wars between Otho and Vitellius. The Lombards crossed over in 547, the French under Charlemagne in 773, and the Emperor Frederick Barbarossa in the twelfth century. What made Bonaparte's undertaking more remarkable was that his army was accompanied by cavalry and artillery.

In the Middle Ages this was the main route for pilgrims and other travellers coming from the north-west of Europe, being the most direct way to Rome. Its height renders it more dangerous in winter than the other passes.

In the Alps, the snowy season is reckoned to last nearly nine months. On the mountain the cold is excessive, even in the middle of summer. The prospect is monotonous and cheerless. Of vegetation there is none, not a tree or shrub exists to gladden the eye, no herb, no green leaf of any kind. Precipitous heights, dashing torrents, sloping valleys, succeed each other with disheartening frequency. All is wild and barren, rocks of a grayish tint, and great heaps of ice. The birds never haunt those regions, nor do they alight there for rest in their flight. Solemn

N

silence reigns supreme, and even in the fairest season of the year the sun brightens up the valleys for the shortest possible time during the day.

It was across these inhospitable regions that Bonaparte decided to carry an army, and, by a masterly strategy, to regain all the fruits of his celebrated campaign of 1796 in Italy. Always a great reader of history and an ardent admirer of the deeds of the renowned captains of antiquity, what was more natural than for him to take as his model Hannibal's famous crossing of the Alps ?

No one seems to have explained in a really satisfactory manner what made Bonaparte set little value on the Little Saint Bernard route, which just as much as the route over the Great Saint Bernard leads to Aosta, but with less difficulties and with a road good enough for artillery and supplies. De Cugnac observes that there were special advantages on the route selected by the First Consul which evidently recommended its adoption. These were the transport of provisions by water through Lake Leman, and the central position of Lausanne, which permitted the Army of Reserve to march north or south, leaving the Austrians in a state of tormenting uncertainty.

Four more columns were to descend into the valley of the Po by treading other passes, none, however, so lofty as the Saint Bernard.

The route allotted to Chabran, who had to come from Montmelian in Savoy, was by way of the Little Saint Bernard.[*] This pass is 7176 feet in height, situated between Savoy and the valley of Aosta, to the south-west of the Great Saint Bernard, on a road which goes from the valley of the Isére to that of the Dora.

Béthencourt, with 3000 men, was to descend to Domo d'Ossola, on the shores of Lago Maggiore, where, narrowing its expanse, the lake permits the waters of the Ticino to flow from it. He was to pass over the Simplon, which is 6590 feet above sea-level, and lies between the Valais and Lombardy, 53 kilometres south-west of the Saint Gothard.

The height of the Saint Gothard pass is 6935 feet. The

* Which of the passes Hannibal used to descend into Italy is a matter of dispute. May not the fact of Scipio having waited for him on the Ticino point to the Carthaginian having crossed by the Little Saint Bernard, and entered Italy by the valley of Aosta? See De Cugnac, p. 363.

Saint Gothard gives rise to the Reuss on the north and the Ticino on the south; in its neighbourhood are also the sources of the Rhone and the Rhine. It was by this route that the division drawn from Moreau's army was to wend its way and descend from Switzerland into Lombardy.

Turreau, coming from Briançon, was to lead a column over the Mont Cenis, advance to Susa, and threaten Turin. His column consisted of some 4000 men, and was to constitute the right of the Army of Reserve. This small division of Turreau, borrowed from the Army of Italy, exercised a very useful diversion.

The campaign of Marengo was very short. Bonaparte, as we have said, quitted Paris after midnight on the 6th of May. In this and in other instances he did not leave the capital until all the preparations for taking the field were in a very forward state. In this manner he was able to impose on his adversary.

Bonaparte, who had conceived the whole plan of campaign, who had organized the army, who had rearranged matters in the interior of France, proceeded to Dijon, there he inspected a mass of conscripts and some isolated companies of regulars, with the object of creating a firm disbelief in the existence of an Army of Reserve. This done, he started from Dijon, leaving France ignorant of his immense projects. In the early morning of the 9th of May, he was in Geneva.[*]

Well aware that nothing could disclose his plans so much as his presence, Bonaparte did all in his power to foster the idea that he purposed remaining in Geneva for a time. He himself inspected several residences, and found every owner only too anxious to put his property at his disposal. Rumours of this were too eagerly believed in Switzerland. He spread a report that an insurrection which had broken out in Paris had compelled him to return to the capital, when in reality he was already on the southern side of the Saint Bernard.

By Bonaparte's directions Berthier availed himself of the local knowledge of Colombini, a road-contractor, and of Major Pavetti, an officer of the Italian Legion well acquainted with the

---

[*] At Nyon, where he arrived at five in the evening, he heard of the grand preparations made at Geneva for his reception. He did not relish all this fuss, so he supped and went to bed. At three in the morning he suddenly appeared before the Cornawin gate. He resided from the 9th to the 11th of May in the house of one Defaussure, professor of meteorology and chemistry.

roads in the Valais. Writing to Berthier on the 28th of April, the First Consul had bidden him, "Call to your side an individual named Colombini, who resides at Vienne in the Dauphiné, a contractor for roads, who knows the Great and Little Saint Bernard and all their issues perfectly. Call likewise to you citizen Pavetti, major in the Italian Legion, who is at present at the depôt, and knows this neighbourhood thoroughly." Pavetti hailed from Romano in the Canavese province. He was a young man of a generous nature, who exerted himself with zeal in the cause of liberty.

Pavetti had warned Berthier that the passage of the Saint Bernard was not yet practicable. It was on this warning that the First Consul caused the demonstrations ordered in the direction of Aosta to be suspended.

At that season the falling of avalanches is common. When the snow begins to melt in the spring, the soil beneath becomes loose and slippery. By its own weight the snow slides down the declivities, carrying with it soil, rocks, and trees.

General Marescot, who commanded the engineers, and General Mainoni, an officer of Italian origin, who had paid great attention to the military topography of the Higher Alps, had been directed to undertake a reconnaissance of the mountains on the left bank of the Rhone.

At Geneva, Bonaparte received General Marescot's report of the reconnaissance made of the Saint Bernard. Marescot had with great difficulty climbed the mountain as far as the Hospice, and had taken into account all the hardships of the ascent. After he had completed his narrative, Bonaparte asked but one question, "Is it possible to pass?" "Yes," replied Marescot, "it is possible." "Well, then, let us start." Bonaparte was a man of strong resolution, and not likely to be turned by anything. The simple possibility of being overtaken by bad weather in the passes was not enough to divert him from his purpose. It was necessary, after all, to hasten, for Massena was known to be in a dire condition.

On the 12th of May, the First Consul reviewed the divisions of Loison and Chambarlhac, on the following day Boudet's division at Vevey, and at Villeneuve the artillery of the three divisions of the main body.

Writing to Moreau on the 14th of May from Lausanne, Bonaparte states: "The Army of Reserve commences to pass the Saint Bernard. The army is weak, and there will be some obstacles to overcome; it is this which decides me to pass myself into Italy for a fortnight."

In the Upper Valais, situated on the river Drance, at the turning of the splendid Rhone valley, 32 miles from the Hospice of Mount Saint Bernard, lies the village of Martigny, which recent excavations prove to have been in olden days a Roman city. It is dominated by the imposing ruins of the ancient castle of "the Batiaz." On account of its proximity to the mountains, Bonaparte chose this village as a suitable place for completing his preparations and for superintending the advance of his army. On the 17th of May, he came from Lausanne, and took up his abode in the house of convalescence belonging to the good monks of Mount Saint Bernard, where the aged and sick of that community, or those whose constitution has been injured by the rigorous climate of the mountain-tops, are sent to recover their health.

Before his departure from Lausanne, Bonaparte had received a report of Massena's dire condition in Genova, the gist of which was the hope that some one would speedily march to his relief.

On the 29th of April, Monsieur Lescuyer, sent by General Massena to the First Consul, succeeded in getting out of Genova, though, by the contents of his letter, he appears to have become incapacitated by a wound.

From Marseilles on the 8th of May he writes to the First Consul :—

" GENERAL CONSUL,

"I got out of Genova at midnight of the 9th instant (29th of April).

"Here is what Massena's situation was at that time: he enjoined me to set it forth to the First Consul. A despatch which I handed, as I was passing through, to General Oudinot, whom I found at Alessio,* made him acquainted with everything. He will doubtlessly have communicated every particular to you, General, also of the verbal instructions with which the General-in-Chief had charged me, of which the most pressing

---

* It is not quite clear how Lescuyer could have come across Oudinot at Alessio. Oudinot was Massena's chief of the staff, serving at that date in Genova with his chief. Possibly it was Suchet, and not Oudinot.

and the one to be most often repeated was : ' That he may come to set me free ; say that some one may come to set me free.'

" As my way through was encompassed by risks, he entrusted me with no despatches for the First Consul; but he recommended me to speak in strong terms to him, as well as to any generals of divisions with whom I might fall in on my way.

" After all, he concluded, everything would be summed up in this : ' That some one may come to relieve me ; the city is blockaded by land and by sea; I fight almost every day, and every day I beat the enemy, but his resources are immense : as for me, I have everything to conquer.

" ' I have 12,000 men ; their state is too well known. I have provisions for thirty days, and up to this moment the Genovese have kept quiet.'

" The hope of an army which is about to effect a diversion keeps up the spirit of the French, intimidates the agitators, and serves to contain the multitude, whom the dearness of the provisions, the vicinity and the insinuations of the enemy tend to excite into rebellion.

" At the break of day Massena is seen passing through the town to inspect the posts; his presence is equal to an army."

The contemplated operation was risky, and demanded the greatest daring in the general who conceived it. To cross a high snow-covered mountain at a season of the year ill adapted for the passage of the Higher Alps, in the perilous period of avalanches; to carry over nearly inaccessible summits all the materials which an army ready to take the field must have ; to step ten leagues over tracks bordered by precipices, and more than forty without finding either bread for the soldiers or forage for the animals, was an uncommon undertaking.

Bonaparte's accomplishment of this stupendous enterprise of crossing the Alps must command admiration alike as a whole and in all its details. The mere conception of swooping down on the rear of Melas's victorious army with a force borrowed and compounded from fractions of various others could have emanated only from the brain of a great captain. In no way inferior to the conception was the personal attention with which all the details necessary to a happy result were planned and carried into execution, nor the genius that succeeded in wringing resources so great from a country apparently exhausted by war and internal dissensions; and last, but by no means least, our wonder is commanded by the art that successfully concealed up to the critical moment all this movement of the invading host. The success of the operation depended entirely on celerity, for the Alpine regions were noted for their sterility. The valley of Aosta was poor, and unequal to supporting an army for which no adequate supplies had been prepared. On this account it was necessary to descend at once to the plains; for this there was besides a more important reason, viz. not to afford Melas time to anticipate the arrival of the Army of Reserve.

At the time when Bonaparte was preparing to swoop down upon Italy, all the outlets of the Alps were being watched by small detachments of Austrians, and these were deemed quite sufficient to prevent a surprise. In the direction of the Great Saint Bernard a body of 2000 men guarded the valley of Aosta, with an outpost at Saint Rémy, only about two hours' marching from the Hospice on the mountain.

After alighting at Martigny on the 18th of May, we find Bonaparte writing to Berthier as follows: "All the cavalry are here. I delay their march for a while, so as not to clog you on the other side until I hear of the capture of that vile castle of Bard." It was on that very same evening that Lannes' advanced guard halted a league from the walls of Bard.

The advanced guard of the Army of Reserve remained some days about Martigny, and that small place was crowded with troops of all arms. All the available horses and mules in the neighbourhood had been requisitioned, and the country people came in crowds to assist the army in its passage over the Alps, either by carrying loads or by repairing the roads, which were in anything but good condition.

Half a league beyond the village of Martigny, the ascent begins. Even at the end of the eighteenth century, the road as far as the little hamlet of Saint Pierre, 13 kilometres (8 miles) below the Hospice, was fairly good and practicable for vehicles.* General Malher, who commanded one of Watrin's brigades, had ordered the municipality of Martigny to repair and strengthen all the bridges up to Sembrancher. The authorities of Orsières were similarly enjoined to do the same to all the bridges up

* De Cugnac puts the height of the Hospice at 2472 metres, and that of Saint Pierre at 1630, giving a difference of 842 metres.

to Saint Pierre, so that they might be in a state to bear the passage of the artillery.

From the 13th of May of the previous year, when Suwarroff had moved forward to besiege Alessandria, three companies of the 3rd battalion of the 28th half-brigade and two small guns, under the command of Major Vivenot, had occupied the summit of the pass. The Austrians had a detachment at Saint Rémy, and this detachment on the 13th of April, 1800, had moved to attack the French, being bent on driving them entirely from the pass. But the Austrians advanced in a careless manner, and were belaboured by the fire of canister and musketry of the French, who were carefully concealed. The attackers were dismayed and disconcerted, and speedily compelled to beat an ignominious retreat.

Malher now suggested making some attempt on the garrison of Saint Rémy, but, rightly enough, he was directed to abstain from doing so, for fear the attention of the enemy should be aroused.

Lannes, owing to his well-established boldness and ardour, had been chosen by the First Consul to lead the enterprise— an honourable distinction which he anxiously sought.

Lannes was born on the 11th of April, 1769, in the same year as Wellington, Ney, and other distinguished commanders. He was one of the greatest generals the Revolution produced. He was one of the first to rush to the frontier in 1792, and owed his advancement and renown simply to his talent and bravery. Whatever may have been his private character, no one has ever denied him the brilliant military qualities with which nature had endowed him. Like Bonaparte and Massena, he was deprived of his command owing to his intimacy with the younger Robespierre. At Dego Bonaparte had been struck by the gallantry of young Lannes, and he promoted him colonel on the spot.

From Geneva, on the 10th of May, Dupont, Chief of the Staff of the Army of Reserve, issued his instructions to Lannes :—

"In conformity with the orders of the General-in-Chief, Citizen General, with the advanced guard which you will command, you will proceed on the 13th of May to Saint Maurice and Villeneuve. At Villeneuve, you will order the troops to furnish themselves with bread for the 13th, 14th, 15th, and 16th of May. During the day on the 14th, you will find

yourself six leagues on the further side of Saint Maurice, and
on the 15th you will be at the foot of the Great Saint Bernard.
In passing by Saint Pierre you will pick up biscuit for three
days—17th, 18th, and 19th inclusive.

" General Mainoni will bring together on the 14th, at the
Hospice of the Saint Bernard, the three battalions of the 28th,
the Swiss and the Italian battalions, and will have them provided with biscuit for four days. You will accordingly give him
his orders.

" You will take every necessary precaution for hastening the
transport of your artillery up to the Saint Bernard, and you will
cause the sleighs for the gun-carriages which are destined for
you to move forward with the greatest speed, so that they may
reach the foot of the mountain before the head of the column.

" You will calculate your march with sufficient precision
so that you may have passed the Saint Bernard an hour before
daybreak on the 16th, and that you will find yourself approaching the enemy's advanced posts, which you will overpower.

" You will order the 12th Regiment of Hussars and the
21st Regiment of Chasseurs to be at Vevey by the 13th.

" The movements of the army will conform to those
of the advanced guard, and on this you will receive further
instructions."

Lannes issued his orders :—

" The advanced guard will pass the Great Saint Bernard on
the night of the 15-16th of May, whatever may be the difficulties encountered on the mountain. The head of the column
will set out from the little valley of Proz at midnight, and
will follow in rear of the last boxes of ammunition sent to the
Hospice by the arrangements of General Marmont.

" The men will be marshalled in two ranks : mounted officers
will go on foot, leading their horses by the bridle, or having
them led.

" No shouts or loud calls will be uttered, because such may
bring down avalanches. In localities difficult to surmount, the
soldiers are authorized to lean on their muskets. No one will
be permitted to quit the road indicated.

" Fifty lanterns will be distributed through the half-brigades
to light up the march of the troops up to the Hospice buildings.
General Marescot will locate some pontoniers between the
battalions—pontoniers who may have to throw bridges over

the Drance should it become necessary. Every man will carry a thousand grammes of biscuit. Peasants from Saint Pierre and mules will carry supplies.

" On arriving at the Hospice the 6th Light will receive some refreshments from the monks, will deposit the ordnance, and will advance rapidly on the Austrian posts. The enemy driven out of its positions, the half-brigade will march with all possible speed on Aosta, which must be taken at any price.

" The general commanding in chief of the advanced guard appeals to the devotedness of the soldiers of the Republic, to get over a passage looked upon by our enemies as inaccessible.

" It is twenty centuries ago that the Carthaginian soldiers overcame it to go and fight the Roman legions.

" Europe will be astonished in hearing that you have marched with cannon and baggage on the footsteps of these heroes.

" Officers and soldiers of France! without hesitation the First Consul has placed confidence in your courage. And at the moment of marching on the enemy do not forget that our brothers-in-arms are waiting in Genova, in the midst of the most cruel sufferings of famine, the deliverance which you are about to bring them, after having at a run crossed Piedmont and Lombardy."

Bonaparte was always bent on deceiving and mystifying his enemies. He wrote to the Consuls about this time to have inserted in the *Journal Officiel* how he had gone through Switzerland and on to Bâle, when in reality he was at Lausanne. With the same purpose, evidently, when about to ascend the Alps, Berthier wrote to Lannes to recommend that Major Pavetti be made to circulate some proclamations giving out the coming of an army of 100,000 men.

According to the records kept at the Hospice of the Grand Saint Bernard, the French staff had established three rest-camps on the road between Liddes and the village of Saint Pierre. The principal object for this arrangement was to enable the troops to commence the ascension of the mountain at an early hour in the morning; that they might recover their vigour was only a secondary consideration.

The track being so narrow as to compel the troops to advance in file, only a certain number were detailed to march each day —from 5000 to 6000 men. In this way the rear-guard could always reach Etroubles before nightfall.

Of these camps one was at Pratz about halfway between Liddes and Saint Pierre, close to the bank of a torrent which fell into the Drance. Another was just below the village of Liddes. The advance-guard placed under Lannes's command was composed of the 6th Light, the 28th, 22nd, and 40th of the line —in all about 6648 men—to which was added Rivaud's cavalry brigade, the 12th Hussars, and 21st Chasseurs, some 700 sabres. Lannes set out from Saint Pierre at 2 a.m. on the 15th of May. This early hour for a start had been chosen for the simple reason of avoiding as much as possible the danger from avalanches, as they fall less frequently in the cool hours of the day.

The novelty and the hardihood of the enterprise appealed to the imagination of the troops. Animated to great exertions, they vied with each other in their efforts, and the activity of the officers was well seconded by the willingness of the men. Berthier issued the following proclamation to the army :—

"The soldiers of the Rhine have signalized themselves by glorious triumphs; those of the Army of Italy struggle with invincible perseverance against a superior enemy. Emulating their virtues, go forth and reconquer the plains beyond the Alps which were the first theatre of French glory. Conscripts! you behold the emblems of victory : march and emulate the veterans who have won so many triumphs ; learn from them how to bear and overcome the fatigues inseparable from war. Bonaparte is with you; he has come to witness your first triumph. Prove to him that you are the same men whom he formerly led in these regions of immortal renown."

The French accounts relate how the soldiers were in high spirits, how they were pleased in being led by such a chief as Bonaparte, and how confident they were of success. The majority of the writers are quite silent on the absence of discipline and mutinous behaviour of some of the troops. The 9th Light, which so distinguished themselves at Marengo as to receive the designation of the *incomparable*, had been recruited in Paris, and was in a high state of insubordination. Rivaud's cavalry had also shown signs of insubordination, so much so that for a while they were put out of orders, and it was only by their protesting their devotion to the Republic and to Bonaparte that they were allowed to take part in the campaign. What caused them to break out was the want of provisions and forage. In passing through Martigny-bourg, Sembrancher, and Orsières the closed doors of the houses added to their discontent, and a voice was heard calling, "At least give us a village to pillage." The brigadier recommended a little patience, declaring that in the evening the supplies would arrive. The brigade halted at Saint Pierre, and whilst Rivaud was away conferring with General Lannes, the soldiers having heard that the biscuit would not start from Villeneuve before the morrow, ransacked the houses for provisions. They carried bread and cheese to the officers, who accepted these simple provisions without making any remonstrance. In one cellar a large supply of spirits was found; an immense punch was improvised, and many of the soldiers partook too freely of it.

The pillage had been going on for two hours when Rivaud galloped back and entered Saint Pierre. The disorder was too great to be stayed by his voice, so the general sounded the boot and saddle. The troops were speedily recalled to their sense of duty, and having got some way out of Saint Pierre, Rivaud halted them and abused them for having violated the sacred laws of hospitality. An old soldier replied, "Citizen General, you were always promising us provisions; we were as hungry as wolves. Now that we are full you may conduct us into the snows and to the enemy. We shall go gaily. Forward, and long live the Republic!"

Berthier ordered Rivaud to punish the squadron commanders severely. This he refused to do, alleging that they had done more than their duty, and that he would rather resign. His words conveyed conviction to Berthier when he told him that if at any time his men were entitled to make a good meal it was on the eve of crossing the Alps, and this they had made.

The discipline of the troops evidently left much to be desired. Coignet relates how General Chambarlhac tried to make the men quicken their pace as they were dragging the guns up the mountain. The gunner who was in command of the detachment told him, "It is not you who command my gun; I am the responsible person. So please move on. At this moment these grenadiers do not belong to you; it is only I who command them." The general stepped towards the gunner, but the latter called a halt. "If you," he then said, "do not move away from my piece I will knock you down with a blow from my lever. Move on, or I will cast you over the precipice." This seems insubordinate language enough, and evidently the general had to comply, for there Coignet's story ends.

In the first editions of Coignet there is a passage to the effect that at the battle of Montebello the 24th Regiment, as they came under fire, shot all their officers but one. Also that, with a view to punish them for this deed, the First Consul placed the regiment in a very exposed position at Marengo. It may have been so, but such heavy mortality in officers in one regiment would surely have drawn comments.

Bonaparte had, amongst other elements of success, soldiers eager to undertake what he might wish, and generals brave, enterprising, and expert. Of the troops he says, "We were all young in those days, soldiers as well as generals. We disdained fatigues as much as dangers. We were careless of everything except glory." Courage and daring often make up for want of caution, and that fortune favours the brave is, after all, in nowise an empty boast.

Lannes commenced his march on the 15th of May with the 22nd and 40th of the line. He set out from Saint Maurice with the intention of reaching Saint Pierre the same day. The troops advanced in the following order. The 22nd opened the march. At their head were the drums of its three battalions. Following that regiment came twenty waggons loaded with hospital equipment and baggage appertaining to the staff and to sutlers. The 40th brought up the rear.

The column, having crossed the Drance by a wooden bridge, entered Martigny-ville, where it halted in the main square. The inhabitants offered some wine to the men of the 22nd, but of this the 40th, being too far in the rear, could not partake. A kilometre further on is the village of Martigny-bourg. Lannes, wishing that the 40th should in their turn partake of the hospitality of the place, made the 22nd double through the village and halted the 40th, but his object was frustrated, as all the doors remained closed. Coignet speaks of these villages as being the most pitiful that one could behold.

The ascent to be surmounted was considerable. In the windings of the tortuous path which led to the summit, the troops were lost to sight, and now and again came in view. Those who were below were cheered and animated by those who had first surmounted the steeps. They answered in turn, and in this manner they encouraged each other in their laborious task ; the valleys on every side re-echoed their voices.

The soldiers gazed in wonderment at the snow-clad summits of the lofty mountains. Extraordinary was their ardour, wonderful their gaiety of spirits, astonishing their activity and energy. Laughter and song lightened their toil, good humour and raillery sped from mouth to mouth, and bitter sarcasm was levelled against the unsuspicious Austrians. The silence of those solitary and deserted regions was replaced by many sounds and voices gay and warlike, sounds which were given back from hill to hill. The more the troops laboured the more did the merriment of their jests and the wit of their repartee increase. Often the roll of the war-drum was added to this, beating a charge when the difficulties of the road presented greater obstacles to the advance.

Beyond Saint Pierre skill or courage seemed as nothing against the potency of nature ; for up to the summit there was no beaten road whatever, only narrow and winding paths over steep and rugged mountains succeeded each other. A determination to conquer all obstacles, however, prevailed. The artillery and baggage were dragged, were drawn, were pushed up by main force until the difficult ascent was accomplished. The officers roused the courage of the men, and all working with a will made what seemed at first sight impossible a comparatively easy matter.

The loftiest pinnacle being within reach, the soldiers hailed the extreme point, the termination of their labours, with shouts of transport, and were soon congratulating each other. Their labours found a reward in the good cheer which by the care of the First Consul awaited them, for the good self-sacrificing monks of the Hospice had spread tables on which were bread, cheese, and wine.*

All the artillery had been directed *viâ* Lausanne, Villeneuve, and Martigny on Saint Pierre. At this last place commenced all the heavy work for moving the guns. This was carried out

---

* The records of the Great Saint Bernard show that from the 13th of May, 1799, when three companies of the 21st half-brigade took up their quarters at the Hospice, to the 9th of July, 1800, 27,703 bottles of wine, 1758 lbs. of meat, and 495 lbs. of bread were distributed.

In conversing with the monks, Bonaparte, it is stated, showed himself desirous of peace.

under the direction of Marmont, who was accompanied by a number of able and promising artillery officers.

To draw the artillery up and down the broken and narrow paths, choked up with snow and ice, the guns and carriages were taken to pieces. This was done at Saint Pierre, where a company of artificers dismounted the guns, the ammunition-waggons, the forges, etc., into suitable parts so as to be easily dragged or carried by hand. Every regiment as it passed received a given quantity of ordnance material in proportion to its strength. Artillery officers were distributed along the column, and were to superintend its transport and prevent any wilful damage being done to the materials on the way.

Gassendi, inspector of ordnance, caused a number of sledges on rollers to be constructed at Auxonne for the carriage of the pieces. In the most narrow parts of the route these sledges were not quite under control, and were found too dangerous. They had, therefore, to be given up, being replaced by fir trees hollowed out so as to form a trough, or receptacle, for the guns. The bottom had been levelled and the front part rounded off so that the trunk might slide without sticking into the ground. A lever inserted into the mouth of the piece and held by a gunner prevented it from turning upside down.

The guns were placed in these hollowed trunks and dragged up by 500 or 600 men according to the weight of the metal. The wheels were rolled on poles. Sledges had been purposely contrived at Auxonne by order of Gassendi for the conveyance of the axle-trees and ammunition-boxes. These latter were emptied and the ammunition transferred to special chests which were carried by men or by mules. The gun-carriages were carried by mules, except the more heavy ones, which men carried on hand-barrows. The transport of the ammunition-waggons gave more trouble than that of the guns, whilst they also suffered greater deterioration.

By order of the First Consul, General Marmont, who was the chief commander of the artillery, had by beat of drum notified at Saint Pierre and in all the surrounding villages that each gun with its carriage and gun-waggons conveyed up the mountain and down the southern side as far as Etroubles would be paid for at the rate of 600, 800, or 1000 francs according to the calibre and weight of the piece. Thereupon a crowd of peasants at once came forward with their horses and mules.

Some thousand soldiers joined them, and thus in less than two days 20 pieces were taken to Etroubles.*

The labour was so tiring that after a first haul all the peasants withdrew, not one was found willing to come forward for a second trip. Marmont on the 19th of May tells the First Consul, "The peasants have abandoned us, disgusted with the severity of the work."

When an entire battalion undertook to transport a field-piece with its ammunition, one-half of the battalion was employed in that work, the other half carried the knapsacks, firelocks, cartridge-cases, canteens, kettles and provisions of their comrades. It was computed that the whole of these necessaries did not weigh less than from 30 to 35 kilogrammes (from 60 to 70 lbs.).

One of the greatest difficulties was to get the artillery over the mountain. It was not easy to drag the weighty ordnance for several leagues over a track practicable only for pedestrians and mules, which in many places did not measure in breadth above $1\frac{1}{2}$ foot, with nothing to prevent a false step to be followed by a fall down a precipice. †

* "Passage of the Artillery:" see p. 339 of "Extraits des Mémoires inedits de feu Claude Victor Pierion, Duc de Belluno."

† Charles VIII. was the first who led artillery on their waggons into Italy. Later Trivulzio passed the artillery of Francis I. through the Cottian Alps to Saluzzo by way of the valley of Barcellonette, Rocca Sparviera, St. Paolo, and L'Argentiera. During a lengthy stay at Embrun, that expert leader had discovered a route for passing an army from France into Italy. The difficulties met on the way were such as would have discouraged any captain less daring than Trivulzio. The rocks had to be broken or moved by the pick and lever, and the guns were carried by soldiers on their shoulders where horses could not draw them. Machines for raising weights were also used, and in this manner the guns were passed from rock to rock. With great ability on the part of the artificers, and with singular toil on the part of the soldiers, all the artillery and baggage was carried over the Val d'Argentiera.

When a general is determined he can make his artillery pass anywhere. The march of Wellington's artillery, when descending the mountainous district where the Ebro takes its rise, and making for the great road of Bilbao in 1813, as described by Napier, was a fine illustration of this fact. "Neither the winter gullies or the ravines, nor the precipitous passes amongst the rocks, retarded even the march of the artillery. Where horses could not draw, men hauled; when the wheels would not roll, the guns were let down or lifted up with ropes, and strongly did the rough veteran infantry work their way through those wild but beautiful regions. Six days they toiled unceasingly; on the seventh, swelled by the junction of Longa's division, and all the small bands which came trickling from the mountains, they burst like raging streams from every defile, and went foaming into the basin of Vitoria."— Napier's "Peninsular War," Book XX. chap. vii.

Prompt efforts were every instant demanded from the soldiers to save the various contrivances which held the artillery from rolling over the precipitous sides; and now supporting, now heaving and dragging their load, they laboured unceasingly. The ascent of the mountain is hard enough for pedestrians free from encumbrances. What must it have been for men heavily weighted, tugging away at a load on ground often covered with snow and ice? Add to this that the majority of the men were not accustomed to hill-climbing.

Coignet describes the labour of drawing the guns, in which he took a share. He states that their three guns, for each half-brigade had its own artillery, were placed in a trough; at one extremity of the trough was inserted a stout bar, to control the movements of the piece, held by a very intelligent gunner who was in command of forty grenadiers. With absolute silence these were bound to obey him, conforming to all the movements which the pieces might make. If the leader called out " Halt ! " all were obliged to remain still and not to budge; when he commanded "Forward!" the march had to be instantly resumed. On every point he was absolute master. The soldiers were ranged by twenty, ten on each side; two more carried the gun-carriage ; two were detailed to each of the wheels ; four were allotted to the upper part of the gun-waggon, eight to the body; eight more carried the muskets of the rest. Every one had his work cut out for him—every one was at his post.

When the snow was reached the work became trying. The track was covered with ice, which destroyed the shoes, and the master-gunner could with great difficulty control his gun, which slid at every turn. It had then to be brought back, and it demanded all the strength and pluck of the men to keep it in the track.

All was sent over in this manner. On the south side of the mountain the ordnance had to be put together, but it was much deteriorated ; as, notwithstanding the closest supervision, it had been impossible to prevent a considerable amount of injury.

Much to their credit, several regiments refused to accept the money they were entitled to for drawing the guns.

The troops marched in single file, ascending and descending one by one; no one attempted to outstrip his comrade, for to have done so would have been highly dangerous. There was

o

indeed enough in this novel experience to awe the soldier, but he was made of hard stuff, and was not easily deterred.

Below Liddes the Drance stream was crossed by two trunks of trees, a rapid rushing torrent flowed 300 feet below. The cavalry had to make a *détour* to reach a better point of passage, which, by the care of General Marescot, who commanded the engineers, had been improved and made practicable. It took five hours to climb from Saint Pierre to the Hospice; then followed a descent of six leagues, or eighteen miles.

Saint Pierre is not quite at the foot of the mountain, as Petit puts it, it is at the foot of the last portion of the ascent. Two-thirds of the way from Martigny, the starting-point of the ascent, have been done before getting there. The altitude at Bourg Saint Pierre is 5348 feet, at the Hospice 8109 feet, at Aosta 1165 feet. The distance by road from Saint Pierre to the Hospice is 8⅛ miles—which could be walked with a good deal of labour in about three hours—from the Hospice to Aosta nearly 22 miles, from Aosta on to Bard 23⅛ miles. In 1800, there existed a carriage-road only as far as Saint Pierre, but even this was not fit for the passage of anything beyond ordinary country carts.*

Though an excellent country road now exists between Bourg Saint Pierre and the summit of the Great Saint Bernard, judging by the configuration of the ground and the remains of the old road, it does not seem to me that on the Valais side of the mountain the difficulty of the ascent could have been very great. Mount Saint Bernard has its glaciers and some precipices, like all the rest of the Alps; but there is nothing which can prevent an army full of ardour and devotion from ascending in good order and crossing its summit, above all when there is no enemy to dispute the passage. With a little experience of hill-climbing most difficulties disappear. On the Italian side the hills are much more steep and rough, and the tracks for two-thirds of the way to Saint Rémy are now pretty much in the same condition as they were in 1800. This section is very trying, and must have been more so at the end of May, when there was still much snow on the ground.

The soldiers, as they arrived at the Hospice, received a glass of wine, a ration of bread, and one of cheese. Professor Rolando

---

* The old road has disappeared in many places. At Orsières it has been made more easy for carriages, though much more winding.

states that Bonaparte had sent 24,000 francs to the monks of the Hospice to collect provisions. This is denied by Silvan Lucat, though he acknowledges that after the victory of Marengo the good fathers were reimbursed for what they had laid out. Rolando could not have been correct when he wrote that the monks got most of the food from Aosta, for the purchase of such unusually large quantities of provisions would have put the Austrians on their guard, and given them some warning of what was about to happen. This was not the case in the Valais, where there was no fear of arousing suspicion of any kind.

The troops, having had a slight rest and partaken of their food, resumed the march. The descent to Saint Rémy was steep and rough, so it is not at all surprising to find Petit recording that the officers arrived at Aosta without boots.

In crossing the Alps, Bonaparte had no other opponent to contend with beyond the obstacles of nature. The difficulties of the ascent and of the descent, together with the roughness of the road, constituted the only serious impediments to the march. But it is not always so, for often in May storms of snow and sleet rage about the Hospice and on the higher reaches of the path. De Cayrol,* who crossed the Alps with the headquarters of the Army of Reserve, states that magnificent weather favoured the undertaking throughout. Bonaparte, writing to Berthier from Martigny on the 19th of May, declares that the day was superb, which would facilitate very much the transport of the artillery. As a proof of the mildness of the weather, the ice on the little lake in front of the Hospice was broken, and it was stated by one of the monks that such a thing at that early season had not been known for forty years.†

At the time the French crossed, there was a bright moon, which was a very fortunate circumstance, as it assisted in marching by night.

For a fortnight, commencing from the 14th of May, the day when General Mainoni with a portion of the troops of the advanced guard set out for the Saint Bernard, to the 25th of that month, the Saint Bernard route was the main route of

---

* De Cayrol had the organizing of the hospitals and the enrolling of wardsmen and sick-bearers.

† Bonaparte's guide, Dorsaz, told him that long habit and old experience had taught the inhabitants to foretell the good and bad weather so accurately that they rarely made a mistake.—Bourrienne.

communication between Italy and France. Fortune gave Bonaparte sufficiently fine weather for several days, and for some really splendid.* A hurricane, a severe storm, a heavy fall of snow, might have turned the enterprise into a huge disaster. Nothing of the kind, however, occurred, and the weather for the ten days from the 15th to the 25th of May, in which 35,000 men, 3000 and more horses and mules, and 40 guns filed over the Great Saint Bernard, was uniformly fair and all that could be desired.†

An avalanche, which fell on the artillery of the advanced guard, buried and carried away an 8-pr. gun with three men. This unfortunate accident instantly gave rise to a number of reports, which were naturally grossly exaggerated. Scared by the report of this mishap, the troops moved forward taking excessive precautions. Lannes, alive to the fact that if this were countenanced it would very likely retard the advance, strove thereupon to reassure the troops, and reminded them that up to that moment no other accident had marred the march, and very possibly this would be the only one.

Soon the snow-clad Alps, which had so lately rung with the merry voices and rude oaths of the passing army, were to lie silent and forbidding. On the 16th, Lannes's vanguard reached the beautiful valley of Aosta, then delightful in its spring greenness, offering a marked contrast to the ice and snow of the Saint Bernard. The difficulty in the descent on the Italian side of the Alps was greater than the distress experienced in the ascent, for the slope of the mountain on that side, as we have said, is considerably steeper than it is on the Swiss side. However, notwithstanding all the difficulties experienced, very few accidents occurred. The horses, mules, and guns had to be carefully let down one slippery step after another. Where the slope was steepest some of the soldiers, sitting down, allowed themselves to slide for a long way. Some of the chiefs performed the descent *en ramasse*—that is, sliding on a sort of sledge down the snow-covered hill.‡

* " *Le temps enfin est devenu beau, ce qui nous était bien nécessaire pour activer le passage de notre artillerie par le Saint-Bernard.*"—Bonaparte to the Consuls, Martigny, le 29 Floréal, an 8.

† In a discourse which Bonaparte delivered at the French National Institute in the month of August he stated, " The monks of the Saint Bernard assured me that the snows had melted this year twenty days sooner than usual."

‡ To the tourist who now makes the ascent of the Great Saint Bernard from

On the 17th, the advanced guard halted at Aosta to pull itself together and to complete in all necessaries. Its advanced posts were pushed well forward towards Villefranche. On the 18th, it quitted Aosta and marched for Châtillon. The Austrians under Colonel Rakitkvich had quitted Villefranche on the previous day, and taken up a position at Châtillon, leaving advanced posts at Chambave.

In the afternoon of the 18th (Berthier says at 6 p.m., and, in the same despatch, one hour before night—the Austrian account makes it 2 p.m.), Lannes was confronted by 1500 Austrians with two guns, intrenched at Châtillon and the neighbouring heights. Though unprovided with guns to prepare an attack, he assailed them with the bayonet in front and in flank, routed them and captured 250 prisoners and two guns. Commandant Brossier says that three guns and three ammunition-waggons were captured. The prisoners belonged to the regiment Deutschbanat. The contest hardly lasted one hour, and the enemy retired in great haste, pursued by 100 men of the 12th Hussars.

The Austrians made a very poor defence of the valley of Aosta. In rear of Châtillon by Saint Vincent lies the Montjovet defile, a very difficult piece of ground, which might have been easily contested. The exit of the pass is commanded by the ruined castle of Montjovet, or Saint Germain, showing that the aptitude of the locality for defence had been recognized many years before. No steps whatsoever were taken to defend La Chiusa della Dora, possibly because the Austrians were too much alarmed to undertake a vigorous resistance.

There were from 1000 to 1500 Austrians at Châtillon, and of these it is stated that those who escaped first made for Bard, and afterwards marched on to Ivrea. One may well ask why this precipitate retreat? Would they not have made a better show at Bard, or by being posted at Donnaz as a reserve, where they might have attacked any of the French who might have tried to turn the position of Bard?

On the morning of the 19th, General Watrin, with the brigades of Gency and Rivaud, marched for Ivrea. Up to that moment, neither the difficulties of nature nor the resistance of the enemy

the Valais side, it may appear an easy matter to march an army that way up. It is only when he begins to descend into the valley of Aosta, between the Hospice and Saint Rémy, that he will begin to appreciate the difficulty.

had been able to arrest the progress of the French. Now, however, they came face to face with a still greater obstacle, for the
fort of Bard, garrisoned by some 400 Austrians, barred the way.
This fort lies eleven leagues from Aosta and four from Ivrea.

In a narrow gorge, where two lofty mountains approach very
near to each other, lies the pyramidal rock of Bard. This
isolated rock was planted seemingly by a slipping down of a
part of Mount Albaredo, which one might suppose had been
purposely precipitated into the valley with the intent of closing
it hermetically. Situated between the Dora and the village of
Bard, it fills with its bulk almost the entire space of the gorge.
In its longitudinal construction it leaves on one of its sides
nothing else but the narrow bed of the river, from the right
bank of which rise the steep slopes of the mountains of Porcil.
On the opposite side lies the village.

The village of Bard is formed of a double range of houses,
and between this defile runs the main road from Aosta to Ivrea.*
The houses on the south side rest on the steep rocky slopes of
the Albaredo. The ingress to the village was through four
drawbridges commanded by the guns of the defences.

The rock was crowned with military works, which, though
of inferior construction, commanded the walled village and
closed to an army the main thoroughfare leading into Piedmont.
The rushing waters of the Dora form a semicircle at the base
of the rock, and in a certain manner constitute a natural line
of defence. From its position and the strength of the works,
the fort could not be carried by assault; it needed artillery to
batter down the walls and open a passage.

The general idea is that the French had only a most vague
notion about the fort. Some have even called it an unforeseen
obstacle. Nothing, however, is less exact, and everything tends
to show that Bard, after all, did not come quite as a surprise
to the French, as many suppose. In January, 1800, a committee had gone round inspecting the frontier, and with regard
to Bard had reported that the fort appeared difficult to be
carried.† It was only by turning it by the valley of Cham-
porcher that the enemy could be induced to abandon it.

---

* The new road, avoiding the village, runs round the base of the rock and on to
Donnaz.

† On the 11th of February, an inspector-general, Lacombe Saint Michel, received
an order to ascertain personally the state of all the strong places on the frontier of
the Alps and of the Jura from Barcelonnette above Nice to Besançon.

Writing on the 10th of May to General Lacuée, councillor of state, Dupont, chief of the staff of the Army of Reserve, states : " We shall be at Ivrea on the 28th, if the fort of Bard does not detain us." In the report of the reconnaissance of the Saint Bernard by Generals Marescot and Watrin occurs the following passage : " You will find enclosed a return of the troops which the enemy has on the reverse slope of the Alps. . . . He appears inclined to make a display of resistance at the castle of Bard, but this obstacle cannot be but a slight one."

Writing to Dupont on the 15th of May, Berthier informs him that the question of supplies has given him considerable thought. That as nothing may possibly be found in the valley of Aosta, being arrested by the fort of Bard would be very embarrassing.

On the same day, writing from Lausanne to General Berthier, then at Villeneuve, Bonaparte observes : " Lauriston has just arrived ; he informs me that all the artillery of General Lannes' division has crossed the Great Saint Bernard. Bid General Duhesme's corps (Boudet and Loison's divisions) cross one after the other, and proceed as quickly as they can to the fort of Bard. Should General Chabran have been able to bring the 12-prs., have them taken there. You will understand that the fort of Bard cannot be taken too soon.

" I imagine that Lannes has to-day occupied Aosta. I hope that at the latest you will be master of Bard by the 17th of May."

Berthier, writing to Lannes from Saint Pierre on the 16th of May, tells him how he will essentially need artillery for an attack of Fort Bard.

General Olivero gave it as his opinion that Bonaparte knew too well the obstacles which the fort of Bard presented to the march of the Army of Reserve, but that evidently they did not appear to his mind to be sufficiently formidable to stop him in his designs.*

---

* In his "Mémoires" Napoleon writes : " The First Consul knew too well of the existence of the fort of Bard ; but all the plans and all the information on this subject fostered the supposition that it would be captured with ease."

Botta relates that Pavetti had represented the reduction of Bard as an easy undertaking, so sanguine was he to see his native district once more restored to liberty.

General Marescot submitted to Bonaparte a report and description of Fort Bard. De Cugnac states there are very good grounds to believe that this report had been prepared by General Herbin, one of Chambarlhac's brigadiers.

In the face of what has been said of the foreknowledge con-
cerning the fort of Bard, it is strange that Marmont could write
in his " Mémoires," " He (Bonaparte) came across an obstacle
on the way which certainly had not been foreseen, because the
First Consul had never said a word to me about it ; consequently no preparations had been made to overcome it." This
statement appears incredible, that no preparations should have
been made when there was every prospect of having to attack
a fort.

Marescot ends his report on the fort of Bard by the following
sentence : "It is not in the least astonishing that the fort of
Bard has not been known ; this being the first time it has had
an occasion of making itself appreciated. Never had an army
passed over the col of the Great Saint Bernard. The engineer
who has planned it and constructed it has fully grasped the
natural strength of its position, and has applied to it the kind
of fortification best adapted to it." This sounds very strange,
for how could the general overlook the fact that after their
conquest of Italy in 1796 the French had occupied the fort,
and that in 1798 many thousands of men were sent into Italy
by the way of the Great Saint Bernard ? De Cugnac has
gathered from the records of the Great Saint Bernard that,
from the 24th of May to the 12th of November, 1798, no less
than 43,000 men had passed the Hospice, going to Italy. The
French, on the 1st of September, 1799, made an irruption into
the valley of Aosta by the Col de Mont. Their force consisted
of 3000 men, under the command of General Mallet. They
overcame the defenders of the Valgrisanche, and occupied Aosta,
pushing after as far as Bard, which fort, for want of materials,
they were unable to capture.

The fort followed the general conformation of the rock. It
was not of any great extent, but several towers and batteries
had been added to the original works. These works were carried
some way down the slope, and were sheltered by splinter-
proofs and bomb-proofs from the commanding height of the
Albaredo. Vaulted galleries afforded safe communication between the more advanced batteries and the upper reaches of
the fort.

The real strength of Bard lay in its position, for the works
in themselves were nothing in particular. The three main
ramparts encircling the fort were simple walls, not strengthened

at the back by any terreplein ; nevertheless, on every side the fort was bounded by steep rocks, which promised to be very unfavourable in any attempt made at escalading.

The rock being so shut in between two mountains very near to each other and very high, the fort was commanded at a close distance. Nevertheless, from these very circumstances, any action taken against it was not likely to prove of serious consequence, for on the Albaredo and Porcil mountains it was difficult to find a suitable locality for establishing a battery. Even then the guns would have had to fire at a too-depressed angle of inclination, which would render the firing too plunging and uncertain, and of little effect against masonry.

Bard commanded the road from Aosta to Turin, which runs under its ramparts between the fort and inaccessible rocks. The fort was well armed, and defended by a garrison of about 400 men. The *Œstreichische Militärische Zeitschrift* states that the garrison was furnished by two companies of grenadiers belonging to the Kinsky regiment. Chabran reports that, when Bernkopf capitulated, 18 guns and 400 prisoners fell into the hands of the French.

General Olivero states that, far from foreseeing the coming of a French army by the valley of Aosta, Melas had some time before their irruption caused a large quantity of artillery and provisions to be removed from Bard and from Ivrea, and to be conveyed to Turin.

What an immense consequence a small obstacle is capable of exercising ! Had the road in this instance gone through, and not by the fort, nothing, not a gun, not a waggon, not a cart, could have passed along the road until the fort had been captured.

The gravity of the obstacle which the fort of Bard presented had not been entirely provided for. There was more to be done than *marcher sur Bard au pas de course.* The passage of the artillery onwards to Ivrea was what constituted the main difficulty. It seemed next to impossible to let it go by without having first command of the fort.

In a letter written to Berthier on the 21st of May, Bonaparte says : " The best-informed people here (at Aosta) believe that if some thirty shells were fired into the fort, if the Albaredo battery opened with some degree of activity, and there were ladders to attempt an assault, especially on the

San Martino side, the fort of Bard could be carried." All conspired to make the capture of the fort appear an easy undertaking.

Berthier's letter to the First Consul, written from Verrès on the 24th of May, gives a good idea of the strength of Fort Bard. "The fort of Bard seems to me likely to hold out for a long time. . . . The castle of Bard is a very provoking obstacle for our operations. The ammunition we spend is wasted, seeing the little injury which we do to it. A direct attack seems to me doubtful in its result." The previous day he had written: "If I saw a chance of succeeding in an assault, I would not hesitate."

"The coming face to face with an obstacle of which little account had been taken went very near to upsetting the brilliant projects of the modern Hannibal. All the reconnaissances revealed that this fort, of which so little notice had been taken, constructed of masonry on a pointed mamelon, and armed with twenty guns, could not be carried by assault, and that it was impossible to hoist cannon up to a sufficiently high point to batter it." *

The little fort of Bard accordingly stopped the advance of the Army of Reserve, and pent it up, as it were, in a narrow neck. The French found themselves in a critical position, for, as the provisions they had with them were calculated to last only for four more days, the danger of the situation from a commissariat point of view will be readily understood. But not only with regard to provisions was this stoppage awkward and unfortunate; it was likewise calculated to give warning to Melas, and by rousing him to the danger which threatened him, would afford him time to come and oppose the French as they tried to issue out into the open country.

In this serious predicament, Bonaparte's steadfastness of character stood forth pre-eminently. Embarked in his glorious enterprise, he stubbornly refused to move a single step backward; nothing could induce him even to entertain such a thought. Bard must either be carried or turned, and the army must march onwards to Ivrea on the border of the plain. Even if the fort held back the artillery, the French could find guns by capturing those of the enemy. Faith in their bravery suggested to him this course as not at all difficult. In a few

* Jomini, "Histoire des Guerres de la Révolution," vol. xiii. p. 185.

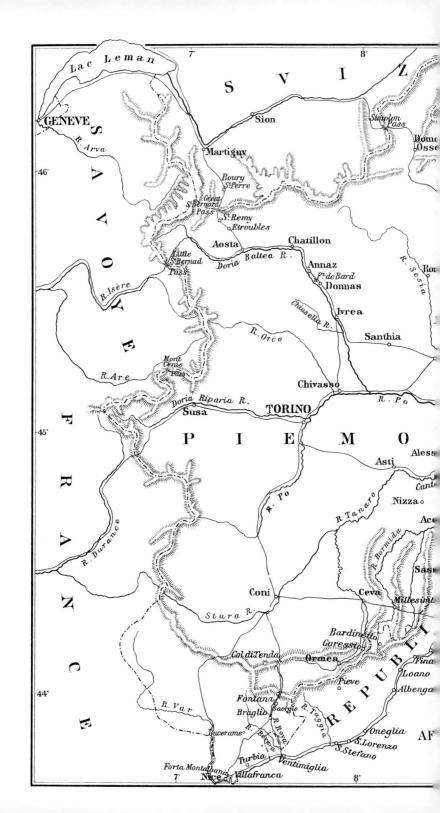

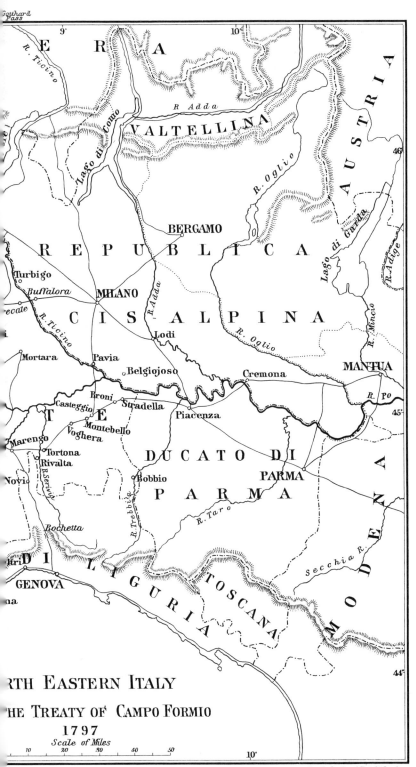

Gotthard Pass

R. Ticino

R. Adda

VALTELLINA

AUSTRIA

Lago di Como

R. Oglio

Lago di Garda

R. Adige

BERGAMO

R E P U B L I C A

Turbigo

Buffalora

MILANO

R. Adda

C I S   A L P I N A

Lodi

R. Oglio

R. Mincio

MANTUA

Mortara

Pavia

Belgiojoso

Cremona

R. Po

Broni

Stradella

Piacenza

Casteggio

Montebello

Voghera

Marengo

Tortona

Rivalta

Bobbio

DUCATO DI

PARMA

Novi

R. Serivia

P A R M A

R. Trebbia

R. Taro

Rochetta

D I   L I G U R I A

MODENA

Secchia R.

GENOVA

L I G U R I A

T O S C A N A

RTH EASTERN ITALY

HE TREATY OF CAMPO FORMIO

1797

Scale of Miles

10   20   30   40   50

10°

Stanford's Geog.l Estab.t London.

days he wrote many able and foreseeing letters to Berthier, through all of which runs the same idea, not to stay the forward movement of the army, to study closely the ground round Bard, to bid Lannes proceed to Ivrea across the Albaredo, to hold the gate of the plain, and to defend that post with all his might against any troops that the enemy might send to confront the Army of Reserve.

Joseph Stockard Bernkopf, who held the place with 400 Austrians, was summoned to surrender, but, like a gallant soldier, he replied that he would never consent to do so. He was told how the infantry were already marching on Ivrea, how Bard was invested on every side, and how part of the artillery was already in position to batter the fort. Resistance, he was assured, would be of no avail, and could only lead to useless blood-shedding. Berthier declares that Bernkopf had been summoned twice, and appeared determined to defend the place up to the very last.

There remained nothing else to be done but either to carry the fort by assault or to seek for some other route by which the fort could be avoided. Either of these measures, at first, appeared almost hopeless.

An army which commences a campaign without provisions and ammunition stands a very good chance of being beaten. The situation of the French, in consequence of the unexpected resistance of the fort of Bard, was really a very serious matter. The question of supply was a difficult one; for what had been collected by the forethought of the First Consul was not much. To obtain the provisions they needed, the French were compelled to keep on the move, and any enforced halt would have placed them in a serious predicament. We find Watrin writing to Dupont, "All this country does not absolutely contain any means of subsistence. The greatest part of the inhabitants have taken to flight." Berthier, in communicating his first impressions on Fort Bard, writes to the First Consul: "You cannot form an idea of the poverty of the people." And it was not surprising, for, as ever since 1792 the valley of Aosta had been compelled to provide supplies for several armies, in 1800 it was in a deplorable condition. The forests had been destroyed by fire or by the axe, the cottages had been burnt, the cattle had been almost swept away, the fields were uncultivated, and the people were subjected to heavy and fatiguing toil. Sickness, poverty, and want were at every door.

Requisitions beyond measure had been levied on Aosta, and other decrees were threatened; the municipality did its best, and in this was helped by the most wealthy citizens. Sub-committees, of three individuals each, were constituted, and these were enjoined to search a certain number of houses and lay hands on all articles of food, leaving to the people only what they considered absolutely necessary.

As a rule, the valleys at the foot of the Alps do not produce much beyond what is required for feeding the inhabitants. In any case what there was left around Aosta could not have been much, as the Austro-Russians had occupied the valley the previous year, and the records show how very heavily their rule had pressed on the population.

Fresh needs incessantly arise to hamper an army in the field. The army must be always at its best as a fighting machine. It must renew its men to repair the waste brought about by battle and disease. It needs horses to replace such as are killed, get maimed or disabled, or fall into low condition. Its arms, its equipment, its clothing, its boots, get destroyed, damaged, or lost. The ammunition must be constantly replenished, for such is the expenditure of it that an army has seldom present much beyond what will suffice for one single battle. To secure the life of an army it is imperative to accumulate in its rear a mass of provisions and forage to last for a fair number of days.

To secure all possible calls being readily met, and to prevent the presence of a too large accumulation of things about the troops, which would interfere with their freedom of action, a chain of large and small magazines, or depôts, is formed in rear of an army. These magazines, or depôts, are located at convenient distances in places of security, and guarded against any attempt by the enemy, by partisan corps, or by the armed population. All these places of storage naturally enough require proper shelter and an adequate garrison. Besides all this, the army must be master of the country to be in a position to draw from it all the resources it contains.

The connection between these magazines must never be interrupted, so that the convoys may never cease to arrive. The roads by which this connection is kept up, and which lead back towards the resources of the *base,* are termed the *lines of communication.* These roads ultimately would in most cases constitute the principal lines of retreat of an army. Let us suppose that the Austrians had been in sufficient strength to occupy the already prepared entrenchments on Mount Albaredo and the Col de la Cou, or that Bernkopf, reinforced by the troops which had retired from Châtillon, could have adequately occupied the outer defences of Bard, the guard-house, etc. Let us imagine that, instead of being so easily driven into the fort, the Austrians had held the village for three or four days longer, and absolutely barred the passage; what incalculable consequences might not have been the result! Already at Verrès on the 23rd it had been found necessary to place the troops upon half rations. Berthier declared to Bonaparte that the resistance of Bard kept him without provisions and ammunition. He pithily summed up the situation when he wrote, "But the provisions are for the moment a terrible obstacle to overcome." "If this letter," he added, "reaches you in some place where you can issue orders for some biscuit to be sent us, nothing is more urgent, for the valley is destitute of everything, above all in the immediate neighbourhood of Bard, where it is very narrow and uncultivated."

Berthier made a careful examination of the mountains. The result showed that, of four possible ways of turning the obstacle, one which left the village of Arnaz and passed by the Col de la Cou, regaining the main road near Donnaz, was the best. The people of the country did not dare to send their mules by this track; but the French improved it, and made it passable even for cavalry and artillery horses.

What very little faith can be placed in much of what Montholon and Gourgaud have written, can be judged from this incident. According to the "Mémoires de Sainte Hélène," the credit for having discovered the Albaredo path is assigned to Bonaparte. Nevertheless, the documents existing in the Bureau de la Guerre show that it was the work of Berthier. We are inclined to think that it was not even Berthier who discovered the way over the Albaredo, but the impetuous Lannes.

The Albaredo track would not have been long undiscovered, for the first action of the advanced guard on the 19th was to send four companies of the 40th to Hone for the purpose of locating skirmishers on the mountain on the right, while another detachment also established skirmishers on the mountain on the left, overlooking the village.

It is so true that where a goat can pass a man can, and where a man can so can an entire corps. Though the path had hitherto only been trodden by single hunters and mountaineers, it was decided that an army which had overcome the difficulties of the Saint Bernard might, by the display of a somewhat similar effort, make its way here also. The order was given, and the troops began the difficult ascent. Marmont states that a track over the mountain to turn the fort, and out of reach of its guns, was made, and that Lannes took his cavalry and infantry that way.

"The route which I have employed to turn the castle of Bard," writes Berthier, "is a track just practicable for men on foot, across rocks and precipices. The first part, about 1200 yards from the place, is climbed in about two hours, in order to reach Albaredo, from whence the fort is commanded. The descent is by a pretty fair road to reach Donnaz in two hours, when the main road from Bard to Ivrea is again struck."

On the 19th and 20th of May, 1500 men worked with zeal to ameliorate the path on the Albaredo. In less than two days steps were cut in the steepest and hardest rocks, at points where the slope was too abrupt. Where the track was very narrow, bordered by precipices, parapet walls were constructed to protect the soldiers from a fall. Small bridges were thrown across chasms and points where the rocks were separated by dips and hollows. This was a really astonishing work, worthy of finding a record in the history of this stupendous campaign.

In this manner, over a mountain which had hitherto been regarded by the inhabitants as almost inaccessible, the infantry, cavalry, and baggage of an army effected their passage. By order of General Berthier, the path over the Albaredo was to be repaired daily, and maintained in good order.

If the infantry found it arduous to clamber up the side of the Albaredo, what must it have been for the cavalry, when the horses in many places had to leap from stone to stone? For all that, very few animals were lost. The path, nevertheless, was considered too narrow for the artillery—some other way for overcoming the difficulty of getting it past Fort Bard had, therefore, to be devised.

On the whole, there was little time lost. Writing to Bonaparte on the 20th, Berthier states that the infantry and cavalry can turn the obstacle by following a mule-track which went from Arnaz to Perloz. In point of fact, Lannes' infantry had already gone past Bard, and that day was at Carema, 1¼ mile beyond Saint Martin. The advanced guard had not been spared, it had marched quickly. It had an affair on the 15th of May at Etroubles, one on the 16th at Aosta; it fought on the 18th at Châtillon, and on the 20th at Donnaz and Saint Martin. On the 21st it drove the Austrians out of Montestrutto, and it captured Ivrea on the 22nd.

Guns were hauled up the Albaredo to batter the defences of the fort. On the 20th, Marescot had a strong battery ready to receive the guns, and, as the transport of the ordnance could be done better by manual labour than by mules, Dupont issued orders for collecting a body of peasants to be employed in helping the soldiers to carry the guns up the mountain. To do this required immense labour. Berthier wrote to the First Consul : " It is impossible to form an idea of the acclivities across which the soldiers have succeeded in dragging the pieces for sixty hours." Possibly there was some exaggeration in this, for in his report, written subsequently, on the 28th of May, he states that it took the soldiers thirty hours to carry the two 4-prs. to the Col de la Cou.

Nothing, however, came out of all this fatigue. The firing of the guns placed on the mountain did not produce the result that was expected. It produced little effect on the bomb-proof batteries and vaulted casements which sheltered the garrison.

The First Consul was still at Martigny; he was very uneasy, anxious for the arrival of news of the fall of Bard, and of the arrival of the advance-guard at Ivrea. Restless on account of the non-arrival of the couriers, he decided to start and meet them on the way. At two o'clock on the morning of the 20th, he set out. With him were his aide-de-camp, Duroc; his secretary, Bourrienne; two monks of the Great Saint Bernard—the Rev. Fathers Murith and Ferretaz—one the prior, the other the procurator, of the house of the order at Martigny.

Most of us are familiar with the picture by the eminent

painter David, in which the First Consul is represented riding a fiery steed, which is in the act of rearing on the border of a precipice. The artist was very far from the truth, which was by no means so sensational, for Bonaparte, enveloped in his cloak, slowly ascended to the summit of the Saint Bernard, partly on foot and partly astride of a very sure-footed mule. The mule was led by a youthful guide, Pierre Nicholas Dorsaz, a native of Bourg Saint Pierre, with whom Bonaparte entertained himself by inquiring into his family affairs.

The romantic part of the story is that young Dorsaz, totally unaware who the officer he was guiding might be, informed the First Consul how his poverty prevented his marrying the girl of his choice, one Leonora Geneoud, and was made happy by a *cadeau* of 1200 francs. The story is quite true, the fact being corroborated by documents, and by the traditions handed down from father to son in the Dorsaz family.

As he gradually advanced up the mountain and overtook detachments of troops, Bonaparte kept turning his eyes on the soldiers, who were toiling and combating against the difficulties of the ascent. A look, a smile, a word would suffice to make them forget their fatigues, to make them laugh at their difficulties and double their exertions.

Conversing with the fathers, he inquired what was the general opinion regarding Fort Bard. The reply he received was that it was considered by every one as impregnable. This was indeed cheerless news, for what would it avail him to have, at the cost of such extraordinary exertions, brought his army to the crest of the Alps, if it were only to plunge it into a narrow valley which was utterly depleted of provisions?

A short halt was made at Liddes, at the house of the parish priest; a frugal breakfast was eaten some miles further on, at the village of Saint Pierre. In the afternoon, the First Consul arrived at the Hospice, where he was welcomed by the head of the establishment, Father D'Allèves. It was there that Bonaparte received Berthier's letter relative to the serious obstacle that Fort Bard was found to be.

He was very tired, but after having warmed himself at a fire and partaken of a modest repast, he started again and made for Etroubles. In all, the party did not stop more than two hours at the Hospice.

To commemorate Bonaparte's passage of the Alps, a stone

was erected in the Hospice by the Republic of the Valais some years later, on the day of the emperor's coronation. It bears the following inscription :—

"NAPOLEONI PRIMO FRANCORUM IMPERATORI
SEMPER AUGUSTO
REIPUBLICÆ VALESIANÆ RESTAURATORI SEMPER
OPTIMO
ÆGYPTIACO, BIS ITALICO SEMPER INVICTO,
IN MONTE JOVIS ET SEMPRONII SEMPER MEMORANDO
RESPUBLICA VALESIÆ GRATA II DECEMBRIS,
ANNI MDCCCIV."

At Etroubles, where he arrived on the evening of the 20th, he took up his abode in the house of the Rev. Vesendaz, which was the best in the country at that time.* There he received the two letters which Berthier had written to him on the evening of the 19th and the morning of the 20th. The First Consul sent pressing instructions for the siege of Bard, for the reparations of the track by which the army was to pass, and for the positions at the opening of the valley which would have to be held.

The next day, the 21st, he moved on to Aosta. The sindic, Signor D. Bianco, went as far as Bibian to meet him, and presented to him the keys of the city. Bonaparte was well received in Aosta, and there was a general illumination at night in his honour.

Bonaparte was always remarkable for the correctness with which he grasped the situation, even when at a distance from the theatre of war. The fertility of his brain can be judged from the letter which he despatched to Berthier from Aosta on the 21st. This epistle of itself gives us an insight into his immense forethought, his talent for forming a just estimate of the situation, and his great care in pointing out to his subordinates every precaution that prudence demands. Certainly Bonaparte shows in the same letter that he had formed a wrong conception of the resistance he might expect from Bard. Still, the opinion he expressed had been gathered by consulting the best-informed individuals in Aosta.

Bernkopf's resistance was very galling to the French. As

* The house no longer exists, having been destroyed by fire.

P

a first preliminary it was considered necessary to gain possession of the village of Bard, through which ran the main road.
This was effected on the night of the 21st and 22nd of May.

Four companies of grenadiers belonging to the 58th Regiment (a regiment which formed part of Loison's division), accompanied by a small squad of engineers and led by General
Gobert, descended into the village of Bard by letting themselves
down from the rocks and by a narrow cleft in which lay the
waterpipe. These troops burst in the Aosta gate, lowered the
drawbridge, and opened communication with the valley. They
then chased the Austrians out of the village, and made for the
gate on the Ivrea side. There, also, they forced the gate open
and lowered the drawbridge. By their action a through communication was opened between Arnaz and Donnaz. Though
the main road had thus been secured, it still remained exposed
to the fire of the fort batteries.* The Austrian garrison, driven
out of the village, withdrew into the fort, from which it opened a
murderous fire. As to the French, they made good their footing
in Bard by taking shelter in the houses, the walls of which
were speedily loopholed.

There were some forty guns and about a hundred vehicles to
be got through Bard. Berthier several times recommended that
the guns should be dismounted. In his letter of the 24th of
May, he urges the dismounting of the artillery and dragging it
up by the new road he had caused to be constructed. He
states it would take but an hour and a half to ascend, and one
to descend. Marmont, however, was strongly opposed to the
artillery being again taken to pieces. He declared it had
suffered very much by being so treated once, in coming over
the Saint Bernard, and that the guns and waggons would be
rendered totally useless were they to be again dismounted.†

Marmont takes credit to himself for the happy idea by
which the difficulty of the artillery was surmounted. His
remonstrances against dismounting the guns a second time
having prevailed, arrangements were made for passing them
stealthily during the night past the walls of the fort. The wheels
of the guns and waggons were covered with twisted hay, and

---

* Some of the attacking party in their eagerness pushed on as far as Donnaz,
and were fired upon by Boudet's troops, as nothing was known there of this intended
night operation.

† Marmont, "Mémoires," book ii. p. 118.

every jingling or rattling part was made fast or covered to deaden the sound. The road itself was covered with mattresses and thickly strewn with manure.

Men replaced the horses, for it was considered that not only would the horses make greater noise, but that if any were struck, killed, or wounded, the whole convoy would be brought to a standstill; whereas the men would go on, careful not to make a sound of any kind, and, not being in harness, if killed or wounded would simply drop out without thereby delaying the march of the rest.

An artillery officer was to be in command of each gun, and 10 louis were promised to the soldiers for each gun taken beyond sight of the fort. This was anything but an easy matter, for Bernkopf was on the alert, and as night came on let off some fire-balls in the village so as to discover the doings of the enemy. Then as soon as the French got into motion he opened on them with grape and canister, rolled on them hand-grenades, and plied them with musketry.

Thiers relates that the first gun sent through Bard was discovered by the noise it made, that the Austrians opened a brisk fire, and that of thirteen artillerymen who were drawing it seven were killed or wounded. He states that it was after this failure that litter and straw were strewn on the roadway and straw wound round the wheels. De Cugnac does not hide the fact that the first and second attempts ended in failure.

Berthier, in fact, admits these two failures, for he writes on the 24th, "To-night, for the third time, an attempt will be made to pass the guns under the cannon of the fort; however, it is an operation which always presents serious difficulties."

From a report written by Berthier to the First Consul, we learn that on the night of the 24-25th of May two guns, 4-prs., and a gun-waggon had passed under the fire of the defenders of Bard without any of the men being hit. Two 8-prs. and two howitzers passed through the town of Bard on the night of the 25-26th of May, and reached Ivrea on the evening of the 26th.

All the horses, and the gun-ammunition, carried on mules, went over the Albaredo. Dampierre writes: "The artillery convoys pass by night under the guns of the fort, but not without losing many men. Marmont sets down the loss at five or six men killed or wounded for each vehicle. The report of the transport of the artillery through Bard sent for insertion in the *Moniteur* was not a true version, for it was silent respecting the difficulties, the hesitations, and the losses incurred.

The passage was carried out with great prudence. The most favourable moment was chosen; the march was conducted in profound silence; and a few guns only were sent across at every attempt. It was also in favour of the French that the noise of the rush of water in the Dora drowned the sound of the guns moving, and that the Austrians could not depress their pieces sufficiently. Trucco states that in moving their guns the French profited by a terrible storm; the noise of the thunder and a sudden rise of the Dora, all assisted to deaden the sound. The storm, however, appears to have occurred on the night of the first failure. The staff officer sent by Berthier to report on the passage of the guns, Captain Menou of the artillery, complained, amongst other difficulties, of very heavy rain and a very dark night.

The operation of passing the guns through the village of Bard was dangerous, nevertheless the Austrians were unable to prevent a certain amount of success.

In the mean while, the infantry and cavalry were moving steadily onwards by the Albaredo route. First went Lannes, then Boudet, then Champeaux, Monnier, Murat, Loison, and Chambarlhac.

Bonaparte, writing to General Lacombe Saint Michel, testifies to the ease with which the artillery had passed over the Little Saint Bernard. Somehow he does not appear to have been fully aware of the practicability of this pass. Mainoni, however, had written in favour of it as follows :—

"If you desire to cross the Saint Bernard, which is not at all impossible, you will have to climb for eight hours (from Orsières) to reach the Hospice, and to allow two hours to descend to Saint Rémy. The road by the Saint Bernard to my mind is the easiest and above all others preferable if conjointly with it a column is directed to march over the Little Saint Bernard, furnished with cannon and howitzers, so that the two together may attack the fort of Bard and subdue it, thus overcoming at once all obstacles which might retard the combination and the completeness of the operations. I venture to assure you, General, that if there is actually going to be an expedition, that it is well seconded from the side of the Saint Gothard and pushed on at every point, it cannot but meet with complete success."

Marmont remarks that, had special guns been prepared for attacking Fort Bard, it would have surrendered in one day, and all the trouble would have been at an end. He also believes that all the labour of dismounting and remounting the artillery might have been avoided by a diligent reconnaissance, for the Little Saint Bernard was practicable for carriages, and six 12-prs. sent later from Chambery crossed by that pass on their carriages.

In reality the Little Saint Bernard had been insufficiently reconnoitred. Marescot had only four or five days allowed him for reconnoitring all the Alpine passes, and we may take it for certain that he had not sufficient time to perform his duty in a thorough manner.

Generals Marescot and Loison having made a careful survey of the fort of Bard, an assault was ordered by General Berthier to take place on the 26th of May at 2.30 in the morning. The direction of the attack was committed to the care of General Loison, the troops being divided into three columns.

One column, composed of 300 men of the 13th Light, led by an officer of known bravery, was to attack the first enclosure from the side of Donnaz. This column was to be accompanied by an officer of engineers with fifteen men, all carrying hatchets, who were to collect all the ladders procurable in Donnaz. After escalading the walls, this column was to move in two directions, one part going to the right to take possession of the gate of the fort, the other to the left to turn the heights.

Brigadier Dufour, with the three grenadier companies of the 58th, and three of the 60th, was directed to assault the entrance of the fort, break through the barriers, escalade the first wall, ascend the rock which commanded the gate, lower the drawbridge, burst open the gates, and penetrate by the rear into the lower battery, and into the upper either by climbing through the embrasures or by turning it by its left.

The third column was to consist of three companies which were at that time on the right bank of the Dora. They were to make a false attack, threatening to cross the river, and thus drawing the enemy's attention to that side.

Mathieu Dumas states that Bonaparte, having explained to a superior officer, chosen amongst the bravest to lead the principal attack, how he had to carry out his orders, took General Marescot aside and told him, "This officer does not understand at all what he will have to do, and the assault will consequently fail." It seems strange that the assault should still have been carried into effect notwithstanding such a hopeless forecast, and that many gallant lives should have been uselessly sacrificed.

As the signal was given, the grenadiers advanced in the most complete silence, and reached the walls. They broke down some palisades, and even began penetrating into the fort; but the alarm was given, Bernkopf directed all his batteries to open fire with case-shot, whilst hand-grenades and a murderous fire of musketry met the assailants at all points. The French were soon in disorder and forced to abandon the attack. The attempt had failed; the enemy, who had not been sufficiently harassed by the labour of the defence, was very much on the alert, and offered a vigorous resistance. The ladders also were found too short, for there had been no opportunity for measuring the depth of the ditch.

This failure proved the correctness of General Marescot's estimate. For, when called for to furnish a report on Fort Bard, he had expressed a conviction that an escalade offered a very slight prospect of success.

Bonaparte, who was present at the assault, tried to minimize this repulse, or otherwise to leave a vague idea that the attack had succeeded. The Austrian sources relate that the French retired in disorder with a total loss of 270 in killed and wounded. At any rate, on the same day (the 26th) Berthier issued an order for General Chabran to assume command of the valley of Aosta * and of the siege of Bard. As long as the fort remained in the hands of the Austrians, it constituted an obstruction in the lines of communication with France. Chabran's corps was consequently left to blockade it. This had been done in succession by the divisions of Watrin, Boudet, and Loison. It was not a pleasant prospect for General Chabran. His corps was composed principally of conscripts, and many of these, frightened by the look of the fort, deserted.

The attack, at first delayed on account of a scarcity of ammunition, was ordered to take place on the 1st of June.

---

* Chabran calls the valley of Aosta, " cette chétive vallée" (this pitiful valley). —De Cugnac, vol. i. pp. 525, 527, 533.

Everything had been done to insure success. Two 12-prs. placed by the village church opened fire at very short distance, and succeeded in demolishing the palisades, the works about the main entrance, and the lower lines; the place could hold out no longer, and capitulated that evening.

General Olivero makes the Austrian officer capitulate on an order sent to him by Melas through a spy (Giuseppe Cornaglia), when it became too evident that a prolonged defence would be of no further avail. He really capitulated—whether under orders or not—when the object of his resistance had passed, when the whole of the French army had gone by.

Professor Rolando seems to infer that since the French artillery managed to pass through Bard, a suspicion attaches to Bernkopf of having connived at the enterprise. We may more than doubt the insinuation that there was any collusion on his part. His defence was very spirited, and has met with a well-merited reward by the prominent place given to his name in all the narratives of the campaign.

The historians, who have always deep admiration for the conquerors alone, have tried to lower the reputation of the brave captain by contesting his fidelity. With a small number of men Bernkopf had for a fortnight offered a stubborn resistance, and placed the French army within an inch of destruction.

The bombardment had every day increased in intensity. Small breaches had been opened, and the walls had been so pounded that in places it was not practicable to put them into a state of repair. Nothing remained to do but to lower the flag.

The Austrian account would certainly have attributed the surrender to treachery had there been the slightest suspicion on that score. But as on this point the Austrians are absolutely silent, historians and other writers have no warrant for bringing such a cruel accusation against a brave soldier.

CHAPTER IX.

FROM IVREA TO MILAN.

Lannes attacks and carries Ivrea—The Austrians defeated on the Chiusella—They
withdraw behind the Orco—Turreau advances on Susa, but is driven back at
Avigliana—Three alternatives open to Bonaparte—Determines to march on
Milan—Expected that the news of his arrival would have extricated Massena—
Murat advances to the Sesia—Moncey's troops commence to cross the Saint
Gothard—Crossing of the Ticino—Capture of Turbigo—Some deficiencies of
the French army—The French enter Milan—Bonaparte receives an enthusiastic
reception—Unfortunate condition of Lombardy—Plan proposed by some Austrian
officers.

THE small town of Ivrea, situated on the Dora Baltea, at its
issue from the mountains, is, by the fertility of the soil, purposely
made for an army to recover after the severe toil of crossing the
Alps.   In years gone by it was of considerable strength, but it
had been gradually allowed to fall into decay.   In 1800, the
walls were in ruins, and the defences but partially armed.   As
the Austrians were far from believing that Italy could be invaded
from that side, they had made no adequate preparation for its
defence.   Nor did they attempt a combat in front of the city,
by reason of the ground being hilly and broken, which would
have necessitated a great expansion of their forces, so that, had
things not gone well, a complete rout would have speedily
followed.

Watrin was ordered to march from his position at Montestrutto on the 22nd of May, and to carry Ivrea ; for this city,
situated as it is at the opening of the valley of Aosta, was a most
important position to secure.

Ivrea is picturesquely situated on the edge of a hill crowned
by an extensive old castle with three lofty towers.   It was the
ancient Eporedia, which the Romans colonized 100 B.C., in
order to command the Alpine routes over the Great and Little
Saint Bernard.   For the last century it had not seen an enemy;
that was since it had been captured by the Duc de Vendôme in

1704. The Austrians had only thought of re-victualling it when the French were at the gates. They held the town and citadel with some 6000 men, infantry and cavalry.*

Such had been the result of the obstruction offered by Fort Bard, that when Lannes might justly have expected to meet with imposing forces, he had to attack a walled town without having a single cannon.

The attack was very brisk, and after two hours' fighting, notwithstanding a vigorous resistance, a battalion of the 22nd, led by Captain Cochet, escaladed the citadel and carried it by a bold dash with the bayonet. Its fall led to the capture of the town. Attacked in three points, the defences were soon broken down and the gates blown open. The 22nd and 40th Regiments rushed in *en masse* from all sides, and captured 300 prisoners. Lannes himself carried the gate on the right. All the Austrian guns, fourteen in number by their own account, remained in the hands of the French.

The operation lasted one day. Ivrea fell on the 22nd of May, in proof of which can be cited the fact that Hulin addressed a letter to the municipality of Ivrea that day, stating that the war commissary, Barmal, alone was authorized to serve requisitions.

The town of Ivrea was surrounded by a rampart and ditch. The citadel, situated on a height, defended the bridge over the Dora Baltea. The French found it in a tolerable state of repair. The Austrians had taken some slight steps towards placing Ivrea in a state of defence, for the loopholes showed that they had been repaired, and a large quantity of gabions and fascines were found in the citadel. There were fourteen cast guns, mounted on serviceable carriages, many rounds of gun ammunition, and a considerable quantity of powder and artillery materials. Dupont, in his report to the minister of war, states that the captured guns had been spiked by the Austrians previous to their retreat.

The citadel needed only provisions, and had Lannes arrived before the town one day later the enemy would have strongly occupied it, and nothing then but a regular siege would have put the French in possession of it.

It must naturally strike the reader with astonishment that no means were adopted by the Austrian commanders to obstruct

* General Watrin's report to General Lannes, Ivrea, 22nd of May, 1800.

the progress of the French and stop their issue from the valley of Aosta. To this supineness they owed their defeat; for it dispirited their soldiers, while it inspired the enemy with courage, and gave the French time to recover from their fatigues and complete the re-organization of their forces.

The many complaints Lannes received from the inhabitants made him issue some very stringent orders against pillaging, as it only estranged the friendship of the people, which it was so desirable to cultivate. Every delinquent was to be brought before a drumhead court-martial and sentenced to death.

Subsequent to its capture, and as the French army concentrated at Ivrea, the French detailed a field officer to command the place, to whom were attached a captain of engineers and a captain of artillery. On the 25th of May, Bonaparte named Brigadier Vignolles to assume the command of the town and district. The citadel was to be garrisoned by a battalion of Chabran's division; the 12th of the line occupied the town. A hospital for the sick and wounded was established in the citadel, where a fifteen-days' supply of provisions for 500 men was collected.

It was laid down that, should Ivrea be attacked by considerable forces, the troops in the town were to withdraw and fall back on Bard, after having placed the necessary reinforcements in the citadel.

When driven out of Ivrea, the Austrians retired on the Chiusella, where General Haddick, who had been ordered to cover Turin, met them. The general had a large force at his disposal, with a strong contingent of cavalry under the orders of Pilatti and Count Palfy. Haddick had hitherto shown himself particularly prudent; his patrols had been scouring the country, still taking great care not to be drawn into an engagement. Lannes was impatient to act, but he was restrained by the peremptory orders which he had received from Berthier.

In war, to make a good beginning is all-important. From the 22nd of May, the advanced guard of the Army of Reserve was in occupation of Ivrea, and the entry of the army into the plains of Piedmont was now secure. The First Consul was still at Aosta, and the little fort of Bard continued to offer an energetic resistance, and barred the way to the artillery.

On the morning of the 25th of May, an order was sent to Lannes to assume the offensive to the south of Ivrea, and to drive the enemy beyond Chivasso. The French troops at Ivrea were at the time disposed as follows : The advanced guard was beyond the bridge of Ivrea, its right holding the heights of Fiorano, and the left resting on the Dora. Boudet's division was on the left bank of the Dora Baltea on the road to Vercelli. All that Lannes had been able to gather about the enemy was that Haddick and De Briey were posted on the heights of Mersenasco, about two leagues beyond Ivrea, with some 5000 infantry and 4000 cavalry. Bonaparte calculated that the Austrians had at the most from 7000 to 8000 men in that direction. He hoped that by beating them it would be possible for Lannes to gather some precise news of Turreau.

Watrin's division—supported by Boudet's division with the 12th Hussars and 21st Chasseurs—set out at break of day on the 26th of May to attack the enemy strongly intrenched on the right bank of the Chiusella. To cover Turin, Haddick had occupied a very good position along the Chiusella; his right resting on the Dora, the left—passing by San Martino—went as far as Baldissero. He had established a battery of four guns to sweep the bridge, whilst other guns were placed here and there along the front. The position was also strengthened with redoubts. The Austrian troops were under De Briey, Pilatti, and Palfy, Haddick being in chief command. The regiments of Kinsky, Bannats, Tuscany, Wallis, and the King of Sardinia's guards were present in the field. The cavalry consisted of De la Tour's dragoons, several regiments of hussars, and some heavy cavalry.

The stone bridge over the Chiusella was very long and narrow ; to obtain possession of it was no easy matter. Lannes ordered his bravest men to capture it. The 6th Light attacked it boldly, but the enemy defended it with the greatest determination. Their four guns plied the attacking column with shot, whilst a musketry fire belaboured it on the flanks. The 6th got possession of it, when the regiments of Franz-Kinsky and of the Bannats rushed on them and compelled the French to abandon the bridge for a short period.

In his corps Lannes had an officer, Pavetti, already mentioned in the previous chapter. His home was at Romano, and he was consequently intimately acquainted with the locality. This officer informed Lannes that to the left of the bridge there existed a very practicable ford, and offered to lead the troops across.

After having attempted several times, but in vain, to cross the bridge under the deadly fire of the enemy's guns, the French crossed by this ford. Macon's brigade with the 6th Light rushed into the river, the water reaching nearly up to their necks, and, notwithstanding the grape and musketry which poured thick on all sides, gained the opposite shore, attacked the right of the Austrian position, and opened a heavy fire. At the same time the 28th, led by General Gency, charged the bridge in close column and compelled the Austrians to give way. Palfy, who was close to the bridge charging with some squadrons of cavalry, received a mortal wound. He was carried to Romano, where he died.

Haddick possibly believed it dangerous to bring on a general action against what he imagined a superior enemy; so he ordered a retreat. The French followed up their first advantage, and pursued the Austrians up to Romano, where the latter had taken post on the heights. The Austrians, who had found the ground close to the Chiusella very unsuited for cavalry, as it was covered with bushes and underwood, had withdrawn to a better position in the plain, which extends between Romano and the hills of Montalengo. It was there that 4000 cavalry rushed at the French. The Austrians executed several brilliant charges, but all void of results. The 40th under Malher, and the 22nd directed by Brigadier-General Schreiber, having forded the river on the right of the original position and some way below the bridge, came up in time, and met the several charges with the bayonet, until the arrival of the 12th Hussars and the 21st Chasseurs, who rushed on the enemy and put an end to the combat.

Boudet, who with his division had supported Watrin, and had moved up to Romano, was ordered to pursue, which he did up to the top of the mountains near Foglizzo. The Austrians retired very speedily, and it was found impossible to come up with them.

A point worth noticing in this engagement is the diversity of statements regarding the losses sustained by the French. Watrin, who regrets that the troops suffered heavily, sets down the number of killed and wounded at 300. Hulin estimates the casualties in killed and wounded at 400. Berthier reduces the figures to 250, and Bonaparte to 200! The Austrian account makes out the loss on their side to have been 348 men and

216 horses, against a loss of 1700 men on the French side. A staff officer of the Austrian army, who simply signs himself W., in a narrative, "La Campagne des Français en Italie en 1800," published at Leipzig in 1801, goes further. He gives 400 men as the losses of the Austrians, and makes the French casualties amount to 2500 men, 300 prisoners, and 300 horses. Troops which retire precipitately, as Boudet relates that the Austrians did, rarely inflict such a heavy loss on their opponents. On the other hand, had the Austrians so maltreated the French, they had no excuse for hurrying away from the battlefield. If we assume that their figures are correct, they show that the Austrians lacked that spirit of tenacity which is the highest quality in fighting men, whilst the French marched on to victory, entirely heedless of its cost.

An indirect proof that the French losses were nothing like the Austrian accounts would make us believe, is that Lannes, who made such a fuss about his losses at Montebello, was silent on this point. Surely he would have said something had they been extraordinarily heavy.

Haddick could not be made to believe that he had had to contend only with Bonaparte's advanced guard. He thought he had before him at least 20,000 men, so he sent word to Melas that, if he did not come to his assistance, Piedmont and Lombardy would fall into the hands of the French. This was on the 26th of May, and on this very day Melas arrived in Turin, where he was greeted with the announcement of Haddick's defeat at Chiusella.

In the narratives of this memorable campaign, the dates are very contradictory. The extract of the *Œstreichische Militärische Zeitschrift*, quoted by De Cugnac, vol. ii. p. 27, states that Bonaparte and Berthier had arrived at Ivrea, and that the battle of the Chiusella commenced at four in the morning of the 26th of May. Gachot goes even further, for he states on page 200, "Behind the 40th, Bonaparte, Berthier, Duhesme, Boudet, and the staffs of these generals, at one moment threatened, drew their swords and prepared to charge the enemy, who, being fired upon at point blank, and sabred on the left by the Chasseurs, retired." * He also states that the First Consul re-entered Ivrea at six in the evening, . . . that an officer of La Tour's dragoons had recognized Bonaparte,

* Edouard Gachot, "La Deuxième Campagne d'Italie," pp. 220, 222, 224.

having been very close to him in the neighbourhood of Romano.

In opposition to all this, we find Bonaparte writing a letter to the Consuls from Ivrea on the 27th of May, in which he informs them, "I arrived yesterday evening at Ivrea." Statements from other officers fix the same date. On the 26th of May, the day of the engagement on the Chiusella, an attempt was made to carry Fort Bard by assault, at which the First Consul and Berthier were present. It was after this attempt had failed that the two officers left for Ivrea, where the headquarters of the army were only established on the evening of the 26th. General Marescot, in his order-book, writes from d'Arnaz, under date of the 26th of May, " The Headquarters left this morning."

It appears very strange that Marmont, in his " Mémoires," should pass over in silence the engagements at the Chiusella or at Turbigo. He states : " We entered Milan without striking a blow " ("Et nous entrâmes à Milan sans coup férir").—Livre v. p. 122.

Bonaparte ordered Lannes to remain in observation in front of Chivasso. Lannes appears to have been keen to occupy Turin and to push on as far as Asti ; the object of such a move being evidently to effect Massena's deliverance. It had, nevertheless, the great inconvenience of leaving the Austrians masters of Lombardy and of abandoning Moncey, Béthencourt, and Lechi, who might be attacked and overpowered by superior forces. This Bonaparte was loth to do. He had resolved first to occupy the left bank of the Po, to sweep the enemy out of the north of Italy, then to concentrate four or five divisions at Piacenza, and to hasten to Genova.

Lannes on the 27th heard the thunder of cannon in the rear of Turin ; it was the combat at Avigliano.

Haddick had retired to the right bank of the Orco, leaving Lobkowitz's regiment of dragoons on the left bank. Melas had given him orders to dispute every inch of ground, and to fall back on Turin as slowly as possible ; always keeping up close communication with Field-Marshal Kaim.

On the 28th Lannes descended from Foglizzo and made for the banks of the Orco ; under a brisk cannonade, he approached closer and closer to the bridge on that river. The Austrian dragoons withdrew across the bridge, to which they set fire as they abandoned it. This move of the French added strength to the already-formed opinion that Bonaparte intended to advance in the direction of Turin, with a view of effecting a junction with Turreau. The Austrians expected to be attacked by the French the following day ; but Lannes made no move on the 29th, and remained quietly at Chivasso. On the Po he found a very large number of boats loaded with rice and corn, and these he appropriated.

Bonaparte himself proceeded to Chivasso, where he held a review of the advanced guard, and praised the troops for all the services they had rendered. He told them how the French cavalry was about to be concentrated ; how it would attack the Austrian cavalry, so as to wrench from it its pretended superiority in bravery and in manœuvring. By his presence at Chivasso he evidently sought to lead Melas astray, and to strengthen more and more the idea that the French were bent on marching on Turin. The Austrians were to be mystified ; the veritable project was to be concealed from them. Appearances were to lead them to believe that the French army intended to act in the direction of Turin—a belief which gained strength from Turreau's operations on the 22nd and on the 24th of May.

According to the bulletin of the 30th of August, the Austrians were led to conceive that the French intended to cross the Po in the neighbourhood of Chivasso, so as to get to Asti and intercept the troops retiring from Nice. To frustrate this object their troops at Chivasso had been strongly reinforced from Turin. One can form a good idea of the embarrassment of the Austrian general, and also his astonishment when the impending attack was not delivered.

Melas, however, was not as easily led into error as Napoleon in his correspondence would wish us to believe. He had sent reconnaissances in various quarters, and made use of reliable spies, by which measures he had on the 28th come to learn of the evacuation of the country round Ivrea and the march of the French on Vercelli.

Whilst Lannes with the advanced guard was directed to threaten Turin, Murat was receiving orders to send reconnaissances in the direction of Biella and Santhia, being supported by Monnier, who was to take post on the main road to Santhia, at a point three leagues from Ivrea.

Berthier, when he was at Ivrea, looking at the many rivers

which water the plains of Piedmont and Lombardy, and disturbed by the absence of a bridging equipage—for it had been considered impracticable to bring the pontoons over the Alps —devised the formation of a corps of pontoniers, to be under the command of the chief engineer. For this service every division was made to contribute fifty men, taken from those who in ordinary life had been accustomed to the navigation of rivers.

All Bonaparte's generals were contributing their share towards the success of the campaign. Turreau, advancing from Savoy by the Mont Cenis route, opened a way for his column to Susa.*

He attacked the Austrians under Lamarsaille at the village of Gravière on the 22nd of May. A very spirited combat ensued, and victory for a time was uncertain. Led by Adjutant-General Liebault, the French, after several attempts, at last turned in a very able manner the Fort Saint François, carried all the positions by assault, and remained masters of the village of Gravière. The same evening at ten o'clock the garrison of Fort la Brunette capitulated.

Bonaparte had sent to inform Turreau that he expected to be at Ivrea on the 18th of May; that should the Austrians concentrate their forces they would necessarily reduce the troops in his front; and that he should then gather as many men as possible and push on to Susa. Turreau was to place himself in communication with the Army of Reserve by way of Largo and Ponte, to which towns reconnaissances would be sent to seek news of his column.

The intention was to call up Turreau's column to Ivrea, and unite it with the rest of the army. Turreau was to march by his left, keeping as clear as possible of Turin, still selecting a road practicable for artillery. On the 22nd of May, Bonaparte, writing to Berthier, enjoins him to send country people forward to ascertain if there was any news of General Turreau.

The general had planted his column between Susa and Turin, watching the Austrians, who occupied that corner of Piedmont.

---

* In p. 27 of his narrative of the battle of Marengo, Berthier states that Turreau had 2500 men, which he had gathered from the garrisons of the Dauphiné, and with whom he had gone in the direction of Susa, after having forced the pass of Cabrières.

On the 24th, he made a forward movement as far as Avigliano, but he had to contend against superior numbers, and was beaten. After this he took up a defensive position some few miles to the east of Susa.

Turreau's force by the nature of the country was separated from the main army throughout the campaign. Nevertheless, it rendered important services in leading the enemy to a false conclusion.

When, on the 22nd of May, the head of Turreau's column showed itself descending from the Mont Cenis, it was but natural that the Austrians would have considered it to be the advanced guard of the main French army, which was advancing by one of the most practicable passes—that of Mont Cenis. Lannes's party they would regard only as a detachment intended for the purpose of effecting a diversion. In this they were naturally led by the fact that the Mont Cenis road was more direct for troops intended for the relief of Genova than the one which led over the Saint Bernard. Being more practicable for artillery, they believed it was the one Bonaparte would have selected above all others for the passage of his main army.

The Austrians had sufficient troops round Turin to check Turreau and crush Lannes, thus laying bare the rear of the French army. It may, however, be even more than doubted if Bonaparte at any time intended to retire by the way of the Great Saint Bernard. He certainly left a small garrison at the Hospice, but that did not mean anything, for he had the Simplon and the Saint Gothard routes open to him, and occupied by Béthencourt and Moncey.

As to the future of Bard, the First Consul had written to Berthier: "When you will have mastered it, do not suffer the supplies to be wasted; they should be placed under guard with an able commander. You understand that should we change our line of operations, it will be extremely important to have this small fort, which closes the valley and assures us the means of resuming when we like the line of communications by Aosta. When the campaign will have taken a different character, then we may get rid of it by having it razed."

What Bonaparte had most to fear was a rapid concentration of the Austrian army. The danger, however, was not great. The Austrians were pretty well scattered, and, Genova being at the last gasps, the Austrians were evidently loth to raise the

siege. The orders for the concentration were issued on the
31st of May. Ott probably received his on the 2nd of June,
and had he obeyed at once without waiting for the capitulation,
he might have been at Montebello on the 7th, instead of on the
9th. On the latter day Lannes was already across the Po.
Ott's delay was disastrous.

The Austrian staff at Turin had shown little enterprise in
gathering information, and had readily come to believe that the
strength of the French in the valley of Aosta did not exceed
6000 men. When Melas returned from Nice he was dissatisfied
with their sluggishness, and it is stated that he reprimanded
them severely.

The French army was at Ivrea, the Alps had been surmounted, and Bonaparte had left behind him only the fort of
Bard, which Chabran, with his 5000 men, was directed to blockade
and reduce. It remained now for Bonaparte to decide as to
his future movements. Three plans were open to him. The
first was to move to his right, to form a junction with Turreau
and attack the Austrians. The second plan was to cross the
Po by means of the boats which Lannes had secured, and to
advance to the relief of Massena, who was still holding out at
Genova. The third was to march eastward across the Ticino,
to form a junction with Moncey, and to capture Milan and all
the stores and reserve parks of the Austrians.

The first plan was rejected because Bonaparte had somehow
or other come to the conclusion that he was not strong enough
to cope with Melas, and that it was hazardous to expose himself
to a defeat with no safe line of retreat as long as Fort Bard
continued to hold out. Bonaparte knew, nevertheless, that a
large Austrian force was blockading Genova, and that another
was in front of Suchet, on the Var; consequently, that if he
made a junction with Turreau he would be stronger than Melas,
having besides a line of retreat by the Mont Cenis open to him;
a line easier by far than that of the Saint Bernard.

On the 24th of May, Bonaparte wrote a letter to General
Brune, who was then at Dijon, which shows how utterly un-
founded was the opinion that Melas could bring larger numbers
against him, and how by rapid movements, of which no one
was a greater master than himself, he could have beaten in
detail the various parties of the Austrian army as they retired
from Genova and the Var.

" You will find enclosed," wrote Bonaparte, " the bulletin of the army.

" The enemy appears surprised by our progress. He barely believes it. He hardly knows where he is. You can judge for yourself. Look at the enemy's situation on the 18th of May : 12,000 men at Nice ; 6000 at Savona and along the Genovese Riviera ; 25,000 in front of Genova ; 8000 at Susa, Pinerolo, etc. ; 3000 in the valley of Aosta ; 8000 opposite the Simplon and the Saint Gothard—all that are infantry; two regiments of hussars at Genova and at Nice; four regiments close to Turin ; the remainder cantoned at Acqui and in the interior of Lombardy.

" He has remained thus up to the moment when we arrived at Ivrea.

" The 3000 men who were in the valley have been beaten and scattered. All the corps which were on the side of Susa and of Pinerolo have moved to between Turin and Ivrea. Nice, therefore, has in all probability been evacuated at the present moment. They even write to me that Melas must have arrived at Turin ; but that is not certain.[*]

"I calculate on having all the army concentrated at Ivrea by the 26th or the 27th, forming altogether about 33,000 men. I shall be master of the whole country from the Dora Baltea up to the Sesia.

" The same day Moncey will cross the Saint Gothard with 15,000 men.

" Suchet and Massena, who have been apprised of the movement, will follow the enemy as soon as they see him getting weak in front of them.

" The castle and the town of Ivrea are ours, as much as the outer fort of Bard. The Hungarian captain, with his 400 Croats, has retired into a keep, where he has a dozen guns which defend the road ; we are going to bombard him.

" Should we have some success, this will only be a beginning. You are going to organize an efficient army corps, with which at the beginning of July you will have to play a fine *rôle.*

[*] Bonaparte was well informed. On the 24th of May, from Aosta, we find him writing to the Consuls, " A despatch which I have received from Nice and the news which comes to me from Ivrea show me that on the 19th Melas was at Nice, not alarmed by anything. . . . I am assured that he arrived by diligence at Turin yesterday in all haste."

" Push forward without remissness the arming and clothing of the conscripts as they arrive.

" You will find yourself commanding the Army of Reserve the moment it effects its junction with the Army of Italy."

It is well to look at Melas's movements in consequence of an intercepted despatch of Massena's, which spoke of expecting to be delivered by Berthier's army. On this information Melas, who was on the Var, ordered three brigades to reascend the Col di Tenda and march on Turin—an order which was cancelled the following day on the receipt of a contradictory letter, which stated that Berthier was marching on the Var with the object of reinforcing Suchet. On the 18th, however, all doubt was removed by reason of a report sent by Kaim. This announced the approach of a considerable corps coming from the Valais. On the receipt of this news, Melas returned to his original project; he sent Knesevich's brigade to reinforce Kaim, and directed Zach to repair to Turin. He himself quitted Nice for Turin, and was to be followed there by Auersberg's brigade. O'Reilly's cavalry division, composed of Palfy's and Nobile's brigades, was also attached to Kaim.

It would be hard to explain why Bonaparte, who was so quick to discern the right move in a campaign, neglected to take advantage of his initiative and abstained from falling on the Austrians whilst they were occupied in effecting their concentration. Of the state of dispersion of the enemy he must have been fully aware, and the best proof is the above letter to Brune. Without counting Turreau's forces, he would have had 33,000 men with whom to meet about 11,000 of the enemy.

In what Napoleon wrote at Saint Helena, he argues that, of the three alternatives open to him, the first was contrary to the real principles of war because it amounted to attacking Melas, who had with him considerable forces. But by his own showing, by his letter to General Brune, Melas had no more than from 11,000 to 15,000 men, who could have been easily dealt with by Bonaparte's army before they had time to be reinforced by any troops coming up from Nice or Genova.

When making a study of the alternative roads leading from Switzerland into Italy, Bonaparte had given up the Simplon and Saint Gothard routes simply with the object of shortening his line of operations. This was because the dire condition of Massena's forces called for a speedy arrival of the Army of

Reserve. The great parade made to hasten to Massena's assistance seems to have been all of a sudden forgotten; possibly owing to the risk of dipping into Piedmontese territory, where all the strong places were held by Austrian garrisons, without having any safe line of communications. This may have been deemed a risk hardly worth incurring, considering Bonaparte's uncertainty whether Massena could hold out for a sufficient time or not.

Massena agreed to evacuate Genova on the 4th of June. So, as it eventually turned out, Bonaparte would have had plenty of time had he adopted the second alternative open to him, and might have saved his lieutenant from the humiliation of an evacuation. Seeing that, as it was, Melas, though not imminently threatened, sent orders to Ott to raise the siege, it is fair to believe that the order would have been despatched sooner had the French made any move in the direction of the Maritime Alps.

The second alternative was dangerous because of the uncertainty whether Massena still held out at Genova, and of the ignorance of the enemy's movements.

The two first projects having been rejected, the third remained. This Bonaparte evidently considered the most promising—the junction of his army with the corps Moncey was bringing from the Rhine, which was calculated to raise the Army of Reserve to over 50,000 effective men. It was on this that he had so much calculated from the very beginning of the campaign.

Bonaparte's aim was more vast than the simple raising of the blockade of Genova—the rescue of a few thousand starving troops—it was to make the Army of Reserve strong by uniting the two main forces—those he had brought over the Great Saint Bernard and those that Moncey was bringing from the Army of the Rhine; to capture the enemy's magazines and sources of supply, and to cut off Melas entirely from his base and the Austrian empire.

The strategic aim of Bonaparte's operations was to gain possession of the enemy's line of communications. The great danger in such a manœuvre, generally speaking, is that the assailant lays himself open to lose his own. It was this consideration, possibly, which prevented Bonaparte from operating against Melas when he got to Chivasso.

He has been reproached for having gone to Milan, and thus deserted Massena and left Genova to its fate. But he may have calculated that he would have effected the raising of the blockade indirectly by threatening the rear of the Austrians, and that Melas would have withdrawn his troops from Genova the moment the Army of Reserve appeared in Lombardy and threatened his line of communications. This withdrawal would have enabled Massena to gather together all his disposable forces, and pass from the defensive to the offensive.

The First Consul's great aim was to sever the Austrian communications with the Mincio. This he was resolved to do, and then to compel his adversary to fight at a disadvantage when he had no longer a secure line of retreat. He thought there was little to be gained by saving Genova, whereas by beating Melas he could at one single stroke recover the greater portion of his former conquests in Italy.

Up to the 24th of May, it was fair to imagine that Bonaparte intended to concentrate his army at Ivrea; and that, having effected this, he would assail the Austrian forces nearest to him in Piedmont, and then the rest in succession. All at once, he altered his plans; the Army of Reserve was made to march on Milan. Acting in concert with Moncey and Béthencourt, the army was to clear the Milanese provinces of the enemy, capture his magazines, besiege his fortresses, and then attend on the Po till Melas came to recover his communications.*

When at Saint Helena, the fallen emperor, who knew well how his strategy in the Marengo campaign had been criticized, pleaded hard in favour of his march to Milan. It is interesting to examine these arguments.†

"The headquarters of the Austrian army were at Turin. But half of the enemy's forces were in front of Genova, and the other half was supposed to be, and was, indeed, on the march, coming by way of the Col di Tenda to reinforce such as were at Turin. Under this circumstance, what action will the First Consul take? Will he march on Turin to drive Melas out of it, combine with Turreau, and in this manner find safe communications with France and its arsenals of Grenoble and Briançon?

---

* "Mémoires de Napoléon—Correspondence de Napoléon," cxxx. pp. 375–377.

† Melas did not dream of a French march on Milan. Writing to Lord Keith on the 23rd of May, he states: "The enemy has surrounded the fort of Bard, and has advanced as far as Ivrea. It is pretty clear that his aim is to deliver Massena."

Or will he construct a bridge at Chivasso, profiting by the boats which fortune has thrown into his hands, and make direct for Genova to raise the blockade of that important place ? Or else, leaving Melas in his rear, will he cross the Sesia and the Ticino, go to Milan, and on the Adda make his junction with Moncey's corps, amounting to 15,000 men, which was then coming from the Army of the Rhine and had descended from the Saint Gothard ?

"Of these three alternatives, the first was contrary to the real principles of war, because Melas had with him very considerable forces. Consequently the French army ran the risk of giving battle, having no safe retreat, inasmuch as the fort of Bard had not yet been captured. Besides, supposing that Melas had abandoned Turin and fallen back on Alessandria, the campaign had failed; either army would have found itself in a natural position, the French army resting on Mont Blanc and the Dauphiné, whilst that of Melas would have had its left at Genova and in her rear the important places of Mantua, Piacenza, and Milan.

"The second alternative did not appear practicable. How venture in the midst of an army as powerful as the Austrian was, between the Po and Genova, without having any line of operation, any safe line of retreat ?

"The third alternative, on the contrary, offered every advantage. The French army, mistress of Milan, could lay hands on all the magazines, on all the depôts, on all the hospitals of the hostile army; * it formed a junction with the left, which was commanded by General Moncey; there was a safe line of retreat by the Simplon and the Saint Gothard. The Simplon led through the Valais and on to Sion, where all the depôts of supplies for the army had been directed. The Saint Gothard led to Switzerland, of which we had been in possession for the last two years, and which covered the Army of the Rhine, at ʋhat moment on the Iller. In such a position the French general could act according to his will. Were Melas with his united army to march from Turin on the Sesia and on

---

* Bonaparte always counted on the supplies accumulated by his adversary. He acted in accordance with his answer given as a boy at an examination, when he was proposed the following question : "What measures would you adopt, in case you were besieged in a fortified place and destitute of provisions ? " "As long," he replied, " as there were any in the enemy's camp, I should never be at a loss for a supply."

the Ticino, the French army could deliver battle with the immense advantage that, should it come off victorious, Melas, without retreat, would be pursued and thrown back on Savoy, and, in the case of the French army being beaten, it would retire by the Simplon and the Saint Gothard. Should Melas, as it was natural to suppose, move in the direction of Alessandria to combine there with the army coming from Genova, it was to be expected, in advancing to meet him, and in crossing the Po, to anticipate him and to deliver battle, the French army having its rear safe on the river and Milan, the Simplon and the Saint Gothard ; whilst the Austrian army, having its retreat cut off and having no communication with Mantua and Austria, would be exposed to be hurled back on the mountains of the Riviera di Ponente, and to be totally destroyed or captured at the foot of the Alps, at the Col di Tenda or in the neighbourhood of Nice.

"Lastly, by adopting the third alternative, if, once master of Milan, it suited the French general to let Melas go by, and to remain between the Po, the Adda, and the Ticino, he had in this way, without fighting a battle, reconquered Lombardy and Piedmont, the Maritime Alps, the Riviera di Genova, and caused the blockade of this latter city to be raised : these were very important results."

An ordinary general would most probably have taken the first alternative. Bonaparte selected the third, and in this he was greatly favoured by the slowness of his adversary.

The Duc de Valmy, in his "Histoire de la Campagne de 1800," offers the following observations : Arrived on Italian soil, and at two or three marches at most from the enemy, the First Consul began to entertain doubts ; he was tormented by anxieties. Where was the Army of Italy? What were Massena and Suchet about ? Where was Melas ? What plans was he likely to adopt? Nothing was absolutely certain ; the only thing that appeared most probable was that the Austrian commander-in-chief would manœuvre so as to escape from the Army of Reserve, and evade fighting a general engagement which would restore Italy to Bonaparte.

In this state of uncertainty, Bonaparte determined to guard at the same time all the passages of which Melas might avail himself in order to regain the line of the Mincio and Mantua, and to observe the left of the Po, towards which Melas must work back. He adopted the plan of capturing Milan, of watching the main road from Genova by which the Austrian army was bound to come, placing himself at Stradella in the centre of the communications which he intended to close.

Some writers have admired these dispositions of General Bonaparte, others have blamed this unusual dispersion of his forces when the moment was fast approaching when he would need all the troops at his disposal. If it was certain that Melas sought to avoid a battle, no objection perhaps could be raised to Bonaparte's plan. But this dispersal was very risky in the opposite alternative; if the Austrian general, intending to offer battle, gathered all his forces around him.

The possession of Milan could not fail to produce a great moral impression both on the Italians and the Imperialists, and to renew and add fresh lustre to the halo of glory which encircled the brow of the First Consul.* The junction with Moncey would raise the French forces to full 50,000 men on one hand, and on the other open a safe retreat over the Saint Gothard and the Simplon in case of disaster. The magazines and reserve parks established by the Austrians lay exposed to immediate capture in the unprotected cities of Lombardy.

It is all very well to applaud Bonaparte's manœuvres, and to approve of his having closed every line of communication the Austrians had before he delivered battle. We should not lose sight, however, of the fact that the occupation of Milan was only a minor operation; that the bulk of the Austrian forces were in Piedmont, and still remained to be beaten; that by his march eastward Bonaparte gave Melas time to concentrate his forces, whereas he should have taken advantage of their state of dispersion to beat them in detail. The march on Milan was time lost, and in effecting that move he was not true to his principles, which were to seek for the main body of the enemy and to beat it in a general action.

A campaign can only be rapidly brought to a conclusion by the complete destruction of the organized forces of the enemy, and, where the circumstances are particularly favourable, it is a grave professional error to undertake unnecessary operations. The question naturally arises: Would a battle fought in the end of May with superior forces have had better ulterior results than the one Bonaparte fought on the 14th of June?

A commentator holds, with good reason, that, had the First

---

* Rose calls the march on Milan a dramatic stroke.

Consul waited for Moncey so as to operate with one compact body of 50,000 men, the plan he followed might have seemed the most preferable. But if he had afterwards to cross the Po with only 29,000 men, as he did on the 7th of June, he could have done that just as well in May, whilst Elsnitz and Ott, being busy in Liguria, were not to be feared. There was nothing then to prevent his crossing the Po with 35,000 men about Cambio, and directing Moncey to come down by forced marches by Varese to Milan and Pavia, to cover the communications by the bridges and to support the army, had such a measure been necessary. In fact, Moncey had nothing to fear from Vukassevich and Laudon, who were both inferior to his two divisions.*

If there is possibly a sound principle in the art of war, it is in the concentration of superior forces at the decisive point. This principle Bonaparte neglected, and it nearly cost him dear.

In 1805, he wrote to Murat, " *On ne doit rien risquer, et la première de toutes les règles est d'avoir la supériorité numérique.*" The Army of Reserve being very badly off with regard to resources, the prospect of appropriating the resources of the enemy was very tempting. The price, however, paid for this —that is to say, the delay in attacking, a delay which Melas could turn to profitable account by concentrating his forces—was very great.

Bonaparte's march on Milan may be described, as some writers have described it, as a stroke of genius, which would not have been conceived by an ordinary general. Still, no ordinary general would have ever come in for any blame had he followed a different course, and sought the enemy's army after the occupation of Ivrea, to beat it before its concentration had been completed.

Gachot makes the new plan of operations by Milan to have been settled at a conference held in the Royal College of Ivrea, on the evening of the 26th of May, at which Bonaparte, Berthier, and Murat were present.† Campana makes Bonaparte take that

---

* See footnote p. 195, vol. xiii., Jomini, " Histoire des Guerres de la Révolution."

† " Il tient, au collége royal, avec Berthier et Murat, une longue conférence. À onze heures, une nouvelle marche de l'armée de réserve est copiée par Bourrienne, et Murat s'eloigne dans la nuit."—Gachot, " La Deuxième Campagne d'Italie," p. 222.

resolution on the 24th of May, and this is borne out by the
following paragraph of a letter which Bonaparte wrote to Moncey
from Aosta on the 24th of May, 1800 : "Attack the 7th or the
8th; go on to Belinzona, to Locarno and Lugano. It is very
possible that we shall be on the Ticino by the 9th."

The idea of undertaking a march on Milan can be traced
further back, even before the route to be followed had been
settled. The intention of doing so is contained in some indications issued to the nominal commander-in-chief of the Army
of Reserve. Bonaparte writes from Paris, under date of the
27th of April: "Besides, it is possible that it may be no longer
Milan where it will be necessary to go, but we may be compelled
to go with all possible speed to Tortona, so as to free Massena,
who, in case he should be beaten, will be shut up in Genova,
where he has provisions for thirty days. It is consequently by
the Saint Bernard that I desire that they shall pass."

The march on Milan was in contemplation when Bonaparte
predicted to Bourrienne, before the commencement of the
campaign, where he would beat Melas.

As we have already seen, the First Consul made a great
point of drawing a body of troops from Moreau's army with
which to complete his own. It was only natural, therefore,
that he should wish to effect a junction with this force. This he
could only do by going before it, and meeting it as it descended
into Lombardy.

In a letter of instructions issued by Berthier to General
Dupont, his chief of the staff, dated the 14th of May, Berthier
says : " You will instruct the general officer commanding at the
Simplon that the army now at Ivrea will probably march by
its left on the Ticino, when he must impose on the enemy with
regard to the number of his forces, and harass him by attacking
his posts, though all this should be done without imprudence.
Moncey will likewise have to be informed that the army will go
direct from Ivrea to Milan by the shortest route."

All this and more appears to show that the movement on
Milan was part of a settled purpose, and had been decided before
the troops actually began to climb the slopes of the Alps.

Bonaparte's march on Milan has been very severely criticized
by some writers. Bulow, on the other hand, calls it one of the
most able manœuvres which have ever been made.

Jomini writes : " Leaving an observing screen before Chivasso and Trino, Bonaparte determined to cross the Ticino, to inundate Lombardy like a torrent, to drive back up to the guns of Mantua the corps which held it, so as to facilitate a junction with Moncey, who, on the 27th of May, was already descending from the Saint Gothard. This daring plan, calculated with rare precision of the time needed for its execution, met with a complete success, notwithstanding the divergent marches which it led to afterwards."

Rocquancourt holds that a march through Piedmont, with the avowed object of proceeding to the relief of Massena, overcoming all the troops Bonaparte might come across on the way, could only lead to moderate results, by no means commensurate with the greatness of the enterprise and the difficulties already overcome. It was for this reason that the First Consul, in place of manœuvring by his right, and approaching Turin, accorded the preference to an advance on Milan and Piacenza, which would place him on the most direct communications of his adversary, whilst at the same time it was calculated to hasten his much-desired junction with Moncey. By following this course he would acquire a large base and all sorts of resources and means.[*]

Thiers believes that the march on Milan was conceived with the principal object of concentrating the French forces before blocking Melas's communications.[†]

Hamley views the flank march on Milan in this guise. Bonaparte's intention was to drive back that portion of the Austrian army which lay north of the Po, and to effect a junction with Moncey's corps. He hoped to be able to keep his design from the enemy till he had thrown a force across the Po at Piacenza. Then the Austrians would be cut off entirely from the Mincio, and any concentration of their forces, which must ensue for the recovery of their communications, would go towards relieving Genova, and at the same time would enable Suchet to form a junction with Massena. Genova, however, was known to be *in extremis;* it might have fallen any day, thus rendering the last part of the plan of no avail.

Humanity and gratitude, if nothing else, should have made Bonaparte, one would think, overcome every difficulty, and get

* J. Rocquancourt, "Cours Complet d'Art et Histoire Militaires," tome ii. p. 460.

† Thiers, "Consulat et Empire," vol. ii. p. 386.

to Genova. But he turned to his left, and thus put off for eight or ten days the relief of that city.

A man like Bonaparte, who was endowed with such extraordinary insight, whose calculations were so far-reaching, whose intentions were so distinct, and whose intellect was so clear, cannot be judged on the same lines as ordinary men. The object he had in view was to interpose between Melas and Vienna, and to cut him from his base on the Mincio. This was the real scope of his move to Milan.

If he exaggerated anything it was Massena's power of resistance. He would not, otherwise, have sent repeated instructions to him as well as to Suchet, urging them to pursue the Austrians vigorously on the first indication of a backward movement.

The recall of the Austrian troops from Genova as part of the general concentration of the Austrian army was what Bonaparte calculated upon for the relief of Massena. What more natural than for him to believe that the Austrians would have been withdrawn from Genova as soon as they found that their rear was dangerously threatened? This withdrawal did come, but it came too late.

In war, what has to be looked for is an adequate result. Bonaparte's aim was not to relieve the troops of the Army of Italy blockaded in Genova, it was a much higher one : to recover as quickly as possible all the possessions in Italy secured to France by the Treaty of Campo Formio.

It was just the difference between genius and mediocrity. Genius will often overlook small results when it beholds greater ones further ahead. The relief of the Army of Italy, desirable as it was, was for him an object of only secondary consideration. If we look at the campaign carried out in 1800 in this light, we are bound to admit that the march to Milan was in conformity with the dictates of war. It aimed not only at cutting Melas from his base of operations, but in placing him in a dire position between the Army of Italy and the Army of Reserve.

The magnitude of the enterprise justified, we think, Bonaparte's neglect of his gallant comrade struggling against all kinds of difficulties at Genova, and the non-fulfilment of the promise which he had made to him. There can be no doubt that he trusted too much to the news of his arrival in Italy alone sufficing to liberate Massena, in consequence of the scare produced by the sudden apparition of the derided Army of Reserve. And this it would have done, if Melas had not delayed too long the concentration of his army.

Bonaparte never for a moment realized the pitiable state to which famine and the horrors of the siege had reduced Massena's troops. Were such troops capable of undertaking fresh efforts? Granted that their courage was still unimpaired when they proudly marched out of the city they had so gallantly held, they were nevertheless in a state of destitution. Where could the commissariat officers obtain the necessary provisions and forage for a forward movement in a country which had been denuded of everything?

As for Suchet, what effort could he make, considering the exhausted state of the country through which he had to move? —a narrow belt of land, with the mountains on one side and the sea on the other. This is fully exposed by the statement made by Massena to the First Consul in the early part of February—

"The army is absolutely bare and shoeless. . . . We have not a grain of forage, nor provisions of any description, no means of transport whatever. . . . Liguria has no provisions of any kind, everything has gone (*est eperissé*). I have placed the troops on half rations; I myself have set the example." *
Saint Cyr, addressing the mutinous soldiers at the gates of Genova, in the previous December, told them, "Have you forgotten that you have made a desert between your present position and France?"—a fact which of itself alone brought them back to a sense of duty.

If Bonaparte was very keen to keep his communications secure, why should not Suchet have been equally careful? For all that, he has been reproached for having undertaken the siege of Savona. But could he well leave 1000 Austrians there masters of his communications with France? After all, were Gazan's men, the starved garrison of Genova, troops fit for any great exertion?

The presence of Suchet's advanced guard at Acqui, as will be shown hereafter, had a very important effect on the issue of the battle of Marengo; an effect which must be justly estimated, for to the reduction of the Austrian cavalry on the 14th of June Melas could with good reason attribute part of his defeat.

Bonaparte remained insensible to Massena's earnest appeal.

* De Cugnac, vol. i. p. 9.

The general had written on the 23rd of April: "I implore
you, Citizen Consul, come to our assistance! The handful of
brave men that I command here, by its constancy and its
devotedness, well deserves all your solicitude." *

Henri Martin writes on this point: "He had imposed untold
sacrifices on the Army of Liguria, which had been accepted
with an admirable abnegation. But these sacrifices and this
devotedness imposed on him in turn an absolute obligation—
the obligation of saving the defenders of Genova. He was pretty
sure of being able to trample over Melas, and afterwards to overpower the general who directed the siege of Genova. He had
already done something even more difficult.

"Bonaparte, however, did nothing of the kind. He abandoned Massena and his soldiers. He immolated them to the
success of a more grandiose and hazardous plan which he had
conceived. He desired no longer only to beat the Austrian army,
but to annihilate it at a single blow by cutting off every possible
retreat." †

Who can say but that the idea contained in the following
words, uttered by Bonaparte, may not have been a reason for
marching on Milan: "But it is necessary to be in force before
going to provoke (*d'aller provoquer*) M. de Melas"?

The scarcity of artillery and ammunition may have been
another of the principal causes which decided him to march
into Lombardy. We find, in fact, on the 24th of May, Berthier
demanding instructions, and soliciting to be informed whether
it was to be a march to the right to join Turreau, or by the left
to join Moncey, so as to get reinforced in guns from the Saint
Gothard or from Susa.

On the same day it was decided to march on Milan. In
conjunction with Moncey's and Béthencourt's troops, which
constituted the left of the French forces, Bonaparte's army
was to sweep the enemy out of Milanese territory, capture his
magazines, besiege his fortresses, and wait on the Po till Melas
should come with his army to recover his lost communications.

There certainly appears some inconsistency between the
march on Milan and the line of route over the Alps chosen for
the Army of Reserve. What decided Bonaparte to select the

* De Cugnac, "Campagne de l'Armée de Réserve en 1800," vol. i. p. 275.
† Henri Martin, "Histoire de France depuis 1789 jusqu'à nos jours," tome iii.
p. 115.

Great Saint Bernard was that, had the choice of the route been allowed to fall on the Simplon or on the Saint Gothard, it would have entailed a longer march and taken more time to go to Massena's aid. Having purposely adopted the shorter route, the object held in view when the selection was made seems, after the Alps had been surmounted, to have been thought no longer of any material consequence.

Bonaparte, at the head of 33,000 men, could have destroyed the force Melas had about Turin, which just came up to one-third of the Army of Reserve—about 11,000 men—and have afterwards dealt with the corps coming up in succession from Nice, 12,000; from Savona, 6000; from Genova, 25,000. By his move eastwards on Milan, he allowed Melas time to concentrate a force round Alessandria numerically superior to his own; owing to which he very nearly suffered a defeat.

Nor was there any reasonable excuse for coming to Moncey's aid. For the information which he had received from Lombardy, as can be seen from a letter written to Bernadotte from Aosta on the 24th of May, proved that the enemy had there only 10,000 men. These Moncey and Béthencourt could easily have disposed of, whilst Bonaparte was free with his centre and right to devote his entire attention to Melas.

By his march on Milan Bonaparte lost the advantage of his first situation; for to accomplish what he intended it became necessary to spread his troops, whilst Melas gained time for concentrating his. The argument is that by an advance from Ivrea he would have very easily beaten the Austrians, at that time in a thorough state of dispersion, though possibly some small corps might have been fortunate enough to escape. But from the very beginning we have stated how Bonaparte craved to do something very brilliant, extraordinarily uncommon; he wished most anxiously, and with good reason, as the events proved, for a battle, a brilliant battle, with which to end the campaign with one stroke.

A series of small defeats inflicted on the Austrians by marching through Piedmont would have dimmed the brilliancy of his great strategic march over the Alps. It would have been a very tame conclusion of a grand operation. The astounding effect of that exploit needed a corresponding *finale*—a pitched, a decisive battle against the entire Austrian army; something that would show to the French nation the full extent of his genius. This is what he so ardently desired, and risked much to obtain. Nevertheless, it was worth risking. He was mindful of the proverb, " Nothing venture, nothing have."

Bonaparte had calculated that he would beat the Austrians on the plain of Marengo, and so he had foretold; but they were not there when he emerged from the valley of Aosta. They had plunged into the Ligurian littoral. Was he, then, not to make an attempt to bar all the roads open to them for regaining the Lombard provinces ? was he to keep his army united, when he was so very uncertain of what course Melas was likely to pursue ?

Bonaparte deemed it a grander plan to draw round the Austrians a net formed by all his divisions, and so close the way that not one of their detachments should escape him. Had he marched on Turin, the Austrians from Nice, Savona, and Genova might have found the roads leading from Genova free. Had he moved in the direction of Genova, in that case the Austrians occupying Turin, Pinerolo, and Susa would have been free to move. In either case a portion of the Austrian army would have been able to escape. He consequently deemed it absolutely necessary to extend the Army of Reserve on one side from Pavia to Piacenza (because this part of the Po, which runs obliquely from west to east, closes the road to Milan), on the other side from Pavia to the Ticino. Thus, advancing with clever manœuvres, he would spread out his army in a semicircle, through which the Austrians had to break.

The move to Milan was so unexpected that all were taken by surprise when Bonaparte discontinued his advance on Genova.

If Massena was sacrificed by this manœuvre, as Lanfry and Michelet hold, none the less was Bonaparte surprised in finding Melas so obstinate as to leave 25,000 men idle before the walls of Genova. This was one of the calculations which miscarried.

It may be questioned if the Army of Reserve did arrive in Italy too late to save Genova. We now know General Ott's hesitation to comply with Melas's orders ; had he complied with them at once Massena would have been saved the disgrace of marching his troops out of Genova. In reality, it resolved itself in the end into a question of a few hours.

The drawback of Bonaparte's plan lay in the extension of the network. The wide dispersion of his forces, so as to guard many points at the same time, made his net dangerously weak. No one, however, knew better than Bonaparte how to make troops march; no commander could have appeared more speedily at any threatened point.

By the move on Milan, the rear of the French army became the advanced guard.

On the 26th of May, Murat advanced on the road to Vercelli, at the head of 1500 cavalry, commanded by Duvignan and Champeaux, and of the 70th regiment, commanded by Monnier. On the 27th, he occupied Vercelli, where he found that the Austrians had burnt the bridge over the Sesia. On the following day, in company with General Duhesme, Murat reconnoitred the fords of the Sesia, and made his dispositions for crossing the river.

During the night of the 28th, two batteries were constructed on the right bank of the Sesia, opposite to the position held by the Austrians. This was done to rivet their attention to that point, whilst Murat attempted to cross the river at a point two leagues further down. Early on the morning of the 29th, at about three o'clock, the Austrians, having discovered that a battery was in course of construction, and that some boats had already been collected under its protection, opened fire from four guns. Detecting a body of infantry concealed in a dike, and believing that these measures indicated an intended crossing, the Austrians opened a heavy fire of musketry, which lasted three hours.

Murat had decided to ford the river close to Palestro, and to turn the Austrian left; whilst Boudet would effect a crossing on the left of Vercelli, with the object of marching on Borgo Vercelli. The current of the Sesia was strong, and Murat experienced some difficulty in crossing, losing a few men, who were drowned. Boudet experienced the same difficulty, and likewise lost some men.

General Festenberg, with between 2000 and 3000 men, was guarding the Sesia; and as soon as it was reported to him by his cavalry patrols that Murat had crossed the river on his left, and Boudet on his right, he ordered a retreat. It was then about 8 a.m. This retreat was molested by Duhesme, who had sent across, in boats, a couple of companies of grenadiers. Festenberg managed to reach the Ticino before the enemy. He was vigorously pursued up to Novara.

Immediately after General Festenberg's retreat, Murat had the bridge re-established, and advanced the same day to Novara. Boudet was directed to take post the following day behind the Agogna, and to extend on the right, whilst Loison's division took post between Palestro and Bobbio. These measures were necessary, considering the fact that the Austrians, who occupied all the right bank of the Po, might suddenly cross to the left bank and harass the French right. Loison was consequently enjoined to guard himself well on the side of Mortara, and at the same time to keep a careful watch on Casale.

Santhia, Crescentino, Biella, Trino, and Masserano, were all occupied by the French, and orders were issued for the rearmost section of the Army of Reserve to close on Vercelli on the 30th.

The bulletin issued on the 29th of May relates that two special couriers had been intercepted during these operations. From them it was ascertained that Melas still remained at Turin, where he had arrived from Nice, travelling by post; that he reproached the generals who had supplied him from Turin with news of the valley of Aosta, and who had insisted that there were not more than 6000 Frenchmen there. The largest portion of his army, which had been operating near Nice, was approaching the Po by forced marches.

On the 30th of May, Murat and Duhesme occupied the right bank of the Ticino. The rest of the army was at that moment crossing the Sesia. Lannes retained his position facing the Austrians at Chivasso. On the same day, Murat wrote a letter to Moncey, informing him that he was striving to throw a bridge over the Ticino at Novara, so as to turn the enemy and facilitate Moncey's junction with the rest of the army. He also informed him that the Austrians appeared to be in full retreat at all points.

Whilst the above movements were in progress, Brigadier-General Lechi, who commanded the Cisalpine Legion, had been directed to cover the left of the army, which had wended its way down the valley of Aosta, coming from the Great Saint Bernard. Quitting Aosta on the 24th of May, the legion marched to Châtillon, where it passed the night. On the 26th it crossed Mount Ranzola and took post at Gressoney. On the 27th it passed the Valdobbia and reached Riva, where it crossed the Sesia. On the 28th it was at Varallo. There, where the Val-Sesia commences to be practicable for vehicles, Prince

Victor de Rohan stopped the way. He was in position with his legion and a gun. Lechi attacked him; the Italians boldly stormed his intrenchments, captured the gun, and made 350 prisoners. After this, Lechi, who was near Romagnano, was ordered to move on the Ticino towards Sesto Calende, at the southern end of the Lago Maggiore, and to lay hands on all available boats.

In the early part of May, Moreau drafted the men who were intended to compose Moncey's corps. By the middle of the month, these were brought together in the valley of the Reuss and in the valley of Unseren, between Lucerne and the northern slopes of the Saint Gothard. At that time, the corps was composed of two divisions, one commanded by Lapoype, the other by Lorge, with a reserve of cavalry. It amounted to 11,510 men. Moncey, writing on the 24th of May on the subject of the strength of his corps, says : " Dont l'effectif n'est encore que de 11,510 hommes; " by which it may be inferred that it was not complete at that date. It was very weak in artillery, which consisted of two 4-prs., 2 howitzers, and five small guns of lesser calibre than 4-prs.

According to a return furnished by Dupont, Moncey brought from the Rhine 12,092 infantry and 1851 cavalry, a total of 13,943 men.[*]

The Saint Gothard route had been surveyed quite recently by Dessoles, chief of Moreau's staff, and by Boutin, a captain in the corps of engineers. The troops commenced to cross the Saint Gothard on the 28th of May, Chabert's brigade of Lapoype's division leading. Chabert occupied Airolo on the morning of the 28th. He met with no difficulty on the march beyond what arose from the bad condition of the roads.

The corps which Melas had left to guard the issues from Switzerland, and two divisions of cavalry and artillery which he had not taken with him to Liguria, were gathered together to defend the passage of the Ticino. On the 31st of May, Murat forced the passage of that river and chased the Austrians out of Turbigo. In the mean while Duhesme had commenced to cross the river at Porto di Buffalora. The Ticino was very broad, deep, and rapid, with steep banks. Bonaparte's words were, " Il est extrémement large et rapide."

On that day part of Boudet's troops took post opposite the

---

[*] De Cugnac, " Campagne de l'Armée de Réserve en 1800," vol. ii. p. 545.

bridge over the Ticino in front of Ponte Buffalora, whilst the other portion followed Murat's advance-guard, which had moved from Novara on to Galliate to effect the passage of the river. General Schilt was to march northwards to draw the enemy's attention to his right flank, as if the French contemplated crossing at Oleggio.

At Galliate the river was defended by intrenchments armed with several pieces of artillery. But the Austrians were principally strong in cavalry. The passage of the river at that point was effected slowly, for the enemy had destroyed the bridge, and there were few boats to be procured on the spot. The French had only two 4-prs. for overcoming the fire of the Austrian battery. These guns, supported later in the day by two pieces of Boudet's division, an 8-pr. and a howitzer, succeeded in silencing the enemy's guns.

Vukassevich had received orders to defend the Ticino as far as lay in his power. The cavalry brigades of Festenberg and Doller were assigned to him. If not able to withstand superior forces, he was instructed to fall back on Pavia, and to cross the Po there. Of Vukassevich's force, a brigade under Dedovich was at Bellinzona striving to hinder Moncey's foremost troops. Laudon, retiring before ¦Béthencourt, had crossed the Lago Maggiore and landed at Angera. This brigade had orders to march on Buffalora. Festenberg's cavalry was nearly all that there was to oppose Murat on the Ticino. The Austrian line of defence from Sesto Calende to Pavia was a very lengthy one, and there were only 5600 men to hold the ground and restrain 30,000 French.

The enemy had withdrawn to the left bank all the boats but a few which the inhabitants of Galliate had hidden in the smaller branch of the Ticino. These four or five boats were offered to the French, and were carried on the shoulder by the infantry to the main branch of the river under fire of the enemy's guns.* By this means some companies of grenadiers were ferried over to a wooded island, whence they could bring an effective fire to bear on the enemy. Murat caused his artillery to move forward so as to take the enemy's in flank. Under the protection of this fire, and availing himself of two

* The Austrian account makes Murat carry on carts all the boats he had been able to find on the Agogna and the Sesia. The French general's reports are silent on this point.

boats, he crossed the river by main strength and compelled the enemy to withdraw his guns. Several small boats found on the left bank provided the means for ferrying a battalion across. Under cover of the bush this body, led by Adjutant-General Girard, who had crossed in the first boat, charged the enemy's cavalry and protected the crossing of the remainder of the corps.

As the French gradually grew stronger on the left bank, they drove the Austrians before them. The latter were weak in infantry; and, as the banks of the Ticino were covered with scrub and brushwood, it was not difficult for the French to gain a firm footing on that side of the river. Festenberg's guns were moved to several positions, from which they strove in vain to hinder the crossing; and were ultimately withdrawn to the village of Turbigo. This village was protected by the Naviglio, of which Festenberg determined to contest the crossing. This canal goes from Oleggio to Milan, and through it flows a great portion of the water of the river.

At Turbigo the Austrians received a considerable reinforcement brought up by General Loudon. Loudon marched to the sound of the guns, and hastened from Gallarate on Castano. With the main body of his troops, he entered the village of Turbigo, and at once charged Girard's foremost troops. Girard, taking advantage of all the accidents of ground, defended the Ponte di Naviglio, and thus gained time for Monnier to come to his assistance. The French crossed the Ticino slowly. The official bulletin stated that in six hours not more than 1500 men and two guns had crossed. Girard had carried the bridge over the Naviglio Grande, where he intrenched himself and cannonaded Turbigo with a 4-pr. gun. Murat saw all the importance of driving the enemy from his position, and night was fast approaching. Monnier at last, having gathered a portion of his troops, crossed the bridge at 8 o'clock, plunged into Turbigo, and attacked it at the point of the bayonet. The village was occupied by a large force, and was obstinately defended, for Loudon had sworn that he would compel the French to recross the Ticino. Monnier, however, carried the position by storm. General Schilt arrived at that moment, turned the village, and surrounded it. By ten that night Turbigo was in the hands of the French.

On the side of Buffalora little could be effected, for the bridges over the two branches of the river had been removed.

Duhesme contrived to secure a small boat, by means of which a few companies of Boudet's division were pushed across.

The crossing of the Ticino was an important operation, and a difficult one to boot. The attack on Turbigo was carried out with considerable vigour, as the possession of that point was necessary to facilitate the passage at Buffalora on the main road. On the left bank of the river were some materials; these were quickly seized by the engineers, and a bridge was constructed. The bridge was re-established on the 1st of June, and the Army of Reserve was at once pushed across the river with its artillery and baggage. The whole of it was on the left bank of the Ticino by the 2nd.

On the last days of May, a junction was made in the north with Lechi and Béthencourt. The former with the Italian legion was at Romagnano, as we have seen, on the 30th, and had on the following day resumed his march on Sesto Calende. Béthencourt had occupied Domodossola on the 29th. These moves opened a fresh line of communication for the Army of Reserve by the way of the Simplon, for at that date the garrison of Fort Bard was still holding out.

The Army of Reserve had now crossed the Ticino, and was on the march for Milan, the capital of Lombardy. At this point it seems desirable to make a few observations on some deficiencies which the march over the Alps and the advance into Lombardy had shown to exist.

Notwithstanding all the pains taken to complete the organization of the Army of Reserve, and in spite of Bonaparte's exceptional mastery of details, the organization of his forces in some important matters was far from thorough. The most essential article, ammunition, was lacking. There was a constant demand for cartridges, of which the soldiers, before coming in contact with the enemy, were reported to be wanting.

Berthier writes to the First Consul on the 20th of May: "What perplexes me most is the question of cartridges; should we have one or two engagements by Ivrea, we should have no way to replace them." On the following day Lannes writes: "I am waiting for cartridges and cavalry." General Watrin asks for some on the 20th, and again on the 25th of May; Lannes does so again on the 27th at Romano. Paulet does so urgently after the first skirmishes which his general, Duhesme, had about Cremona.

Transport for the ammunition seems to have been scarce; for we learn that the troops marching on Ivrea were made to carry ninety rounds apiece, half of which number each soldier was to hand over at Ivrea with the object of forming a small magazine at that place. On the 27th of May, the chief of the staff is ordered by Berthier to see that the 3rd battalion of the 28th takes eighty rounds per man, with the object of handing over a portion of these cartridges to the advanced guard.

The medical arrangements left much to be desired. De Paulet de la Bastide, adjutant-general on the staff of General Duhesme, writes to the chief of the staff on the 29th of May, that the divisions of Boudet and Loison needed everything that was necessary for the dressing of wounds; that the surgeons were too few in number; that there was a dearth of medicines and of lint for bandages; that the attendants were too few, and that in consequence it was difficult to prevent many soldiers from quitting the ranks under pretence of assisting their wounded comrades.

Later still, on the 11th of June, Cæsar Berthier, adjutant-general of Murat's cavalry, reported to the chief of the staff that the cavalry had no hospital.

In this campaign, as in the campaign of 1796, the French were inferior to the Austrians in guns. The artillery for Loison's division was made up of guns captured at Ivrea. This was not the only case in which the retard at Fort Bard made itself felt. Throughout the campaign a dearth of artillery was experienced. Seeing that Bonaparte himself was an artillery officer, this inferiority in guns appears strange.

A regular body of engineers does not seem to have been allotted to each division of infantry, for we find De Paulet asking the chief of the staff, in the name of his general, for one or two officers of engineers and a few sappers to be attached to General Duhesme's division, as none were forthcoming when required.

In an anonymous pamphlet attributed to Kellermann ("Réfutation de M. le duc de Rovigo, ou La vérité sur la bataille de Marengo"), it is stated that Bonaparte harassed Melas with an incomplete fighting equipment.

Notwithstanding that the French army had reached the fertile provinces of Piedmont, still on the 28th of May General Berthier complains to the chief of the staff that Loison's division had been without provisions for three days.

What was at the bottom of all these wants, was neglect and poverty. The Directory, ignorant of all that was needed for the due maintenance of an army in the field, had systematically neglected to look after the wants of their armies in a continuous manner. To do this requires care, forethought, and, above all, money; and of money there was none. Bonaparte had taken the field too soon after having assumed the reins of government for some of his measures of organization to have reached their necessary development.

The difficulty of crossing the Alps with a large animal transport, of itself compelled the French to descend into the plains of Italy accompanied by a modest train; and their supply difficulties would have been very great had not the Austrians been careless in the location of their magazines. The French, excepting those established in Switzerland, had none. They easily obtained possession of those of the enemy, which had been located in open towns instead of being formed in the many fortresses the Austrians held in Lombardy and Piedmont. In all this the Austrians showed the grossest carelessness, for invaluable stores were allowed to fall intact into the enemy's hands, and no steps were taken to set fire to them or otherwise to destroy them.

The very incomplete state of the Army of Reserve is revealed by a letter despatched by the First Consul on the 29th of May to Carnot, minister of war. In this communication, Bonaparte complains that many of the infantry regiments were incomplete, and had at that moment detachments and even battalions in France; some formed part of, and did duty with, the fleet at Brest. Several regiments of cavalry were hardly represented in the army, and the cavalry was much below strength. He adds that the army was most in need of horses for the artillery. Bridge equipment it had none, and trusted to capturing it from the enemy. The total number of artillery artificers required was 200, but there were only thirty of these present with the army. There were no pontoniers, and a battalion of sappers was much needed.

Murat won much honour in leading the bold and swift march on Milan, passing through a country intersected by many rivers, and defended by an enemy brave and well supplied, whereas his own troops were often without bread and ammunition, armed with guns of small calibre, and badly served. He had not as yet given a proof of what he would do a few years hence, of the daring enterprise and relentless pursuit of the enemy which so distinguished him in the campaigns of 1805, 1806, and 1812, nor of the impetuosity which saved the fortune of the emperor on the bloodstained field of Eylau.

Murat, with the advanced guard, had pushed on to Corbetta, three leagues only from Milan. At four o'clock on the evening of the 2nd of June, whilst thunder was rolling in the distance, he entered Milan by the Vercelli gate at the head of six cavalry regiments. Berthier, with Monnier's division, followed the cavalry. Steps were at once taken to blockade the citadel.[*]

Gachot, writing on the subject of Bonaparte's entry into Milan, declares that he was disappointed with the reception he met on entering that city. When he expected to be received with open arms, and to be welcomed with great enthusiasm, he was received in profound silence; the people remained dumb before the future conqueror of Europe. A dense crowd filled the streets, but it was not demonstrative. Bonaparte was furious. However, the people were afraid lest the Austrians should return speedily into power, as had occurred before, and might inflict on them cruel reprisals; for the Austrians had certainly given proof of little conciliating spirit.[†]

Nevertheless, it is strange that most of the writers of those events should state quite the reverse. Gachot says that the First Consul caused Bourrienne to write to his colleagues—men who, after all, had a right to know the truth—"Milan has given him a spontaneous and touching reception." Some of his immediate suite are said to have organized the ovation made to Bonaparte at the Scala Theatre, so as to make him forget the cold reception accorded to him on the 2nd of June, for they well knew how eager the general was for acclamation.

Trolard, who bases his narrative on ocular evidence contained in the local papers of the period, states that there were no cheers. The population, astonished at the sudden change of scenery, abstained from clapping their hands and shouting "*Viva!*" Many of the Milanese simply doffed their hats. The crowd at the Scala on the night of the reception was less than usual.[‡] Again, in another place, he states that, notwith-

---

[*] This was held by General Nicoletti with 2800 men.

[†] Edouard Gachot, "La Deuxième Campagne d'Italie," chap. xvii. p. 244.

[‡] Trolard Eugène, "De Rivoli à Marengo et à Solferino," vol. ii. p. 84

standing the message Bonaparte had sent to the Consuls that he had been received by a population stirred by the greatest enthusiasm, there was on the part of the inhabitants a good deal of deference, but nothing more.

The bulletin issued on the 3rd of June runs as follows : " General Murat entered Milan on the 13th (2nd of June). He caused the citadel to be surrounded at once. Three hours later, the First Consul and all his staff made their entry, passing through a multitude of people animated by the greatest enthusiasm." *

Brossier writes in the diary of the campaign of the Army of Reserve : " 13th Prairial (2nd of June).—Triumphant entry of the French into Milan. By all these measures the occupation of Milan had been rendered safe, the army headquarters went there the same day in the midst of proofs of general joy. The inhabitants, of all ages, of both sexes, bowed before him who for the second time brought them liberty and happiness."

Alison records that Bonaparte made " his triumphant entry into Milan on the 2nd of June, when he was received with transports of joy by the democratic party, and by the inconstant populace with the same applause which they had lavished the year before on Suwarroff." †

Guizot writes in the same sense : " The Lombard populace received the First Consul with transport, happy to see them-selves delivered from the Austrian yoke, and beguiled in anticipation with the hope of liberty." ‡

We read in the " Campagne de Bonaparte en Italie en l'an VIII. de la République " an account published the same year : " The First Consul and all his staff made their entry into the city in the midst of an immense crowd, animated by the greatest enthusiasm." § The same is recorded by the Duc de Valmy : " The First Consul was received with unanimous and sincere enthusiasm." ‖

Dampierre, writing the same day to Mathieu Dumas, states : " The First Consul has been everywhere received with enthu-siasm by the people, but with coldness by the upper class."

* " Correspondence de Napoléon," No. 4854.
† Alison, " History of Europe," chap. xxxi. p. 365.
‡ Guizot, vol. vii. p. 16.
§ Alexandre Foudras, " Campagne de Bonaparte en Italie en l'an VIII. de la République," p. 30.
‖ Duc de Valmy, " Histoire de la Campagne de 1800," p. 128.

Bonaparte's entry into Milan took place in the midst of an immense crowd, which shouted from every side in its semi-Oriental style, "*Ecco il sole, il liberatore della nostra Italia. Viva! viva!*" ("Behold the sun, the liberator of our Italy. Hail! hail!")*

Joseph Petit, the Horse Grenadier of the Consular Guard, could certainly have had no special object in giving too vivid a colouring to Bonaparte's entry into the capital of Lombardy. His words are: "But the finest *coup-d'œil*, the instant most flattering to us as spectators, was when we had reached the Place du Dome, and the hero who had led us enjoyed the supreme gratification which the gratitude of a numerous people exhibited. The vast space was made to ring with reiterated shouts of '*Vive General Bonaparte! Vive l'armée Française!*'" †

A warm reception went to the hearts of the French, for at that period they were more covetous of glory than of pleasure.

Botta, the Italian historian, writes: "I am not able to describe the rejoicings that took place." He says nothing to show that the First Consul met with an enthusiastic reception; but subsequently he declares that "the French were received with pleasure in the districts of Lodi, Cremona, Bergamo, and Crema, in which districts they were welcomed with considerable joy." ‡

Bonaparte had hastened his march and entered Milan when the inhabitants had barely heard that he had left Dijon. Nothing could exceed their wonderment, for none were aware that he had so recently crossed the Alps.

The astonishment of the Milanese was nothing more than natural, for Europe had endeavoured to make it believed that Bonaparte was either dead or held in captivity. Just a little more than a year before, the *Foglio Lombardo*, in its issue of the 22nd of June, 1799, published the following item of news: "General Bonaparte, with the whole of his staff, was compelled to surrender to Admiral Smith. He has been interned for a long time." §

Milan still echoed with the success of Melas on the Var, and

---

* *La Revue de Paris*, June 15, 1900, No. 12, p. 800.
† Joseph Petit, "Marengo ou Campagne d'Italie par l'Armée de Reserve," p. 32.
‡ Botta, "Storia d'Italia," tom. iv. p. 15.
§ "Il Generale Bonaparte fú forzato a consegnarsi con tutto il suo stato maggiore nelle mani dell Ammiraglio Smith. Egli é stato internato per lungo tempo."

the capture of Nice, when behold, like a clap of thunder, Bonaparte appears and rides at the head of his troops into Milan. " The entry of the First Consul," writes Jomini, " into Milan, which was for the Lombards a real *coup de théâtre*, excited amongst them an enthusiasm difficult to express." *

We read in Marelli's *Giornale Storico*, " The population, surprised at this sudden change of scene, did not clap hands, nor shout ' Hurrah!' Many doffed their hats in sign of respect, and he graciously responded." †

The Lombards were more interested in Bonaparte's success than the French themselves, for the behaviour of the Austrians on their return into Lombardy had been immeasurably arbitrary and harsh. A large number of individuals and of families had become compromised, and such as had not thought it prudent to emigrate had been deported to Austria, or were subject to a very vexatious police supervision. Others were even languishing in prison. The Austrians, in short, had occasioned so many vexations in Lombardy that their expulsion from the country came to be regarded as another benefit conferred on the people by the French. Of a host of Lombards, who had been compelled by the rigorous system introduced by the Austrians to cross the frontier and seek a refuge in France, many returned, bearing arms under the First Consul.

The previous year, the news of the arrival of the Austro-Russian army had created great enthusiasm amongst the population of Northern Italy. On their entry into Milan, on the 29th of April, the new-comers were hailed as liberators, for the French and the democrats had disgusted a large section of the population. The illusion, however, soon vanished. The departure of the French did anything but make matters more pleasant; and the so-styled liberators, the harbingers of Providence, were found to be much worse than the former occupiers of Lombardy.

The Italians had soon come to understand all the meaning of the Austrian rule, and, in comparing it with the French, they were not slow in detecting the very marked difference which existed between the two. The contempt with which they had

---

* Jomini, " Histoire des Guerres de la Révolution," liv. xvi. chap. cii.

† " Il popolo, attonito per tale improviso mutamento di scena, non batteva le mani né gridava evviva. Molti rispettosamente levavansi il cappello, ed egli graziosamente rispondeva."

welcomed the cessation of the Republican rule thereupon vanished; and the Gallophobe attacks and libels, of which their Press in the preceding months had been so prolific, from that moment ceased to appear.

The unfortunate country was desolated by all kinds of vexations and of most arbitrary proceedings. The allies came to be dreaded. At the cry, "Behold! here are the Russians!" every one fled for dear life, all the doors were made fast, and all the animals were securely shut up in their stables. The boldest of the men would take up arms and gather together in some building, determined to defend themselves, and did not venture out till after dark. Speaking of the valley of Aosta, the Abbé Fenoil declares that the heavy domination of the Austrians has left a more painful record than that of the soldiers of the Terror.

Lombardy had been made to provide for the allies, as it had previously been made to maintain the French. It was not Bonaparte alone who followed the principle of feeding and maintaining his armies on foreign ground. In eight months alone, the Austrians consumed 30,000,000 of lire worth of victuals and fodder, most of which remained unpaid. The consequence was that wheat rose to 86 lire the sack, and Indian corn to 45. The French had irritated the Lombards by imposing a capitation tax of 7 lire. But during the thirteen months which the Austrians had held the country, since the expulsion of the French, this tax had risen from 7 to 30 lire. From the month of May to the end of 1799, 30,187,280 lire of fundable property were appropriated, besides 13,346,460 for military expenses. Under such circumstances it is not surprising if very great dissatisfaction existed. Nor could the Austrians plead ignorance of the cause of all this discontent. Thugut acknowledges it in a letter to Count Colloredo. He writes: "There is not a shadow of doubt that our army, and the men connected with it, have borne themselves in Italy in such a way that there is not a single Italian who would not prefer the French *régime* or that of the Cisalpine Republic to the vaunted Austrian despotism."

Bonaparte feared lest the Republican party in Italy would resort to reprisals, would break out into acts of revenge, after having been kept down, as it had been, by the Austrians with such a strong hand. He had, therefore, to take measures to provide for the general security. He invited the Milanese to re-establish the National Guard, which should be employed in the defence of their city against attack from small bodies of the enemy. He declared that as soon as the Italian soil was free from the Austrians, he would reconstitute the republic on the firm basis of religion, liberty, equality, and order. Knowing that the clergy were the class most opposed to the French rule and ideas, he strove to dissipate every shadow of suspicion that the religious worship and other practices of the people would be interfered with. He convened an assembly of parish priests, and boldly disowned all the events which had occurred in 1796. "All the changes which occurred then," he said, "above all in the discipline, were against my way of thinking. I, a humble representative of a Government which had no care whatever for the Catholic religion, was not able to prevent in those days the disorders which had been incited purposely with the object of overthrowing it. To-day, furnished with far greater powers, I am firmly resolved to use all the means necessary to guarantee it."

After the enthusiastic reception reported in the bulletin and referred to by many writers of those events, the following letter, written by Monsieur Petiet—who had been intrusted with the new organization of the Lombard territory—to the municipality of Milan reads strangely:—

"*Plusieurs officiers français se plaignent, Citoyens, du peu d'égards qu'ils éprouvent de la part des habitants chez lesquels ils sont logés. L'intention du Premier Consul n'est point sans doute d'autoriser des demandes indiscrètes ou exaggérées, mais il ne peut pas tolérer que les officiers de son armée soient reçus des Cisalpins avec indifférence et souvent avec mépris. Je vous engage, Citoyens, à faire sentir aux habitants de Milan combien leur conduite vis-à-vis des Français pourrait devenir dangereuse pour eux, et que leur intérèt comme leur devoir est de traiter avec plus d'amitié et d'égards les officiers et autres militaires de l'armée auxquels ils donnent l'hospitalité.*

"PETIET."

Master of Lombardy, Bonaparte had secured his communications with Switzerland by the Saint Gothard, from which

Moncey, with about 14,000 men taken from the Army of the Rhine, was descending. At the same time he had interposed between Melas's army and its base of operations on the Mincio and Adige.

On entering Milan, he instantly dismissed the Austrian authorities, and one of his very first acts was to seize all letters found lying at the post-office. Amongst the mass of letters thus captured he found information of some value. But the situation of Bonaparte, reading at Milan the intercepted despatches that had been written by the Austrian Government to the general commanding their army, and the reports made by this general to his Government, was a singular one.

From the letters that came from Vienna for the Austrian commander, and those from the army directed to Vienna, the First Consul gathered a quantity of useful details. He became aware of the amount of the reinforcements which were *en route* for the Austrian army, of the actual situation of the army which was blockading Genova, with the positions it occupied, and of the situation of the parks and of the hospitals. The Austrian minister of war could hardly have furnished a more complete report than that which Bonaparte found at his disposal from the intercepted documents.

In a few hours he had learnt all that he required to know on the moral and material condition of the Austrian forces in Italy.

A letter coming from Genova revealed to him other items. From it he learnt that the city still held out, but that it was at its last gasp, that Massena was still resisting, but that in all probability he would soon be compelled to capitulate.

A courier on his way from Vienna was captured. He was the bearer of orders for the various depôts, parks of artillery and equipments in the Austrian rear. This information was turned to good account, and on the knowledge thus acquired orders were issued to lay hands on all the war materials stored in the neighbourhood.

As Bonaparte gained possession of the Milanese, his first care was to lay hands on all objects useful to his army which his rapid advance had compelled the Austrians to abandon. Orders went forth that everything serviceable which the Austrians had left in their magazines or in their manufacturing establishments should be seized.

Beyond the great moral impression caused by the occupation of the capital of Lombardy, the march to Milan secured no positive advantages, for it did not lead to a concentration of the French forces. On the contrary, it was followed by a dangerous dispersion, for to carry out Bonaparte's plan a large number of troops were required. How otherwise could a line of at least thirty leagues in extent be effectively closed to the enemy?

Melas did not penetrate Bonaparte's design, and strongly believed that the relief of Genova was the principal object of his enterprise. Only when he heard that the French had entered Milan he began to realize how critical was his position.

The Austrian generals had been warned that a large army was concentrating at Dijon. They at first scorned to believe this, and all other rumours that had reached them. When at last these were referred to the Aulic Council, all the answer they received was that the subject was not worthy of consideration.

Melas persisted in disbelieving. On the 28th of May, he had issued orders to his subordinates to rejoin him. Nevertheless, he persisted in refusing to accord credence to what he heard of the doings of the Army of Reserve.

The Austrians might very easily have stopped the French in the valley of Aosta, in the position of Bard, which had already been marked out, and where there existed intrenchments and barracons in a good state. The staff, however, were confident, and the cry was, " Let them come down into the plains, and we shall beat them."

When at last the French columns appeared, having crossed the Alps and traversed the district of Aosta, the Austrians abandoned Ivrea and the Canavesan. As the French marched along the left bank of the Po, the Austrians endeavoured to assemble around Turin all the forces at that time scattered throughout Piedmont. But when they had gathered a goodly number, and offered battle in the direction of Volpian on the left of the Po, the French were too alert to fall into this snare, and followed the course of the Po on the left bank of the river. Zack, when questioned on the situation, is said to have replied, "I have them in a sack." Chevalier Cavour states that from that moment the Austrians lost their head and committed many errors, one greater than the other.

At a council of war it was decided to defend the right bank

s

of the river. This unfortunate decision allowed the enemy complete freedom on the left bank, and plenty of time to be joined by reinforcements. In the end the plan brought about the loss of Italy to the Austrians. There were, nevertheless, at this council of war officers who objected, and who held that it was derogatory for a numerous army to observe a strictly defensive attitude in the face of an army which could not number more than 20,000 combatants, and had to defend the crossing of a river for a very considerable extent—from Turin to Piacenza—which could not have been less than forty leagues. These officers argued that it was preferable to place the heavy artillery in safety in the fortified places, to abandon the heavy baggage, and to follow the enemy on the left bank of the Po, always offering battle, which, by reason of his inferiority as much in point of numbers as in cavalry and artillery, the French commander-in-chief would be precluded from accepting. Once on a level with Vercelli, the army should abandon this manner of proceeding, move on Novara, cross the Ticino at Turbigo, and, leaving Milan on the right, march so as to effect a junction with Vukassevich and the reinforcements coming from Austria. Then it would be time for them to retrace their steps.

The conception was good. The distance from Turin to Vercelli could have been got over in three moderate marches, one march more would have taken the army to Novara, and a longer one have brought it level with Milan. In two or three other marches it could have been within Gallarate and Varese, where Vukassevich's corps was at that time. Possibly Lannes with the advanced guard of the Army of Reserve would have harassed the left flank of the Austrian columns marching towards Vukassevich, still the Austrians had superiority of numbers on their side, and if well handled could have swept Lannes away.

The Austrians did their scouting very badly not to get an idea of the weakness of Lannes's force at Chivasso—this in a country where the feeling was much in their favour. Chabran bears witness, for, writing from Sartirana on the 16th of June, he remarks, "*L'habitant n'est pas pour nous*" ("The people are not in our favour").

The reason given, and very possibly the true one, for Melas having abstained from threatening his adversary's communications by a move on Vercelli, is the sudden news he received of all the disasters on the valley of the Danube. How Kray had suffered several defeats and had taken refuge in the intrenched camp at Ulm; how Moncey had arrived at Bellinzona, and Vukassevich had retreated towards the Adda. All these circumstances demanded, he thought, more cautious measures, such as a concentration of his army under the cannon of Alessandria.

Melas had the choice of three roads by which to regain the Mincio. One leading from Alessandria to Piacenza; a second by Casale, Mortara, and Milan; the third, and most difficult, of Alessandria, Colle della Scoffera, Bobbio, and Piacenza. His dilatoriness and his state of uncertainty allowed Bonaparte to close all three against him.

At the end of May, Melas found himself exposed to be attacked by Bonaparte, and to be beaten in detail while his army was in a thorough state of dispersion. What else could he expect? Nevertheless, there was still time to do something. To concentrate his army he was bound to bow to necessity, to make great sacrifices, to withdraw at once from Genova, to draw back from the Var; in fact, to give up a great part of Piedmont. Melas, however, for a second time fell a victim to Bonaparte's craftiness. He failed to penetrate his adversary's intentions; he believed that with some 30,000 men he could easily dispute the passage of the Po, and prevent a junction with Turreau. He was imposed upon by Lannes's bold attitude, and believed that the necessity had not yet arisen for a complete withdrawal of his troops from Genova and the Var.

When he became actually convinced of the appearance of a formidable army in Italy, he despatched couriers in all directions bearing orders for the concentration of his army. The date given by Campana for the orders sent to Ott and to Elsnitz to march on Alessandria was the 28th of May. Jomini says that the orders sent to Ott were despatched on the 31st of May, and reached him on the 1st of June. Hamley, possibly, is still more correct, for he states that Melas issued his orders for the concentration on the 31st of May, and that Ott probably received them on the 2nd of June. This appears to accord with the date given by General Melas in his letter to Count de Tige.*

It is hard to believe that all the Austrians were badly informed. Amongst the correspondence seized by Murat at

* See De Cugnac, "Campagne de l'Armée de Réserve en 1800," vol. ii. p. 229.

Piacenza was a letter signed " Marqui," evidently written by a superior officer of the Austrian army, and dated Coni, 3rd of June. This letter contained the following passages :—

" My suspicions, with regard to the Army of Reserve, were not without good grounds, notwithstanding that no one would pay attention to them. Berthier has come from the valley of Aosta, and by the valley of the Rhone into that of Domodossola, and from thence to Lago Maggiore.

" General Flavigny, who was in front of me at Barcelonnette, has descended on the side of Susa. He has not more than 3000 men, and cannot undertake anything of serious importance.

" But at this moment I am told that Lecourbe, with a corps coming from Germany, is descending by the Saint Gothard on Bellinzona, so that if Genova does not surrender, it is impossible to foresee how things will turn out." *

* See De Cugnac, " Campagne de l'Armée de Réserve en 1800," vol. ii. p. 232.